Keith Martin on COLLECTING FERRARI

"Buying a Ferrari was the nicest thing I ever did for myself."

You only live once—get the car of your dreams.

Keith Martin on

COLLECTING FERRARI

Featuring **Mike Sheehan, John Apen, Steve Ahlgrim** and the editors of

MOTORBOOKS
INTERNATIONAL

This edition first published in 2004 by Motorbooks International, an imprint of MBI Publishing Company, Galtier Plaza, Suite 200, 380 Jackson Street, St. Paul, MN 55101-3885 USA

Motorbooks International titles are also available at discounts in bulk quantity for industrial or sales-promotional use. For details write to Special Sales Manager at Motorbooks International Wholesalers & Distributors, Galtier Plaza, Suite 200, 380 Jackson Street, St. Paul, MN 55101-3885 USA.

ISBN 0-7603-1971-5

Front cover: *360 and 550 Noses* by Jeff Dorgay.

Designed by LeAnn Kuhlmann and Brenda Canales

Printed in China

Ferrari: Racing as a Way of Life

From the very beginning of my career, I was drawn to Ferrari. They were always right in the thick of things, fighting to prove that they were the best cars in the world. Whether it was the Formula One tracks of Europe or the highways of Mexico, Ferraris have always been ready to go up against anyone.

There's no team in any other sport that has had the constant presence and frequent dominance that Ferrari has had in racing. In Formula One, they have been involved in every season since it began, in 1950. Today, if a football team wins the Super Bowl two out of three years, everyone starts talking about a dynasty; yet Ferrari has won five F1 constructor's championships in a row.

I'm often asked what my most memorable moment with Ferrari has been, and I'd have to say it was my first win at the 24 hours of Le Mans in 1958, driving a 250 Testa Rossa.

Le Mans is this giant monster of a race, one that devours cars and drivers during the course of 24 hours. To win you had to have equal parts good driving, good machinery and good luck. So many times cars that were very fast were sidelined due to equipment malfunctions or accidents.

On that memorable day in 1958, it rained nearly the whole time, and when I finally saw the checkered flag come out I felt an intense jubilation combined with near-total exhaustion.

As I recalled in my biography, *Yankee Champion*: "It was impossible to see the smaller and slower cars in the rain and darkness. I drove down the Mulsanne straight at top speed and waited to hear the resonance of exhaust in front of me. As soon as I could sense the location of a car ahead in the blackness, it was a flash of light, the bare outline of car and driver as I sped past—and then back into the darkness, peering ahead for the next one.

"While no race is won until the finish line is crossed, it was a great feeling when the rain stopped and the sun came out Sunday afternoon. We had some laps in hand, the tension from driving in the wet was gone and we knew we could win. While my winning the 1961 Formula One championship was the biggest event of my career, the 1958 Le Mans remains my favorite race and the most rewarding to me."

Of course, I went on to repeat twice more at Le Mans, but as exciting as each of those victories was, they weren't quite the same as the first one.

For Ferrari, racing has always been the reason for the whole organization to exist. It's well known that early on, Enzo Ferrari viewed his street cars to be merely a way to earn enough money to pay for his race cars. Even today, new Ferraris have the same edgy, passionate sense that the cars have always had, and I would certainly like to have a 550 Maranello in my own garage today. It's no wonder that over the past five-and-a-half decades, Ferraris have become so highly collectible.

I've been a reader of *Sports Car Market* for more than a decade. Keith Martin and I have crossed paths at various concours, like Pebble Beach and Amelia Island, and at vintage racing events including the Mille Miglia and the Tour Auto. He's clearly committed to the hobby and to helping make collectors more informed about the collector car market.

It's nice to have all of these articles from *SCM* combined in once place. We fans of the prancing horse can sit down and immerse ourselves in good writing, tall tales and decent advice about the most passionately built cars in the world. I'm sure you'll have as much fun reading them as I did. *—Phil Hill, Santa Monica, California*

(*Phil Hill is the only American-born Formula One Champion. More information about his career, and information about ordering a copy of his book,* Yankee Champion, *may be found at www.philhill.com.*)

Phil Hill, a true Yankee champion.

CONTENTS

Part II: Mid-Engine Ferraris

Part III: Random Thoughts

A Very Hardworking Group, Indeed

As with our first book, *Keith Martin on Collecting Porsche*, this book about Ferraris is really the result of an extraordinary amount of creative effort by a large cast of individuals. Every contributor to *Sports Car Market* magazine is an enthusiast, and the thoughts they've offered come straight from the heart. At the same time, all the writers in this book have been around Ferraris for decades, and their articles are based on hands-on experiences.

Special thanks to one of my personal heroes as well as a long-time good friend, Phil Hill, for graciously contributing the foreword to this book.

Our featured contributor to *Keith Martin on Collecting Ferarri* is Mike Sheehan, who has been a part of *SCM* since its days as an eight-page mimeographed newsletter. Although he's loath to admit it, Mike got his start in the car world by restoring VW buses for hippies in '70s. Since then, he's owned a restoration shop, raced Ferraris semi-professionally and on the vintage circuit, and now has a sales and brokerage service.

What has set Mike apart from the beginning is his candor. When I was looking at buying my first V12 Ferrari, he told me two things. First, he said, "It's the best thing you'll ever do for yourself." He followed that with, "And if you're lucky, you won't lose more than $20,000 on the car. And that's if nothing breaks."

Our key profile writers are John Apen and Steve Ahlgrim. John used a 330 GT 2+2 as a daily driver when his now-grown children were little, and still has a California Spyder and a 275 GTS in his stable. As the editor of the Manheim Black Book he brings a wealth of knowledge about the entire market to the table.

Steve is the most recent addition to the *SCM* Ferrari gang. He spent 16 years, many as general manager, at the Atlanta-based Ferrari dealership FAF, and is now the general manager of the T. Rutlands and Maranello Auto Parts companies, a premier source of aftermarket parts for Ferraris.

Additional profiles were authored by Michael Duffey, Dave Kinney and Steve Serio.

Our Legal Files columns come from Alex Leventhal, who has driven both a 308 GT4 and a 365GT 2+2 on various vintage rallies.

The market reports were compiled by a much larger cast. The real heart of *SCM*, these stalwart souls spend hours looking at cars all over the world, describing them in detail so you feel like you are there with them, looking over their shoulders. The chances are good that nearly every weekend of the year, there's a collector car auction somewhere, and at that auction you'll find an *SCM* reporter.

It's not practical to list each writer with each car they personally reviewed and photographed, so my thanks goes to everyone below for the everything they have contributed.

The Market Report specialists represented in this book are by John Apen, Carl Bomstead, Dave Brownell, B. Mitchell Carlson, Scott Featherman, Dan Grunwald, Richard Hudson-Evans, Dave Kinney, Terry Parkhurst and John Rogers.

Of course, without auction companies, there would be no auctions to report on. We are especially appreciative of the auction companies listed below, both due to their encouraging us to share our critical analyses with our readers, as well as their support of *SCM* through their advertising. Contact information about each company may be found in the Resource Directory at the back of this book.

The market reports in this book were taken from cars examined at auction conducted by the following companies: Barrett-Jackson, Bonhams Europe, Bonhams USA, Christie's, Coys, H&H Classic Auctions, Kensington, Kruse International, Mecum Auctioneers, RM Auctions, Russo and Steele, and Silver Auctions.

Whenever practical, we have credited the auction companies for the photos we have used in the articles. In the market reports themselves, we are thanking both the auction reporters and the auction companies for the photos used.

It seems as if we had barely gotten *Keith Martin on Colleting Porsche* off to its successful launch when Tim Parker, Senior Vice President of MBI, started pestering us about "the Ferrari book that's coming next." His creative team of Peter Bodensteiner and Jennifer Johnson, editorial, and LeAnn Kuhlmann and Brenda Canales, designers, have again been terrific to work with. We'd like to thank Mandy Iverson for the colorful, easy-to-read format she developed for this series.

I'd like to report that after doing one book, the second one came easier, but in fact it required the same amount of painstaking research, mostly by *SCM*'s production manager, David Slama. He went back through 16 years of Ferrari-related articles, digitized those that existed only in typewritten form, and developed the plan for the overall content of the book.

Adrian Gilles, our technology wizard, facilitated this process by helping round up all the images in their various forms, and converting them to digital format. A new addition to the team this time is Kathleen Karapondo, a first-rate writer and copy editor who went over every single word in this book. Her charge was to bring linguistic correctness and stylistic consistency to the hodge-podge she was given, and she's done the job admirably. The initial copy editing, when the articles first appeared in SCM, was performed by Brian Rabold, Stephen Siegel, Bill Neill and Bengt Halvorson.

Ron Tonkin Ferrari made available the Enzo that accompanies my intro, and John Vincent kindly took the photo. Additional vintage Ferrari photos appear courtesy of Bob Dunsmore.

In any family-owned business like *SCM*, it's really a husband-and-wife team that make everything happen. Cindy Banzer, my spouse and executive editor of *SCM*, has been supportive and offered continued encouragement both as we continue to grow our magazine, and with the production of this book.

If there are any errors or omissions in this book, they are mine alone. Of course, you don't need to read a book to become a fan of Ferraris, but we hope that these articles offer you a little better appreciation of the marque, and will help you look at the next Ferrari that goes by with an enhanced appreciation for just what it is that makes this marque so special.

—*Keith Martin*◆

An Insider's Guide to Collecting Ferrari

There have been more than a few Ferraris that have passed through our lives over the years, and each has created memorable moments. They've included a '50s 212 Barchetta I drove across the Rockies, a '60s 330 America we used on a daily basis for runs to the grocery store and to shuttle kids to soccer games, and now we're in the hunt for a blue 308 GTS.

Ferraris aren't the best cars in the world by any stretch of the imagination, but they are the most evocative. The marque was born and tested on the race track, and that tough-as-nails mechanical nature is a part of every car that carries the prancing horse. With few exceptions, every Ferrari has striking styling that sets them apart, and they all have a memorable exhaust sound as they run through the revs.

Through our ownership experiences, we've also learned about the dark side of Ferrari ownership, the land of $5,000 brake jobs, $15,000 valve jobs and $25,000 engine overhauls. Ferraris have always been expensive when new, and even though the cars generally go down in value over the years, the cost of parts and maintenance is always high.

But Ferraris are exotic, and exotic experiences never come cheaply.

They've come a long way from the almost toy-like roadsters of the 1950s to the world-beating supercars of the 21st century. But through it all, every car built in Maranello has had a piece of Ferrari's competition heritage in it. From the most mundane 400i or 308 GT/4 to the latest 360 Modena or 550 Barchetta, the engine, gearbox and suspension of the cars are always about performance at the very highest level.

Over the years I had my share of rides in Ferraris, six, eight and twelve cylinder models, and marveled at the exotic mechanical sounds they always made. Then, in 1989, Ron Tonkin, owner of the oldest Ferrari dealership in the U.S., asked if I would be interested in being a salesman at his Ferrari – Maserati – Lotus – Alfa Romeo store.

There's no training school you go to when you're selling exotics. You just immerse yourself in the cars; I recall hour after hour sitting with the owner's manuals, teaching myself about every knob and switch in the 308s, 328s and Mondials on the showroom floor. That was followed by time spent in the shop, talking with the technicians and watching as they performed pre-delivery work on the new cars.

In *Keith Martin on Collecting Ferrari*, I've attempted to bring together the best articles about this magnificent marque from the past decade of *Sports Car Market* magazine. Long-time Ferrari owners and enthusiasts John Apen and Steve Ahlgrim have provided most of the model profiles, and our own irascible Mike Sheehan offers his highly informed and opinionated take on many aspects of Ferrari ownership.

Just like *SCM* itself, the articles here are full of insights from those who really know what they are talking about. They don't pull any punches, but give you the good with the bad about every model they examine. At *SCM* we believe this is exactly the information that an informed collector is looking for today, to make a good decision when it comes to buying a collectible. (If you're not already a part of the *SCM* gang, use the post-paid card inside the back cover to give us a try.)

John M. Vincent

This book is not designed to be a buyer's guide, or a complete survey of the marque. It's just some of my favorite articles, about some of my favorite cars. There's no need to read it in a linear fashion from front to rear – just open to the car of your choice and start in.

Ferrari has been building some of the world's best performance cars for over half a century, and if we can help you appreciate and enjoy them a little more, then we've accomplished what we set out to do.

—*Keith Martin*◆

PART I
Front-Engine Ferraris

A 1962 330 America, that I pulled out of a barn in Missoula, Montana, was my first V12 Ferrari. After sweeping all the cobwebs off and chasing the mice out of the engine bay, we got it running. The test drive was memorable, especially when the entire exhaust system dropped off on the freeway. That, along with the carburetors constantly trying to set fire to themselves, convinced me that I was better off trailering the car home than trying to drive it.

The car was primitive, yes, but made the most incredible sounds under acceleration. I don't know if it was really fast (Ferrari claimed 300 horsepower from the four-liter engine, but Italian horses were pretty small in the '60s, and besides, this car's horses were pretty tired), but it *felt* fast as it rocketed down the road.

We ended up spending about $40,000 on this $25,000 car, and chalked up the money we lost as our introduction to Ferrari Economics 101.

The front-engined, V12 Ferraris are the stuff the prancing horse legend is made of. While you can argue the merits of other powertrain configurations all you want, this is the basis for the classic Ferrari design from the 1950s, so much so that it's still being used in the most modern machines being produced today.

The profiles in this section reach back to a 1951 340 America and extend all the way forward to the 550 Barchetta of the 21st Century.

Along the way you'll find our thoughts on the ups and downs of buying, restoring, showing and selling the iconic 275 GTB, Daytona, Lusso, and California Spyder. But in addition to these high-end cars, those that sell for hundreds of thousands or even millions of dollars, we have profiles of more affordable Ferraris like the 400 and the 456.

You'll also get advice on which Ferrari to buy if you want to participate in the Mille Miglia, and why buying any Ferrari with a salvage title should be regarded as a very bad idea indeed.

These V12s truly constitute the backbone of the Ferrari heritage, and our articles, drawn from *SCM*, offer an evaluation of them from a variety of unique, entertaining and educational perspectives.

—Keith Martin◆

1965 275 GTB/6C Berlinetta

Chassis number: 7269
Engine number: 7269

Described by Sergio Pininfarina as having "the heart of a lion and the shape of the wind"

Bonhams

Ferrari's highly successful 250 series was superseded in 1964 by the 275. In Ferrari nomenclature of the period, a model's designation reflected the cubic capacity of an individual cylinder. The newcomer displaced 3.3 liters—up from its predecessor's 3 liters—and was thus called the 275. The V12 engine remained the familiar Colombo type in standard form, producing 280 horsepower at 7,600 rpm. A higher, 300-horsepower state of tune employing six Weber carburetors was available, and this was used for the handful of 275 GTB/C (competition) models built.

Despite its near-perfect appearance, revisions to the original 275 GTB were soon executed: a longer hood, enlarged rear window and external trunk hinges being introduced towards the end of 1965. Mechanically, the only major change was the adoption of torque tube enclosure of the prop shaft.

Sold new in Ferrara, Italy, the car pictured here was supplied in June 1965 to a good client of the factory, who specified the six-carburetor set-up and coachwork in Rosso Chiaro with black leather upholstery. According to the factory, he returned chassis 7269 to the works for regular servicing and went on to own numerous other Ferraris into the current era.

This car has been uprated to "longnose" bodywork and retains its original interior, including even the protective plastic covering over the footwell carpets. The odometer reading of 86,000 kilometers is commensurate with the condition of the car, which appears to be largely original. Recent maintenance has been entrusted to Garage Symbol in Matran.

This car sold for $141,266, including buyer's premium, at the Bonhams Geneva sale, March 11, 2002.

Close your eyes and imagine what a Ferrari looks like. If you're older than 40, chances are your image is a 275 GTB, which was described by Sergio Pininfarina as having "the heart of a lion and the shape of the wind." Its low-profile design with fastback roof, long hood and covered headlights is the quintessential Ferrari shape. The complementing 3.3-liter V12 engine and stylish interior puts the 275 GTB on most Ferrari enthusiasts' short list.

It takes a tally card to decipher the variations of 275 GTB models. They were built with shortnose, longnose, steel and alloy bodywork; as street and comp cars; with two and four cams; with three and six carbs; with open driveshafts, interim driveshafts and finally torque-tube driveshafts. Add a chop top and a few Speciale versions and you need an abacus to compute the variations.

The 275 shortnose is at the bottom of the 275 GTB food chain. Think size doesn't matter? The 2-inch shorter nose makes for a $25,000 reduction in value. S/N 7629 was a shortnose that was uprated to a longnose. Uprating sounds like a good thing, but it takes a pretty big stretch of the imagination to believe someone spent the equivalent of the cost of a small car to replace a perfectly good front clip for the sake of 2 inches. More probable is the scenario that the original nose was irreparably damaged and a shortnose clip was unavailable. The resulting Frankencar is half longnose and half shortnose, and certainly no improvement.

In the fall of 1997, S/N 7269 showed up in the Ferrari Market Letter, *advertised as having new leather, new chrome and new paint. Nothing was mentioned about a converted nose; the asking price was $200,000. The car apparently sold to a German collector who must have transferred the new leather, chrome and paint to a different car—7269's next appearance at the 2001 Bonhams Gstaad auction was with rust-scabbed front quarter panels, pitted chrome and a fair engine compartment. Offered at no reserve and reportedly sold at $147,000, we're told the car was actually bought back by the vendor and re-consigned to Bonhams for their Geneva sale.*

At Geneva the car was reported as having poor chrome, original interior, older paint and shabby carpet, which makes one wonder what the "original protective plastic covering" in the auction company's description was actually protecting. Already hindered by a #3 condition, probable previous accident damage and an incorrect front end, Robert Brooks's podium announcement of a gear selection problem also harmed its value.

Ferrari specialists will want $30,000 plus for the paint, interior, chrome and gearbox repairs. Add in a few more bucks for some suspension and engine work and six months later you're driving a $170,000 GTB. A tidy shortnose pulled a perfect $178,000 at Monterey this year, so it looks like the buyer did fine.

But what about the $25,000 premium six-carb cars receive? You only get the $25k if the setup is original. No proof, no prize. The originality of this setup is questionable so, without build sheets, which apparently were not offered here, the buyer's gain is about equal to what the nose graft takes away.

The vendor was surely disappointed with the bid, but a buyer couldn't be expected to pay much more. There are always a few 275 GTBs available, and their prospective buyers tend to be very well educated about the current market values, as well as costs of repairs and restoration. As long as the vendor had some good times with the car and the buyer has a few more, everyone should go home happy. —Steve Ahlgrim

(Historic data and photo courtesy of auction company.)

From the October 2002 issue of *SCM*.◆

Years produced	1964-66
Alternatives	Ferrari 550 Maranello, Ferrari Daytona
Number produced	450
Original list price	approx. $14,000
SCM Price Guide	$150,000-$180,000; add $25,000 for six-carb version
Tune up/major service	$2,000-$2,500
Distributor cap	$450 (two required)
Chassis #	On chassis by top of right shock mount
Engine #	Lower right side of block by bell housing
Club	Ferrari Club of America, P.O. Box 720597, Atlanta, GA 30358; Ferrari Owner's Club, 8642 Cleta St., Downey, CA 90241
Web sites	www.FerrariClubofAmerica.org; www.FerrariOwnersClub.org
SCM Investment Grade	A

1965 Ferrari 275 GTS Spyder

Chassis number: 08005

If God is in the details, then this car is an agnostic

Independently, the names Ferrari and Pininfarina have a magic all their own. Put together, they signify a machine of rare transcendent beauty. This has never been more true than in the case of the Ferrari 275 GTS.

Christie's

Introduced at the Paris Salon in October, 1964, this lovely open Ferrari mated the marque's legendary 3286-cc single-overhead camshaft V12 and five-speed transmission with a simple and elegant body from Pininfarina. Breathing through a triplet of twin-choke Webers, the lusty V12 made spectacular mechanical noises while churning out a healthy 260 bhp.

The chassis underpinnings of the GTS are typical mid-'60s road-going Ferrari, with independent front suspension by upper and lower A-arms, followed by a leaf-spring live rear axle. When *Road & Track* tested an example in September, 1966, the 3,345-pound Spyder reached 145 mph and covered a quarter mile in 15.7 seconds. *Car and Driver* did even better, with a 14-second sprint at the drag strip.

Although clearly descended from racing Ferraris of the recent past, this product of Italy's most revered automaker was intended for fast long-distance, open-air motoring for two people and plenty of luggage. Although not the most flamboyant of Ferraris, there was no mistaking the classic egg-crate grille or the black prancing horse on the field of bright yellow. Although not the rarest of drop-top Ferraris, just 200 275 GTS Spyders were built between 1964 and 1966.

Rolling on its original center-lock alloy wheels and just as strikingly handsome as it was when first built in 1965, this marvelous example of a desirable Ferrari Spyder has received the best of care and shows just around 48,000 miles on the odometer. Sold new in Los Angeles and a resident of Oregon since 1970, it is finished appropriately in red with an interior trimmed in tan leather and features an original Blaupunkt radio and tool kit. Only needing a driver, it is perfect for show, weekend enjoyment or historic tours such as the Forza 1000 or California Mille.

This Ferrari 275 GTS Spyder sold for $147,700, including buyer's premium, at the Bonhams & Brooks Quail Lodge sale, held August 18, 2001.

If you would consider the 330 GTC as the best "bang for the buck" in a classic 12-cylinder Ferrari coupe, then the 275 GTS has to be the equivalent open car.

The 275 GTS isn't as expensive as its sexier siblings, (California Spyder, 330 GTS or Daytona Spyder) or as rare, but that shouldn't be the barometer for pleasure.

The harshest criticism I can levy is that the 275 GTS suffers from looking like a big Fiat 1500. The plywoodesque veneer-finished dash leaves a little to be desired (leave the wood to the Jaguar guys). But, perhaps the rather staid styling has kept the prices on earth, albeit the earth of Monte Carlo or the Hamptons.

It's true that the better-styled and more glamorous 275 GTB or NART Spyder that were built during the same era better embody the competitive spirit of Enzo Ferrari, but let's talk about what is equally important: the driving experience.

The first V12 Spyder I had the pleasure to drive, 16 years ago, was a 275 GTS and it was impressive. Engine sound, exhaust note and a very smooth, proven transmission overcame the styling flaws for me. The stated 260 horsepower is adequate, wind noise not egregious and the driving position, although not great, was certainly not uncomfortable. As an overall high-speed touring exotic, the 275 GTS has few peers from that time period.

When I gave this particular 275 a visual once-over in Monterey, it had straight and honest lines. The panel fit was excellent and much of the overall car looked and felt original and true. The chassis was unmarked and clean.

However, if God is in the details, then this car is an agnostic. The consignee needed a lesson in vehicle auction preparation because "buyers do care about details." The seats were dyed perhaps three too many times, the mechanical minutiae under the hood lacked respect (nice Pep Boys oil filters and battery), and the cam covers were much too wet from leaking gaskets. All of this added up to a big warning shot about the last owner. What else was overlooked or uncared for? It reeked a bit of the attitude of, "Hell, Marge, I'll fix it myself with my new Craftsman toolset." Furthermore, I feel that red, this car's color, is the least attractive hue on a 275.

Assuming this car was a nice driving example, and that's something we won't know until the engine temperatures are up, the wind is tangling your hair and you watch the odometer roll a bit, $147,700 was all the money for this Spyder. If a host of mechanical needs become evident, and the bill is more than $5,000, then the amount paid should be considered full retail and then some.—Steve Serio

(Historic data and photo courtesy of auction company.)

From the February 2002 issue of *SCM*.◆

Years produced	1965-66
Number produced	200
Original list price	$14,500
SCM Price Guide	$135,000-$185,000
Tune-up/major service	$15,000
Distributor cap	$300
Chassis #	Upper side of the left frame tube; ID plate on the firewall
Engine #	Right rear side of engine block
Club	Ferrari Club of America, Box 720597, Atlanta, GA 30358; Ferrari Owner's Club, 8642 Cleta St., Downey, CA 90241
Web site	www.ferrariclubofamerica.org; www.FerrariOwnersClub.org
Alternatives	Aston Martin DB5 convertible, Jaguar XKE SI roadster, Mercedes-Benz 300SL

1965 Ferrari 500 Superfast

Chassis number: 6043
Engine number: 6043

The wing line, rising gently from the tail before dipping towards the extended nose, gives the sleek Superfast the appearance of being in motion even while at rest

Bonhams & Brooks

Introduced at the 1964 Geneva Salon and produced for only two years, the opulent 500 Superfast, of which only 36 were made, was at the same time Ferrari's fastest, most powerful, most expensive and most exclusive road car. Maranello's flagship and the last of the limited-edition closed Ferraris, the 500 Superfast caught the public imagination in a manner not seen since the creation of the Bugatti Royale.

The Superfast chassis is multi-tubular and initially used a four-speed/overdrive gearbox. With its distinctive flat sides, the Pininfarina body, surely one of the maestro's greatest works, showed influence of the earlier Aerodinamico prototype; the wing line, rising gently from the tail before dipping towards the extended nose, giving the sleek Superfast the appearance of being in motion even while at rest. Ferrari's racing heritage manifested itself in the magnificent, Lampredi-designed five-liter "long block" V12 engine, the largest to power a Ferrari at that time. The competition-derived Tipo 208's 400 bhp made it the most powerful production engine of its day and was sufficient to propel the Superfast to 175 mph.

After just a few examples had been built, a revised Superfast was made available, the most significant change being the adoption of a five-speed, all-synchromesh gearbox. Twelve such cars appear to have been built, outwardly distinguishable by their three-vent engine bay louvers that replaced the earlier eleven-vent style. As each car was built to order, the common reference to Series I and Series II is somewhat misleading, particularly as some of the earlier cars were built with the five-speed gearbox and the three-vent louvers.

Ordered in left-hand drive form for continental touring, this car is finished in a very dark green specially ordered by its British owner and has black leather upholstery with matching carpets. Unique features include: lowered and lengthened driver's seat for its tall owner, special positions for the ashtray and window switches, deletion of the parcel tray and Superfast script, seatbelts, passenger footrest, Blaupunkt Koln radio and electric antenna.

Never restored yet always properly maintained without regard to cost, this one-owner, 12,288-mile example includes other items of great interest to collectors, including the factory warranty book, Italian "Libretto" (log book), last Italian road tax disc and factory tool kit. Almost certainly the finest surviving example of Ferrari's super exclusive 1960s luxury flagship, 500 Superfast #6043 is an exciting proposition in all respects and a genuinely unique opportunity for the serious collector.

The car described here sold for $265,666, including buyer's premium, at the Bonhams & Brooks Gstaad Auction held December 19, 2000.

Years produced	1964-66
Number produced	36 (29 LHD)
Original list price	approx. $20,000
SCM Price Guide	$300,000-$400,000
Tune up/major service	$2,000-$3,000
Distributor cap	$400 (two required)
Chassis #	Right front chassis near upper wishbone
Engine #	Right rear engine block near flywheel
Clubs	Ferrari Club of America, Box 720597, Atlanta, GA 30358; Ferrari Owners Club, 8642 Cleta St., Downey, CA 90241
Web sites	ferrariclubofamerica.org; FerrariOwnersClub.org
Alternatives	Ferrari 400 Superamerica, Maserati 5000GT

Though the name "Superfast" was used by Pininfarina for several show cars based on the Superamerica beginning in the late 1950s, the production Superfast was filled with ingredients associated with early '60s Ferraris. Built on the current production 330 GT chassis, Ferrari installed, with relatively few chassis modifications, a five-liter engine that shared the bore and stroke of the old screw-in liner SA engine but had an altogether new block, one with different bore centers and press-in cylinder liners.

Unlike the various "America" series in which the big engine was installed in an otherwise standard, left-over chassis/body unit, the Superfast utilized different outriggers to support an entirely new body (a two-seater this time) onto the then brand-new 330's 2+2 chassis.

At almost twice the price of a 330 GT 2+2, the well-heeled Ferrari customer had to place a very high value on the additional horsepower (and exclusivity) of one of the fastest road cars of the era. When the 330 GT was upgraded to a five-speed transmission, this change was made more or less concurrently with the Superfast; in fact, the underpinnings were the same spec as the contemporary 330, with the exception of the differential ratio.

The 500 Superfast is an attractive car, but in most enthusiasts' opinion, its styling pales when compared with the Superamerica's, which was pointed at both ends and featured covered headlights. This probably accounts for the higher value of an SA compared to an SF.

In fact, the rule of thumb I have found useful is that a Superfast is worth about the same amount as a comparable 275 GTB/4. So, one needs to ask oneself, "Would I pay $265,666 for a one-owner, 12,000-mile, unrestored four-cam?" My guess is that you would have to pay even more—probably in the low $300,000 range. That makes this purchase, if all the tales are true, a very good one. —*Michael Duffey*

(Historical data and photo courtesy of auction company.)

From the March 2001 issue of *SCM*.◆

1967 Ferrari 330 GTC

He got a firsthand education about the dangers of buying an older, newly painted, good-looking exotic... the 5,300 miles he drove cost approximately $13 a mile

Chassis number: 10673
Engine number: 10673

After being imported from California in 1968, some mechanical work was done to this car and it was repainted. The present vendor purchased it in 1995 with 54,414 miles, and in 1998 spent $58,000 on the engine, chassis and a re-trim of the interior. $34,500 was for rebuilding the engine, including replacement of both heads and rebuild to "unleaded" specifications with all new valves, etc., as well as a rebore and 12 new oversized pistons. Approximately $3,000 each was spent on brakes, suspension, exhaust, electrics, air conditioning and transaxle. Interior refurbishments were $4,000.

Thirty pages of invoices relating to its post-1988 servicing and refurbishment are available. Mileage is now 59,700. Black with matching leather interior and red carpets, this superb Ferrari Grand Routier is presented in very good condition in every respect.

This GTC coupe sold for $71,435, including buyer's premium, at Bonhams' Olympia, London, auction on December 2, 2002. Richard Hudson-Evans, SCM's reporter, judged it 2+ condition with thick but unmarked pre-1995 repaint and with a new, slightly sat-in interior.

None other than Phil Hill and Paul Frère, separately, declared the GTC, in 1966, as one of the best GTs ever made, and over 600 left the factory between 1966 and '68. Even today, those who have owned many Ferraris proclaim the GTC to be the best driving of all the vintage V12s. Cheap by two-seat Ferrari standards, GTCs regularly change owners for $60,000 to $100,000.

Prices of GTCs bottomed in the mid-'70s, and long-term owners have enjoyed modest but not spectacular appreciation. I recall the warning that Mike Gorley, our service manager at FAF (the authorized dealer in Atlanta of which I was the majority owner) and a long-term GTC owner, gave me in 1977: "Better buy a GTC, they will be over $10,000 before the end of the year."

This car was previously sold at a 1995 auction for about $80,000. Assuming that the seller at Bonhams was the earlier purchaser of the car, he got a firsthand education about the dangers of buying an older, newly painted, good-looking "exotic." Prior to his 1995 purchase, he probably realized that most 28-year-old cars that haven't been completely and competently restored have some critical components that need attention, such as worn valve guides, leaky rings, weeping water pumps, weak synchros, etc.

However, it's doubtful that he realized the full extent of his potential liability. From the figures in the catalog, it appears that he "invested" $127,000 in just the purchase and repair bills, and assuming a normal Bonhams 10% seller's commission, he netted about $56,000. So the 5,300 miles he drove cost approximately $71,000, or $13/mile. Which, by the way, makes our Editor's $1.76/mile cost for his recently sold Mondial seem downright reasonable.

How do you avoid the fiscal immolation this hapless owner endured? First, remember that on any under-$100k 12-cylinder exotic, the three most important factors are condition, condition and condition. So if buying in a venue where you can't do a test drive or have your mechanic check out a car, do what the new owner did here: Buy an exotic with a fistful of repair invoices.

Bonhams

You will be much further ahead than if you buy a rat, even a handsome one, and fix it yourself. Why? Well, due to some unexplained law of economics, repairs are much cheaper if you buy them from the previous owner rather than your mechanic. Just as you don't get 100% of your money back for home improvements, so too with car restorations.

This particular car is a prime, although not unusual, example of how the market discounts repairs. The seller bought the car for $80,000, put in $58,000, and got back $56,000. The buyer, on the other hand, bought the car for less than the 1995 price and got all the repairs thrown in for free.

As the car has only covered 1,700 miles since the 1998 engine work, the new owner will probably have to adjust the valves, clean the carbs and fool with the advance weights in the distributors (that's plural). But even with all that, I would have to say he's going to come out just fine on this.

At $71,435, the new owner can put another $10,000 into this car for cosmetic enhancements without going under water.

Sometimes at auctions the forces of audience enthusiasm conspire to push a car to unexpectedly high prices. At other times, lack of the same, and, I would hazard to say in this case, a failing paint job leading to an unexciting visual presentation, means that someone got a good buy.

GTCs will never have the values or visual panache of their predecessor, the 275 GTB. But they are much more satisfying to drive. And this car appears to be ready to give its new owner quite a few good miles of motoring, and maybe even at a reasonable cost per mile. I hope the seller had a business use for his Ferrari so that he can at least use the loss as a write-off.
—John Apen

Years produced	1966-68
Number produced	600
Original list price	Approx. $17,100, with A/C, radio, power windows
SCM Price Guide	$85,000-$125,000
Chassis #	Right front chassis rail, plate on right inner fender
Engine #	Right side, near starter motor, back of block
Tune-up/major service	$3,000-$3,500
Distributor cap	$300+
Club	Ferrari Club of America, P.O. Box 720597, Atlanta, GA 30358
Web site	www.ferrariclubofamerica.org
Alternatives	Maserati Ghibli Spider, Jaguar XKE Series I roadster, Iso Grifo
SCM Investment Grade	B

(Historic and descriptive information courtesy of Bonhams.)
From the July 2003 issue of *SCM*.◆

1971 Ferrari Competition Daytona

Chassis number: 13971
Engine number: 001M

Ferrari's first modern luxury Grand Touring Berlinetta—striking looks, an exhaust note to die for, big horsepower and a top speed few would ever find

From the stable of arch enthusiast and consummate perfectionist, the late Aldo Cudone, comes this fearsome Daytona. It was prepared to competition specification in 1981 for *Signor* Cudone in the workshops of Giuliano Michelotto, the factory-appointed tuner responsible for the 308 Group 4, F40 LM, 333SP and many other Ferrari racing cars. This work was carried out under the supervision of Gaetano Florino, head of *Ferrari Assistenza Clienti* at the time, without regard to expense.

In the modern classic car market, the big four-cam V12 front-engined Ferrari Daytona is rightly regarded as offering a tremendous amount of machinery—and of public road performance—for the money such cars cost. Most sought-after of all, however, are the handful of Daytonas assembled for endurance racing in the *Assistenza Clienti* center neighboring the old pre-war Scuderia Ferrari building.

Acquired from second owner Clementino Borghi by Aldo Cudone in 1981, this Daytona was uprated to full factory specification by Michelotto (mechanics) and Bacchelli & Villa (bodywork). Works drawings were made available—after all, the Daytona had been racing until 1979 and the know-how was still fresh.

The riveted Group 4 bodywork includes six side exhausts, flared arches covering wider competition wheels, full height faired headlamps, air splitters atop front fenders, a chin spoiler, twin exterior fuel fillers, plexiglass side windows and a single pantograph wiper.

Inside, the cabin is trimmed in lightweight materials and there are harnesses for both occupants, plus a fire extinguisher, roll cage and other competition necessities. Nonetheless, the trunk still manages to accommodate a space-saver spare and full tool kit.

Mechanically, the car was fully rebuilt by Michelotto to competition specs. Although we do not have a record of the horsepower figures, the presentation of the engine bay, dominated by the ram air induction box, speaks for itself.

Judging from its still concours condition 20 years later, *Sig.* Cudone's "Comp Daytona" was used most sparingly. We know he drove the car, accompanied by an Italian rally ace, on the 1985 Coppa d'Italia, but since then the car appears to have been carefully stored in climate-controlled conditions. It is offered today by his family with current FIA testament to the enthusiasm and perfectionism of one man and the talent of two great Ferrari specialists.

This car sold for $239,960, including buyer's premium, at the Bonhams & Brooks Monaco sale, May 21, 2001.

The 365 GTB/4 Daytona was Ferrari's first modern luxury Grand Touring Berlinetta, with striking looks, an exhaust note to die for, big horsepower and a top speed few would ever find.

Initially priced at $19,000 in 1969, production ceased in 1974 with a price tag of just over $25,000. As production ended, the first of several gas crises hit and prices plummeted—I bought an alloy Comp Daytona prototype in mid-1974 for a mere $14,000. Daytona prices peaked in 1989 when a good "street" Daytona would easily bring $500,000. Prices dropped below $100,000 by 1995 and have rebounded slightly in the last five years to the $100,000-$125,000 range for a good, clean, no-stories car.

Bonhams & Brooks

Almost 1,400 365 GTB/4s were built, and although never intended to be race cars, a few were indeed prepared by privateers and raced successfully. A mere 15 Competition lightweights were built with factory support and raced very successfully, with multiple class wins at Le Mans, Daytona, the Tour de France and at virtually every other major racing event on the planet. These very desirable factory-built competition cars bring as much as $1,500,000 today for a Le Mans class winner, and sell quickly when on the market.

With the few factory-built competition cars commanding a huge premium, there has long been a demand for non-factory built competition cars for club racing and for those who want the ultimate in a 1970s Ferrari "bad boy" street car.

I know of 33 non-factory Competition 365 GTB/4 Cs built over the years. The very few privateers' cars with period Le Mans, Daytona or Sebring race histories command a substantial premium, while those with no race history are the club racers' bargain basement buy, available as cheaply as $125,000—about the cost of the competition conversion.

When I inspected this car at Aldo Cudone's Padova race shop in October 1997, the quality, authenticity and money spent on its conversion were instantly obvious. With bodywork by Bacchelli & Villa and mechanical and race preparation by Michelotto, the work was to the highest standards in Italy and, bluntly, to higher standards than when the factory-built Competition cars were new.

While this example is a non-factory car and has no race history from the 1970s, and so is not eligible for most first-tier European rally events, it brought a price of almost $100,000 more than recent sales of similar but lesser-quality cars. This is further proof that "the best" will always bring the best prices.—Michael Sheehan

(Historic data and photo courtesy of auction company.)

From the September 2001 issue of *SCM*.◆

Years produced	1969-74
Number produced	1,273
Original price	$19,000 (1969)
SCM Price Guide	$105,000-$140,000
Tune-up/major service	$3,000
Distributor cap	$200
Chassis #	Steering column and on frame near right front suspension pickup points
Engine #	Right side of engine block near flywheel
Clubs	Ferrari Club of America, Box 720597, Atlanta, GA 30358; Ferrari Owners Club, 8642 Cleta St. Downey, CA 90241
Web sites	www.ferrariclubofamerica.org; www.FerrariOwnersClub.org
Alternatives:	Two Maserati Ghiblis, four Ford SVO Mustangs or a single 289 Cobra

1972 365 GTS/4

Chassis number: 15845
Engine number: B1576

I drove all night and most of the next day, enthralled by the wonderful V12 sounds whipping by in the wind

This unique car is that most mythical of beasts, a genuine one-owner-from-new Daytona Spyder. We know of just one other, a North American-specification model resident in the U.S. Ferrari sold just 121 Daytona Spyders. Left-hand drive chassis number 15845 (the car offered here) is one of just 25 built to European specification (seven of which were right-hand drive). This car is one of two sold to Germany. It was delivered finished in classic Rosso Chiaro featuring original black leather upholstery. A total of 52,000 kilometers is displayed on the odometer. 15845 was delivered new via German Ferrari importer Auto-Becker to its first and only owner. Some cosmetic refurbishment of stone chips is reported, but apart from that the paintwork remains original, as does the very presentable leather interior. The engine, never rebuilt, has been properly maintained. The car is presented in commensurately good condition today, having been owned by the same individual for its entire life and thus never exposed to the potential vicissitudes of numerous ownership changes. Over the years, its owner has consistently rejected approaches from would-be purchasers, preferring to offer it today at auction. Although well known, this car has not been exhibited at the usual historic events, thus its new owner will be able to enjoy the privilege of showing it to an appreciative public for the first time. 15845 comes complete with original documentation, warranty card, brown leather owner's wallet, instruction books, tool kit, duplicate keys, sundry service invoices and German registration papers.

The SCM analysis: This car sold for $365,500, including buyer's premium, at Bonhams Europe Nürburgring auction held August 9, 2003.

Convertible versions of newer Ferraris like the 355 Spider and 360 Spider may substantially outsell their closed brothers, but that wasn't always the case. U.S. dealers once struggled to sell ragtop Ferraris like California Spyders and NART Spyders, and European distributors often wouldn't order them at all. The production of any convertible V12 Ferrari seldom broke 100 examples and the total production of all convertible V12s didn't pass 1,000 units until the 550 Barchettas were built in 2001.

In the late 1970s the Daytona Spyder began to break this stigma. As speed limits and insurance costs began to restrict how people drove, beauty and rarity gained greater importance in a Ferrari purchase than ultimate performance. Open Ferraris became more popular and the beautiful Daytona Spyder began to creep into the garages and onto the wish lists of many collectors.

By the early 1980s, the desirability of the Daytona Spyder was high enough to make it an early entry into the speculator's market. This reached a feverish level by the end of the decade and thanks to the fancy trading of some enterprising dealers, prices broke the million-dollar mark. Like many of those '80s high fliers, the Daytona Spyder is worth about a third of that high value today. Unfortunately, along with the deflation in price came a decrease in status. The bubble market for Daytona Spyders led to a proliferation of counterfeits, mostly converted Daytona coupes or rebodied Corvettes. Their existence continues to stifle the desirability of the originals and dilute the market.

The Ferrari Market Letter has records of 113 Daytona coupes that were converted to Spyders. The actual number is probably higher, and may even exceed the 121 factory-built Spyders. Like Cobra replicas and other clones, these conversions are parasites, feeding off the rarity and value of the original models. As this population grows, owners and prospects for original cars are turned off by the loss of exclusivity and the value of the original models is stunted.

I was fortunate enough to drive a Daytona Spyder from Iowa to Atlanta in the early 1980s. It was mid-summer so I threw back the top in the seller's driveway and left it down for the duration of my trip. I drove all night and most of the next day, enthralled by the wonderful V12 sounds whipping by in the wind. Handling, acceleration and comfort were all impressive, though the arduous steering at low speeds and marginal braking performance were notable shortfalls.

This Daytona Spyder's original owner is none other than Dr. Hans Riegel, the German Willy Wonka. Riegel built his personal fortune as the proprietor of confectionery company HARIBO (HAns RIegel from BOnn). While his candy empire may not be a household name in the U.S., you might recognize the logo and packaging of the company's gummi bears. 15845 spent the past few years in a candy warehouse at HARIBO, its existence and location common knowledge in collector circles.

With the provenance and authenticity of the car undeniable, the real question here was the car's condition. It had been driven over 55,000 kilometers (34,000 miles) and although never abused, the car was hardly pampered. The auction house made every effort to exploit the unique one-owner history but in the end it didn't seem to matter—after all, once the car changed hands, it's just another two-owner Daytona Spyder. The selling price was appropriate for the condition of the car and both the buyer and the new owner should be pleased.—Steve Ahlgrim

(Historical and descriptive information courtesy of Bonhams Europe.)

From the December 2003 issue of *SCM*.◆

Years produced:	1970–74
Number produced:	121
Original list price:	approx. $25,000
SCM Price Guide:	$300,000-$375,000
Tune-up/major service:	$3,500
Distributor cap:	$513
Chassis #:	on frame, above right front spring mount
Engine #:	below head on rear passenger's side of block
Club:	Ferrari Club of America, P.O. Box 720597, Atlanta, GA 30358
Web site:	www.FerrariClubofAmerica.com
Alternatives:	1969-1970 Aston Martin DB6 Mk2 Volante, 1971-1972 Maserati Ghibli SS Spider
SCM Investment Grade:	A

2001 550 Barchetta Pininfarina

There is always a good following for convertible Ferraris, especially ones that are attractive and have exceptional performance

Chassis number: 87985

To mark the world-renowned Carrozzeria's 70th anniversary in 2000, Ferrari invited Sergio Pininfarina to submit designs for a front-engined roadster that would capture the spirit of past Maranello classics, such as the 166 Mille Miglia, 250 GT California Spyder and 365 GTS/4 Daytona Spyder. In its manufacturer's own words: "Ferrari has always created very special runs of cars, and the 550 Barchetta Pininfarina was developed with the aim of being a unique Ferrari—one that deliberately seeks to be more provocative and less rational than the rest of the range."

By "less rational" Ferrari was referring to the fact that the car was exclusively intended for open-air use, its only weather protection being a manually erected soft top for emergencies. The Barchetta's stylish interior emphasizes the car's sporting nature, featuring carbon-fiber race seats trimmed in leather, while the rear roll bar and specially strengthened windshield surround provide additional structural reinforcement. The all-alloy, 48-valve, 5.5-liter V12 engine is the same as that of the 550 Maranello, developing 485 hp at 7,000 rpm for a top speed of 185 mph.

As well as Pininfarina's 70th anniversary, the introduction of the 550 Barchetta celebrated 50 years of collaboration between Ferrari and Italy's most famous Carrozzeria. Announced Ferrari: "As such, only a limited run of 448 cars will leave the Maranello factory gates during 2001, each individually numbered and carrying a plaque inside with the car's own serial number and Sergio Pininfarina's signature."

Chassis number 124036 was supplied by Ferrari concessionaire Forza Spa, of Turin, Italy, in May 2001. The total distance traveled to date is 7,500 km. Offered in as-new condition, the car is Italian registered and comes with cover, books and tools.

This car sold for $209,595, including buyer's premium, at the Bonhams Olympia auction held December 2, 2002.

Years produced	2000-02
Number produced	448
Original list price	approx. $258,000
SCM Price guide	$325,000-$350,000
Tune-up/major service	$6,500
Distributor cap	N/A
Chassis #	Frame rail, passenger's side of engine compartment
Engine #	Passenger's side of engine in front, just under where head meets block
Club	Ferrari Club of America, P.O. Box 720597, Atlanta, GA 30358; Ferrari Owner's Club, 8642 Cleta St., Downey, CA 90241
Web site	www.FerrariClubofAmerica.org; www.FerrariOwnersClub.org
Alternatives	Ferrari Daytona Spyder, Lamborghini Diablo SVT roadster, Ferrari 330 GTS
SCM Investment Grade:	B

The 550 Barchetta was introduced with the slickest marketing plan in Ferrari's history. It began with Ferrari announcing plans to make a small run of a convertible version of the 550 Maranello, which would be built in limited numbers and inherit the heritage of the special Spyders before it.

The super-customers who made the list were invited to Italy for tours and events, including a lavish reception and unveiling of the Barchetta at Luca di Montezemolo's personal estate. The marketing plan worked, and the entire Barchetta production was immediately sold out at the list price of approximately $258,000 each.

A darker view of the plan might note that the Barchetta was introduced at the tail end of the 550 Maranello's production. Supply had begun to exceeded demand and prices were sliding. The 550's replacement, the 575 Maranello, was not ready for production yet and something needed to be done to shore up the sales. The marketing department called for a "special edition" and the Barchetta was the answer to the call.

Bonhams

Although these handpicked buyers had to sign an agreement promising not to sell their 550s for one year, or to sell them back to Ferrari, in fact they began changing hands immediately. The feeding frenzy initiated by speculators and "gotta have one" buyers quickly drove prices upwards of $475,000.

Now, two years later, Barchetta spotter Greg Rossier recently noted 38 Barchettas advertised. The turnover is not unreasonably high for an exotic car, but it is more than expected considering Ferrari's customer selection process. The lack of a serious top has been cited as a reason from a few owners who were selling their Barchettas, but it's more likely profit taking and a "been there, done that, what's the next flavor of the month car" attitude that's actually fueling sales.

The price brought by this Barchetta is highly influenced by the fact that Europeans do not have the same appreciation for convertibles as Americans. An open car is an impractical vehicle for high-speed Autobahn travel and a topless car would be almost useless in rainy England. An equivalent Euro-spec Barchetta, with EPA/DOT paperwork, should bring $20,000 to $40,000 more in the US. A US car in the same condition, but with fewer miles, would bring $300,000 to $325,000.

The buyer of this Barchetta appears to have gotten a good deal. His purchase price was at the very low end of the presale estimate and, surprisingly, less than the original purchaser paid for the car. This price trend should cross the pond to the States soon enough, but the sky won't fall completely. There is always a good following for convertible Ferraris, especially ones that are attractive and have exceptional performance, like the Barchetta. It won't be another Daytona Spyder in terms of value or long-term blue-chip standing in the Ferrari pecking order, but neither will it ever be a Straman-cut Testarossa.

As an aside, prior to the Barchetta, Ferrari had built fewer than 1,000 open V12 Ferraris in its entire history, with production runs from just a handful to 200. They have always enjoyed a good following and premium resale values. The Barchetta's production of 448 cars was nearly 50% of the total of all the open-top V12 Ferraris produced in the previous half century, and as we all know, high production numbers and ultra-high values never go hand in hand.—Steve Ahlgrim

(Historic and descriptive information courtesy of Bonhams.)

1951 Ferrari 340 America Berlinetta

Chassis number: 0148A

Think 340 America modified to race in *The Fast and the Furious*

Christie's

Ferrari S/N 0148A is part of a very aristocratic lineage of Ferraris, as it is equipped with the famous Lampredi V12, which would go on to contribute to Ferrari's first victories in F1 in its 375 F1 version. In the 340 version, the 4101-cc engine develops 260 hp at 6500 rpm. It was a legendary motor that was several steps above the standard 250 production unit, and went on to spawn its elder siblings, the 375 MM and 410 Sport, of fearsome reputation for their power. This notoriety is reflected in both the type's rarity and also the famous owners that were destined to enjoy the 340 America series.

This car, bodied by Ghia, was first built for Michel Paul Cavalier, president of a large French industrial concern. The distinguished Monsieur Cavalier became one of Ferrari's first repeat customers—and thus a precious one—as well as a friend. While little is known about him, he became perhaps the only non-Italian member of the early Ferrari board, and it is believed that his industrial savvy was most useful as the factory's growth mushroomed amidst the hectic demands of competition and Maranello's engineering development.

Cavalier owned several very special Ferraris through the years, cars that were tailor-made for him, and it is a measure of his lore in Ferrari history that these cars are now to be found in several of the finest collections. S/N 0148A remained in France after Cavalier sold it to a watch merchant, who in turn passed it on to Michael Dovaz. The latter has a rather infamous private museum in Nemours, France, where it stayed for a number of years before passing on to a Parisian doctor and then a Dutchman.

The current owner bought this car and then subjected it to a frame-off restoration. This was undertaken in Italy by Zagato with the aid of Galbiati, who specializes in aluminum bodies—a definite plus since S/N 0148A is believed to be the only alloy-bodied car in this small series. The engine, which was already in running order, was rebuilt by Michel Magnin.

The 340 was painted in a dark blue, while the interior has fully redone leather seats in a lighter shade of blue with matching carpets. All chrome elements have been impeccably renewed. The car has since taken part in the 1999 Mille Miglia, where it was driven by French connoisseur Marc Souvrain for its current owner.

Historic Ferraris do not come with a much better pedigree than this, and S/N 0148A would make a great road/rally machine or a very prominent concours entry.

This car sold for $391,000, including buyer's premium, at the Christie's Pebble Beach sale, August 19, 2001.

This 340 has been on the market for some time. Last year, the Parisian owner had been asking for about $600k. On December 18, 2000, it was offered at the Poulain Le Fur auction in Paris, where it was supposedly bid to $445k without selling. Obviously, as time passed the owner faced reality and lowered his asking price until he reached an accurate market valuation.

Interestingly enough, the selling price at Christie's was almost exactly mid-way between the $350k-$450k estimate. While very nicely restored, and looking very racy, $391k is all the money for a car that looks faster than it actually is. S/N 0148A is not a race car. It does have an even-numbered chassis, as do most of the early Ferrari race cars. But all Lampredi-engined V12s, as this one is, carry even chassis numbers, whether they were competition cars or boulevard cruisers. This is just another anomaly in the Ferrari chassis numbering sequence.

The Ghia body, regarded as visually-challenged by some, has been improved (or is that customized?) by having its heavy-looking bumpers removed, one-inch wider Borrani wheels fitted at the rear, a boy-racer quick-filler fuel cap added, lightweight competition seats installed and side and hood scoops added. Think 340 America modified to race in "The Fast and the Furious."

The restoration of S/N 0148A was done to a visually stunning standard, although I could have done without the overly generous application of silver paint to its aluminum underhood mechanical components.

Thanks to its alloy body, even chassis number (even if not competition sourced) and its robust, torquey 340 engine, this car will provide its owner with more than adequate performance, decent comfort and entry into everything from the Mille Miglia to the Tour de France and Monterey Historics.

The previous owner paid about $400k for this car, unrestored. We can assume that the restoration cost another $200k, making the seller's "investment" around $600k, coincidentally the same as the original asking price for the car. As the new owner paid just $400k but got a restored car instead of a project, this car should be considered well bought.—Michael Sheehan

(Historic data and photo courtesy of auction company.)

From the December 2001 issue of *SCM*.◆

Year produced	1951
Number produced	12 Berlinettas, 13 Spyders
Original price	N/A
SCM Price Guide	$350,000-$475,000
Tune-up/major service	$5,000
Distributor cap	$800
Chassis #	Driver's side, behind front crossmember, stamped on chassis
Engine #	Middle of block between cylinder heads
Club	Ferrari Club of America, Box 720597, Atlanta, GA 30358; Ferrari Owner's Club, 8642 Cleta St., Downey, CA 90241
Web site	www.ferrariclubofamerica.org; www.FerrariOwnersClub.org
Alternatives	Maserati A6G2000 Zagato coupe, Fiat 8V Zagato

1957 Ferrari 250 GT PF Cabriolet Series I

Chassis number: 0783
Engine number: 0783

For those too young to remember Rubirosa's escapades or too jaded to be impressed, the price is also justified by the aesthetics and rarity of this Pinin Farina design

RM Auctions

Porfirio Rubirosa was an accomplished competition driver, finishing second at Sebring with the Lancia factory team in 1954 and first in class (500 Mondial Spyder) in the Governor's Cup race in Nassau in 1955. He also scored a class win at Sebring in 1956 with Jim Pauley in his 500 Mondial.

The quintessential playboy as well, Rubi dallied exuberantly and publicly with a number of high-profile women, including Zsa Zsa Gabor, Ava Gardner, Kim Novak and Eva Peron. It was only natural that a man who combined serious racing with other, more hedonistic pleasures would want a car that was both sexy and fast. Hence, Rubi commissioned his own version of the SI PF Cabriolet from Ferrari and Pinin Farina.

And this is that very car. It is fitted with a pair of interchangeable windscreens that can be changed in four hours from a cutdown plexiglass racing screen to the stock full height windshield that accepts a folding soft top to protect the occupants from the elements. Its more luxurious accoutrements balance racing type hood catches and a faired headrest.

Restored in its original colors of red and tan leather, and in its dual-purpose configuration by the late George Frochen in 1984, the "Café Racer" has appeared at the Monterey Historic races and Ferrari events since, but has been otherwise little used. With the exception of the prototypes, it is the most personal and unique of this very attractive and desirable series.

RM Auctions sold this car for $671,000, including buyer's premium, in Phoenix, Arizona, January 19, 2001. It was purchased by an SCM *reader whose day job involves the movie industry. This price is 12% over* SCM*'s Price Guide high of $600,000, which itself is up 31% in the last year. It's the highest price paid at auction for a Series I Cabriolet since #0849 was sold by Christie's at their May 1990 Monaco auction for $754,400. (Adjusted for inflation today, that would be $1,029,200.) Rubi's "Café Racer" was itself sold at the Brooks Quail Lodge auction in 1999 for $530,500.*

The high current price may be a reflection of the perceived value of having a car that belonged to one of the great womanizers of history. For those too young to remember Rubirosa's escapades or too jaded or politically correct to be impressed, the price is also justified by the aesthetics and rarity of this Pinin Farina design. Many feel that the elegant, covered-headlight, early Cabriolet is one of the most beautiful open cars Farina ever built. It was the precursor of the even more valuable California Spyder. As a testimony to their desirability, 39 of the 40 SI PF Cabriolets originally built are still thought to exist. Long-time SCM *subscriber John Clinard has owned an SI PF Cabriolet for many years and refused to part with it during the late '80s boom even when offered near Defense Department sums by then flush and world-conquering Japanese collectors.*

Never intended for racing, the Series I Cabriolets were the luxury cars of the 250 Grand Turismos in 1957-62. The Scaglietti-designed California Spyder cost $11,600. The PF Coupe was priced at $12,450, the same price as an alloy-bodied competition Tour de France Berlinetta. The SI Farina Cabriolet cost $14,950. In today's dollars, this would be $89,000, or $20K more than the California. But it included chrome wires, leather interior, a heater, and driving lights. If you had bought yours from John von Neuman's Ferrari Representatives of California, you might have had it serviced by a talented young mechanic named Richie Ginther.

Years produced	1956-59
Number produced	40 (including 4 prototypes)
Original price	$14,950
SCM Price Guide	$450,000-$600,000
Tune-up/major service	$1,000-$1,500
Distributor cap	12 lead, not available
Chassis #	Plate on firewall
Engine #	Right rear engine mount
Clubs	Ferrari Club of America, Box 720597, Atlanta, GA 30358; Ferrari Owners Club, 8642 Cleta St., Downey, CA 90241
Web sites	www.ferrariclubofamerica.org; www.FerrariOwnersClub.org
Registry	jeffreyrowe@compuserve.com
Alternatives	Ferrari 250 LWB California Spyder, Aston Martin DB4GT Zagato

The Series I Cabriolets were in production from 1956 to 1959. There were forty built, including four prototypes. The first three prototypes were true "Spyders" lacking roll-up side windows. The second of these Spyders had many features borrowed from competition cars: a metal tonneau over the passenger seat, a short Plexiglas windshield, and an aerodynamic headrest tapering to the rear. This second prototype was probably the inspiration for Rubi's "Café Racer," which, with its vestigial windshield, outside gas filler cap, and external racing style hood latches, is arguably the sexiest of all the production SI Cabriolets.

The SIs were followed by the Series II PF Cabriolets, with approximately 200 built through 1962. With far more sober styling, including open headlights and clunky bumpers, they are the cheapest V12 open Ferraris, and struggle to reach the $150,000 level.

The SI Cabriolet shown here was restored in the late '80s, to a high standard, and the aerodynamic headrest fairing added. Well sorted, it is ready for immediate use. This is a current new high price for a Series I, but is justified by the beauty of the car and its impeccable history. The Ferrari market today, far wiser than it was a decade ago, is continuing to place ever-higher values on the truly special cars from Maranello, and letting the more common serial production cars languish.—John Apen

(Historical information and photo courtesy of auction company.)

From the May 2001 issue of *SCM*.◆

1958 Ferrari 250 GT Berlinetta TdF

Chassis number: 0911 GT
Engine number: 0911 GT

More than adequate horsepower to quickly run away from virtually any competitor of its time, including Corvettes, 300SLs and Jaguar XK 140s

RM Auctions

Twenty-six-year-old Luigi Taramazzo's first success with S/N 0911 GT (one of the most famous and successful of all Ferrari racing cars) came shortly after taking delivery in 1958. He brought it home second in class and sixth overall at the Coppa delia Consuma, behind the more experienced Eduardo Lualdi, also driving a 250 GT TdF. Three weeks later, he was the overall winner of the 1958 Mille Miglia, with co-driver Gerino Gerini. (The last true open-road Mille Miglia was held in 1957. The 1958 event was modeled after the Tour de France, with wheel-to-wheel competition on closed circuits.) The duo were consistent leaders from the event start and captured first place overall by 1 hour and 25 minutes, beating the team of Villotti/Zampiero, who were also driving a 250 GT.

Taramazzo continued his string of successes with 0911 GT following the Mille Miglia against intense competition in Italian national championship races. Taramazzo and 0911 GT captured the class win in the important Trentio-Bondone hill climb on July 13, where he finished seventh overall. Only a week later Taramazzo and 0911 GT won overall at the Garessio-San Bernardo.

The prestigious and important Coppa Intereuropa, a one-hour timed event, was held at Monza on September 7, the weekend of the Italian GP. On the demanding 4.65-mile Grand Prix course in a race that drew the finest competitors in Italy, Taramazzo brought 0911 GT home first overall and of course, first in GT class. With an average of 107.2 mph, he was only 13.8 mph off the GT-winning speed of Tony Brooks's Van Wall Grand Prix car.

In the Fontedecimo-Giovi hill climb on September 28, Taramazzo and 0911 captured second overall and first in GT. At the Coppa San Ambrocus at Monza, in another contest with his rival Lualdi, Taramazzo came home second overall and in GT. With this podium finish, he garnered enough points to be crowned the Italian National GT champion—one of the most coveted titles in Europe—after a closely contested season.

Taramazzo would race once more in 0911 GT before trading the car back to Ferrari. The list of subsequent owners of 0911 GT is extensive until it found a long-term home with author and Ferrari historian John Starkey in the UK in 1980.

In brilliantly restored condition, and with an unmatched provenance, 0911 GT must be considered one of the most important vintage Ferraris extant.

This car sold for $1.265m, including commission, at the RM Monterey auction, held August 18, 2001.

The 250 GT put Ferrari on the map as the best, fastest and most consistent of the GT racers of its day. Winning the grueling Tour de France in both 1956 and 1957 earned it the popular name of 250 "TdF."

In theory, the 250 TdF was available to anyone with the ability to write a check to the local Ferrari dealer for $12,000. In fact, the very best cars, with the latest camshafts, pistons and lightweight parts were reserved for the best-known and most talented drivers. Even so, a "mildly tuned" 250 TdF was more than adequate to quickly run away from virtually any competitor of its time, including Corvettes, 300SLs and Jaguar XK 140s.

This car had been crashed and repaired during its arduous competition life, and the shape of the front body is certainly open to some questions as to how true it is to the original shape. Nonetheless, its eyeball appeal, superb provenance and first-rate presentation by the auction company helped propel the sale price past expectations.

S/N 0911 GT, consigned by a longtime SCM *subscriber, was well known to the dealer/broker crowd in attendance at the DoubleTree Hotel. They knew it had been bought just a year ago for less than $1 million. Its 30% jump in value brought a collective gasp from those same dealers and brokers, who thought the market for high-end Ferraris might be softening.*

The turmoil in the global economy that resulted from the terrorist attacks on America has not begun to settle. Whether money will flow from stocks into cars, and whether high-end cars will suffer as those who play in that market turn their attention to other things, is yet to be determined. What is clear, however, is that whichever way the market goes, superb cars with documented histories, like this one, will always command a premium when put in front of the right audience.—Michael Sheehan

(Historic data and photo courtesy of auction company.)

From the November 2001 issue of *SCM.*◆

Years produced	1956-59
Number produced	77
Original list price	$12,000
SCM Price Guide	"Standard" TdF $700,000-$900,000; 14-louver comp. $1m-$1.5m; Zagato-bodied $1.5m-$1.75m
Tune-up	$1,500
Distributor cap	$500 for two
Chassis #	Front frame tube
Engine #	Engine rear mount
Club	Ferrari Club of America, Box 720597, Atlanta, GA 30358; Ferrari Owner's Club, 8642 Cleta St., Downey, CA 90241
Web site	www.ferrariclubofamerica.org; www.FerrariOwnersClub.org
Alternatives	250 SWB, 250 MM

1959 250 GT LWB California Spyder

Chassis number: 1581 GT
Engine number: 1581 GT

This California may have run great and driven strong, but it will need at least a complete major service before the new owner tries the Copperstate Rally again

Luigi Chinetti, the famous American importer and driver, convinced Enzo Ferrari to produce an open version of the highly successful competition 250 Berlinetta. The resultant "Spyder California" was clearly aimed at the American market, and the first prototype was completed in December of 1957. Its mechanical specification was very similar to the 250 GT Tour de France. The Pininfarina design was built by Scaglietti and provided an elegant two-seater sports car that has to this day lost none of its appeal.

Including alloy-bodied vehicles, only 51 long-wheelbase Spyder Californias were built, and this was the 41st car produced. It has traveled 25,546 miles since new, the paintwork is polished through in places and there are some minor scratches. The panel fit of the doors is superb and the shut lines are excellent. The interior upholstery—black leather with darker red piping—has been carefully aged and now has that lovely, comfortable feel to it that cannot be replicated. There are some scuffs in one or two places and some of the carpeting has been replaced along the way. The instruments are all intact and the switchgear is original, not a single knob or switch broken or missing. The convertible top is older now and the rear plastic has faded yellow with time, but it fits tight and serves its purpose. The trunk has its original carpeting and the tool roll is mostly original. The wheels are probably the original Borranis and the chrome is fading now, although traces of the original Borrani decals can be seen. The external chromework such as the door handles and trunk lock and handle has also mellowed with age and the bumpers show signs of some parking nudges. Decals on the doors show that the car was driven on the 1994 Copperstate rally, since when it has been dry stored in Arizona.

This is an amazing time-warp Ferrari. It is also a long-wheelbase Spyder California—with disc brakes, covered headlights and documented two-owner history. The opportunity to acquire it is amazing and will probably never be repeated.

This car sold for $1,217,500, including buyer's premium, at Christie's Pebble Beach auction, held August 18, 2002.

My pocket guide to used-car advertising terms says paint that is "polished through in a few places" and has "some minor scratches" means the car needs to be repainted. "Carefully aged" 43-year-old leather means the seat panels have been resewn by hand where the thread has rotted. How is it that a car of dubious merit sells for twice the low estimate of $500,000? Call it Christie's Monterey magic, as well as the growing interest in cars that are original rather than restored.

In all fairness, the car in question was pretty special. It featured disc brakes and an outside spark plug engine found only in the late long-wheelbase Californias. It also had a documented and admirable history. Originally delivered to the highly successful amateur racer, Alfred E. "Erwin" Goldschmidt, the car was passed on to Bill Ruger when Goldschmidt's SWB California Spyder was due to arrive. Ruger was the founder of Sturm, Ruger & Company, the largest gun manufacturer in the US. While he was widely recognized as America's greatest gun designer, he was also an avid car collector with an impressive collection of more than 30 classic cars.

Christie's/Kevin Boegehold

Ruger bought #1581 when it was only about six months old. He used the car sparingly and in the mid-1960s the Spyder was retired and sent to his Arizona home. While certainly very original, this was not a survivor. Its paint was very thin, making the car a sure candidate for a respray—for rust prevention if nothing else. The interior really was starting to come apart and featured sections of Kmart-grade carpet. Even the underhood details, like incorrect spark plug wires and Pep Boys hose clamps, kept the car from being a wash 'n' show example.

Years produced	1957-60
Number produced	42
Original list price	$11,600
SCM Price Guide	$750,000-$1,000,000
Tune-up/major service	$2,000-$3,000
Distributor cap	$225, two needed for late-model LWBs
Chassis #	Left frame tube, front of engine compartment
Engine #	Right rear engine mount
Club	Ferrari Club of America, P.O. Box 720597, Atlanta, GA 30358; Ferrari Owner's Club, 8642 Cleta St., Downey, CA 90241
Web sites	www.FerrariClubofAmerica.org; www.FerrariOwnersClub.org
Alternatives	275 NART Spyder, TdF, PF Spyder Series I, Aston DB4 drophead
SCM Investment Grade	A

Christie's tried to represent the car as oozing with patina, but that wasn't the case. This California may have run great and driven strong, but it will need at least a complete major service before the new owner tries the Copperstate Rally again. The paint and the interior need work and can not be updated without making them noticeably nicer than the rest of the car. Without question, any serious refurbishing done will quickly avalanche into a full-blown restoration.

Good California Spyders are difficult to find. They're relatively rare and most are in the hands of well-heeled owners who simply aren't interested in selling them unless they get a price that exceeds the current market. Admittedly, the pre-auction estimate of $500,000 to $700,000 was low, and seemingly didn't take into account the value-add of the Ruger provenance. The buyer was a phone bidder who must have put a high value on the car's originality. At $1.2 million, he paid full market and then some, but in doing so set the new bar for California Spyder values.

More importantly, the new owner is getting a car with which he can set the standards for the restoration, without having to undo any shadetree body, paint or mechanical work. This is a true no-bad-stories car, and when properly and correctly restored, it will rank as one of the most collectible and desirable of the LWB Cal Spyders.
—Steve Ahlgrim
(Historic data courtesy of auction company.)

1961 Ferrari 250 GT SWB Berlinetta

The SWB is a car you can take to any event and know you brought the right car

Chassis number: 2549GT

By the late '50s it was apparent that Ferrari had perfected the dual-purpose gran turismo automobile with its line of 250 GTs. The Colombo-designed V12 had evolved into a powerful engine. More important in racing, where it's been said, "to finish first, you must first finish," it was reliable. That reliability carried over to 250 GTs that never saw the race track, creating confident, satisfied owners.

By 1961, competition pressure had persuaded Ferrari to create high-performance versions of the 250 GT SWB Berlinetta. Known as the 168 Comp./61s and sometimes called "SEFAC hot rods," one steel-bodied car, built during the construction of many of the Comp./61s, was delivered with a comprehensive selection of Comp./61 performance features, making it a true factory hot rod: 2549GT.

2549GT was built to US specifications. In addition to the Tipo 168F engine, it was built with a cold air box, 40-mm Weber carbs, aluminum front and rear bulkheads, outside fuel filler, ribbed alloy case competition transmission, full Abarth competition exhaust system with SNAP exhaust extractor tips, 8 x 34 (4.25:1) rear axle ratio, black-face competition instruments, a metal dashboard and single floor skins without insulation; all highly specific competition specification items. These features are documented in the Ferrari factory build sheets.

Chinetti sold 2549GT upon receipt to pioneer television entertainer and personality Dave Garroway, creator of The Today Show. He paid $17,900 for 2549GT, a premium of some 40% over the New York price of a standard 250 GT SWB Berlinetta. It was never raced, serving only as a road car for Garroway for a period of six years, until sold through Atlanta Ferrari dealer Don Fong to Terry King in 1967. King used the car as a daily driver for years, and then commenced a restoration that was, sadly, unfinished at the time of his death by cancer.

The engine benefited from improved porting and high-lift cams during its rebuild and now delivers more than the factory-rated 285 hp.

Organically sensual, superbly restored and uniquely configured, 2549GT is unique among the very small club of Ferrari dual-purpose gran turismos.

This Ferrari 250 GT SWB sold for $902,000, including buyer's premium, at the RM Arizona Biltmore sale, held January 18, 2002.

As the '50s came to a close, Enzo Ferrari found he needed to do something to improve the cornering speeds of his sports racers. He shortened his current chassis about eight inches to 2400 mm, and the short-wheelbase chassis was born. Pininfarina was selected to dress the chassis and the result was the impressive 250 GT Berlinetta, commonly called the SWB or Short Wheelbase.

RM Auctions

Years produced	1959-62
Number produced	approx. 90 steel-bodied cars, 75 alloy-bodied
Original list price	approx. $13,500
SCM Price Guide	Steel versions: $750,000-$850,000; Alloy versions: $950,000-$1,200,000; SEFAC hot rods: $1,500,000-$1,800,000
Tune-up/major service	$2,000
Distributor cap	$450 (two required)
Chassis #	Left frame member by steering box
Engine #	Right rear above motor mount
Club	Ferrari Club of America, PO Box 720597 Atlanta, GA 30358; Ferrari Owner's Club, 8642 Cleta St., Downey, CA 90241
Web site	www.FerrariClubofAmerica.com, www.FerrariOwnersClub.org
Alternative	Aston Martin DB4GT

Few Ferraris have the desirability of an SWB. They have a handsome profile that draws attention even when surrounded by more exotic machinery. The SWB is a car you can take to any event and know you brought the right car.

Terry King, a ballroom dance instructor in Atlanta, Georgia, bought this particular car when he was in his early 20s and it was the love of his life. He drove it through college, and, as it became a little tatty, he started taking it apart for refurbishing. One thing led to another and the project became a full-blown restoration. As the paint was removed, a seriously distorted front fender—a remnant of a previous botched repair—proved to be a financial hurdle that moved the restoration to the back burner. Over the next 10 years, as his salary allowed, Terry collected parts and restored pieces in preparation of the eventual reassembly. Unfortunately, as the bodywork was finally being performed, Terry succumbed to cancer and never got to see his beloved SWB in its finished state.

"They have a handsome profile that draws attention even when surrounded by more exotic machinery."

The auction text does an excellent job of portraying the unique virtues of SWB S/N 2549GT, but, at a price so close to the million-dollar mark, a very special car is expected. 2549GT is just a steel-bodied car without competition history. It was built at a time when special features were not uncommon and its performance is unproven. Its condition and pedigree brought a price just over the high end of the SCM *price guide, but $100,000 less than a more worn steel-bodied car with some competition history brought at the Bonhams Gstaad sale a month before.*

However, this was a smart purchase. The car has been out of circulation for decades and was relatively unknown, so the exposure it will get in the next few years will embellish its provenance. Purchased by an SCM *subscriber who uses his cars, we can expect to see the car at future historic events. I think Terry would be pleased.—Steve Ahlgrim*

(Historic data and photo courtesy of auction company.)

From the April 2002 issue of *SCM*.◆

1962 250 GT PF Cabriolet Series II

Chassis number: 3311
Engine number: 3311

Seemingly stored since the early '90s, if the fluids were freshened periodically and corrosion hasn't taken a toll on the block, the car may need only minor mechanical attention. If the storage were less than careful...

Effectively an open-top version of the Pininfarina-built 250GT Coupe, whose chassis and mechanics it shared, the Series II Cabriolet was built beside its closed cousin from its introduction in 1959 though end of production in 1962. It was the first Ferrari production car to use the new V12 developed in the racing division, the 128F engine. The major innovation was a revised cylinder head design, with outside spark plugs allowing 12 port heads and producing 240 hp in street form. The Series II had discs in place of drum brakes, and a new four-speed gearbox with overdrive.

Built towards the end of production, this example was delivered in Europe and subsequently has been in long-term ownership in Atlanta. Red with tan leather interior, it is offered with hardtop. Preserved in substantially original condition, it is reported as having an engine rebuild while in past ownership and is in fundamentally sound condition, though in need of some cosmetic refurbishment.

The SCM *analysis: Despite the entreaties of at least four suitors, this car stalled on the block at Bonhams' August 15, 2003, auction in Carmel, CA, at a reported high bid of $120,000. The after-block sale was reported at $135,000, including buyer's premium.*

Series II Cabriolets, long out of favor, have been increasing in value of late, with some cars fetching twice what they would have just a few years ago. Yet of all the convertible V12 Ferraris, they remain the least expensive. Blame the bland styling, similar to that of the unloved 250 GT coupe, for keeping collectors' interest at a low level.

Ferrari's established practice during the era this car was built was that Pininfarina would build the luxurious and more expensive models, while Scaglietti did the sportier, cheaper cars. The Series II Cabriolet was the most expensive car in the Ferrari line, and its conservative design was intended for older, mature Ferrari enthusiasts. The foil was the Scaglietti-built 250 California Spyder LWB, the Ferrari for the younger, sportier set.

The 250GT Cabriolet Series II carried soundproofing, undercoating and rudimentary corrosion protection and cost $15,000, while the Scaglietti-built California Spyder cost just $11,600. Conjecture has it that Pininfarina's conservative styling was a conscious effort to distinguish the Series II Cabriolet from its sporty sibling. Indeed, one reported reason for ending production of the Series I Cabriolet was that it was often mistaken for the much cheaper Scaglietti-built California, and even then, those who were spending big bucks for an exotic didn't want it mistaken for a less expensive model from the same manufacturer.

This was one of the lowest auction prices for a Series II PF Cab we've seen in the last year, falling at the bottom end of the SCM Price Guide's *$125,000-$245,000 range. Was it a good buy? That depends on whether you're the type who likes to gamble.*

The car had an older re-spray over the original paint, and it was in bad shape. The chrome was thin but the bumpers were fairly straight and the body appeared sound. The original seats were worn and the stuffing had collapsed—as they say, "suitable for patterns." The European instruments and all the knobs and little trim pieces were present and accounted for, and the steering wheel was surprisingly nice. The hardtop is a real plus, however it was not seen at the auction, so its condition could not be determined.

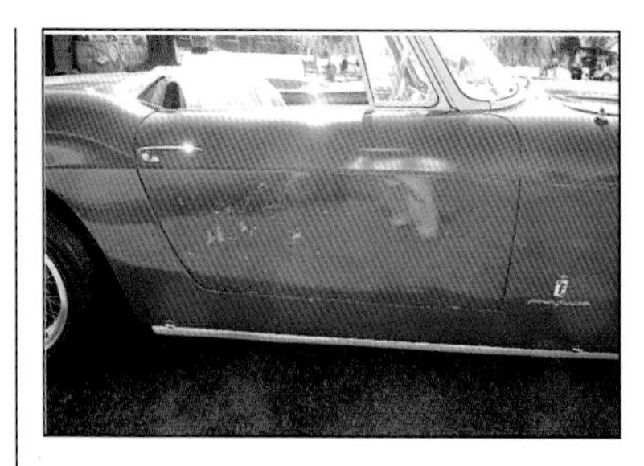

While restoration of the cosmetics would appear to be uncomplicated, requiring only money rather than long frustrating hours chasing missing pieces or rebuilding a rusty body, the mechanicals are much harder to assess.

A previous owner is stated to have had the engine rebuilt, though be careful in your interpretation of what this auction catalog statement means. A little research shows that this car was advertised for the last six months of 1987 by a knowledgeable and reputable North Carolina Ferrari dealer thusly: "Red/tan. Black un-restored hardtop. Two owners from new. Older restoration in beautiful condition. Recently rebuilt engine, no smoke. Drive anywhere. Gerald Roush, publisher of Ferrari Market Letter, drove it to and from National FCA meeting in 1987. $125,000."

So it seems that 16 years ago, in early 1988, the car arrived in Atlanta and was probably a nice driver then. The engine rebuild was likely well done, however, as far as can be determined, no major work has been done on the car since. Seemingly stored since the early '90s, if the fluids were freshened periodically and corrosion hasn't taken a toll on the block, the car may need only minor mechanical attention. If the storage was less than careful...

On the same weekend that this car sold, RM auctioned off a very nice 1- condition PF Cab SII, S/N 3407, for a record price of $258,500. It had been given a complete cosmetic restoration, with no engine work required. It was implied that the owner had recently spent about $100,000 on paint, interior, chroming, complete disassembly, and a rebuilding of the rear end.

So perhaps the buyer of the car pictured here could *achieve a #1 car after a simple paint stripping, re-spray and re-upholstery, for, say, $50,000. He would have then achieved the Holy Grail of the collecting hobby, buying a car where everything was as good or better than it seemed, and ending up with a fully restored car without getting buried. Care to wager?—John Apen*

(Background information courtesy of the auction company.)

From the March 2004 issue of *SCM*.◆

Years produced:	1959-62
Number produced:	200
Original list price:	$15,000
SCM Price Guide:	$125,000-$245,000
Tune-up/major service:	$1,000-$1,500
Distributor cap:	$300
Chassis #:	plate on firewall
Engine #:	right rear engine mount
Club:	Ferrari Club of America, P.O. Box 720597, Atlanta, GA 30358
Web site:	www.ferrariclubofamerica.org; www.ferrariownersclub.org
Alternatives:	1959-64 Maserati 3500GT Vignale Spyder, 1957-63 Mercedes 300SL Roadster, 1952-55 Siata 208S America roadster
SCM Investment Grade:	B

1963 Ferrari 250 GT Lusso

Chassis number: 5251
Engine number: 5251

The Lusso was not just about going fast from point A to point B; it was also about the style in getting there

Arguably the most beautiful product ever to carry the Maranello marque's prancing horse emblem, the 250 GT Lusso Berlinetta debuted at the Paris Salon in October 1962. Styled by Pininfarina and built by Scaglietti, the Lusso (luxury) combined racetrack looks with new high standards of passenger comfort. Beautifully proportioned, the new 250 GT blended a low-slung nose, reminiscent of that of the 400 Superamerica, with a sculpted Kamm tail by means of some of the most exquisite lines yet seen on an automobile. Slim pillars and wide expanses of glass not only enhanced the car's outward appearance but made for excellent visibility and a pleasantly light and airy interior.

Testing the 250 GT Lusso five years after its introduction, *Road & Track* magazine acknowledged that the design had already achieved classic status. "Although there were many variations on the basic Ferrari 250 GT since 1956 when this 3-liter series was first offered, the 1962-64 250 GT Berlinetta Lusso has come to be identifiable by that single word, Lusso. The design of the body was at once elegant and exciting, and no other road Ferrari before or since has earned the same degree of enduring admiration for its aesthetics."

One of just 350 250 GT Lussos made, this superbly presented example has been restored to the highest standards and is finished in classic red with black interior. A California car prior to its acquisition by the present owner, it has enjoyed the benefits of air-conditioned storage and is described by the vendor as in "excellent" condition in every department.

This car sold for $140,000, including buyer's premium, at the Bonhams & Brooks Cavallino auction, January 19, 2001.

The Ferrari 250 GT/L Berlinetta "Lusso" production started at approximately the end of the 250 GT Berlinetta SWB (short-wheelbase) production and the Lusso's production ended at the start of the 275 GTB's run. The Lusso was to be the last of the 250 series cars, and in its short two-year life, only 350 to 355 examples were built.

The 250 GT/L was powered by a Colombo-designed, 60-degree, 2953-cc (180 cubic inch) V12, producing 250 bhp at 7,000 rpm. This engine was mated to a Ferrari-built four-speed transmission. Overdrive was not offered.

The Lusso has been roundly criticized for not being a strong performer on the road. Indeed, it pales when compared to a lighter 250 SWB, or even with the later 330 GT 2+2. But the Lusso was not just about going fast from point A to point B; it was also about the style in getting there.

Inside, the Lusso is among the most distinctive of production Ferraris. The speedometer and tachometer are set in two large pods in the center of the dash, angled towards the driver's view, while the oil pressure, fuel and other gauges are in the driver's direct line of sight between the spokes of the Nardi steering wheel. Other unusual touches (for Ferrari, at least) include a horn button at the end of a stalk within reach of the driver's fingers, a one-piece seat with no articulation (only forward and back adjustment) and a quilted vinyl covering (echoing the underhood pad in many Ferraris) in the rear parcel area. Many owners found the parcel area a welcome addition, as the spare tire largely fills the trunk.

Bonhams & Brooks

Years produced	1963-64
Number produced	350
Original list price	$12,600
SCM Price Guide	$100,000-$135,000
Tune up/major service	$2,000-$2,500, including valve adjustment
Distributor cap	$325
Chassis #	On a plate on the firewall
Engine #	On right rear, under distributor
Clubs	Ferrari Club of America, Box 720597, Atlanta, GA 30358; Ferrari Owners Club, 8642 Cleta St., Downey, CA 90241
Web sites	www.ferrariclubofamerica.org; www.FerrariOwnersClub.org
Alternatives	Aston Martin DB5, Maserati Mistral, Lamborghini 350GTSpyder

Few would disagree that the Lusso is a beautiful car. A Pininfarina design with bodies built by Scaglietti, the organic lines flow from front to rear, devoid of most of the styling clichés that age many sports and GT cars from the early '60s. Practical observers will note that the car also lacks anything but the thinnest suggestion of bumpers, making both the front and rear end of the Lusso extremely vulnerable to the "park by touch" crowd. The construction of the 250GT/L is of steel, with aluminum hood, doors and trunk lid.

In the late '80s days of "Ferrari Fever," the Lusso became a half-million dollar automobile. Since the collapse of '91 and a brief stint below the $100,000 mark, the Lusso has settled in the $120,000 to $150,000 area for a strong #2 or weak #1 condition car. Superb examples have been known to bring more, and "story" cars or those needing attention are occasionally found below a hundred grand. To the investor who feels that because the Lusso was a $500,000 car in the past and will be again in the near future, I can only say don't hold your breath. The Lusso is a satisfying car to drive, and an exhilarating car to look at. The rewards of ownership of a Lusso are best measured in the heart, and not in the wallet.

This particular Lusso was the subject of a top-notch restoration and was therefore a good buy. Spending close to top dollar for a car that promises to be relatively trouble-free in the near future is a better alternative than going bald from the constant headaches that will result from persistent mechanical difficulties that always seem to accompany bargain exotics.

—Dave Kinney

(Historical data and photo courtesy of the auction company.)

From the June 2001 issue of *SCM*.◆

1964 250 GT Lusso

Chassis number: 5883GT

Even in street trim, the Lusso performs in true Ferrari style...quick, agile and very reliable

Arguably the most beautiful product ever to carry the Maranello marque's prancing-horse emblem, the 250 GT Lusso debuted at the Paris Salon in October 1962. Styled by Pininfarina and built by Scaglietti, the Lusso combined race car looks with new standards of passenger comfort. Beautifully proportioned, it blended a low-slung nose, reminiscent of that of the 250 SWB Berlinetta, with a sculpted Kamm tail. Slim pillars and wide expanses of glass enhanced the car's outward appearance.

The Lusso's immediate antecedent had been the 250 SWB, a true dual-purpose car that was capable of coping equally well with the conflicting demands of road and track. The SWB (short-wheelbase) designation arose from a chassis that, at 2,400 mm (94.49 in), was 200 mm (7.87 in) shorter than the standard 250 GTs of the time. Specifications could be varied to suit individual customers' requirements: Models supplied for competition had lightweight aluminum-alloy bodies, while road-going cars enjoyed a fully trimmed interior and softer springing.

Ferrari's policy of building a single, dual-purpose race/road model did not survive long into the 1960s, as the diverging requirements of the two markets necessitated specialization. Thus was born the competition-only 250 GTO and the more luxurious, *Gran Turismo* 250 GT Lusso. Built on a short-wheelbase chassis similar to that of the 250 GT SWB, the Lusso was powered by a 3-liter V12, with three twin-choke Weber carburetors. The two-cam, all-aluminum unit produced 240 hp at 7,500 rpm, producing a top speed of 150 mph and 0-100-mph acceleration time of 19.5 seconds.

One of just 350 250 GT Lussos made, this superb example was supplied new in the US and was re-imported to Italy in 1987, where it was restored in 1989 by Officine Sauro of Bologna. Records indicate that the car was once owned by one Kurt Miska.

The car enjoyed a number of owners in Atlanta in the early 1970s. In 1976 the car was owned by a George Brown of Atlanta, and offered for sale by him in 1979 at 51,000 miles, benefiting from "new paint and leather to original silver/black specification." The car was next owned by Luther Godwin, of Baldwin, New York. It was acquired by its present Italian owner in 1996, who describes its condition as "believed good" in all respects. Finished in the original silver metallic with black interior, the car is Italian registered and comes complete with tool kit, restoration invoices and ASI/FIVA papers.

This car sold for $223,610, including buyer's premium, at Bonhams' Monaco sale May 26, 2003.

Ferrari called the Lusso the 250 GTL—"L" is not found in any other Ferrari designation. Speculation was that the L stood for Lusso, an Italian word meaning luxury. While it was, in fact, more luxurious than the 250 SWB it replaced, it was not in the same league with the Super-America, the true luxury car of the Ferrari line at that time. The Lusso was a step away from the dual-purpose race/street Ferraris that preceded it, but style, not luxury, was its appeal.

Years produced	1962-64
Number produced	350
Original list price	$12,600
SCM Price Guide	$130,000-$160,000
Tune-up/major service	$2,000-$2,500, including valve adjustment
Distributor cap	$450; two required
Chassis #	Left frame member by steering box
Engine #	On right rear, under distributor
Club	Ferrari Club of America, P.O. Box 720597, Atlanta, GA 30358
Web site	www.FerrariClubofAmerica.com
Alternatives	Alfa Romeo TZ-1, Aston Martin DB5 Volante, Bizzarrini Strada, Lamborghini 400 GT
SCM Investment Grade	B

Bonhams & Brooks

Chuck Jordan, former head of styling for General Motors, has been quoted as saying the Ferrari 250 Lusso is the most beautiful car ever built. Jordan backed that statement by buying a Lusso that he kept for many years. If imitation is the most sincere form of flattery, he flattered the Lusso in one of his own designs: The Chevrolet Vega featured a Lusso-style Kamm tail and rear-end treatment. Pininfarina surely noticed imitation, but probably wasn't flattered.

Despite its great looks, the Lusso is not particularly comfortable. The seats are true buckets without back or rake adjustments. High engine revs make it rather loud at normal cruising speeds. Combined with a somewhat noisy gearbox and minimum sound insulation, the Lusso is not a quiet car. The interior is, however, exquisitely trimmed with a large upholstered area behind the seats and a beautiful leather-covered dash.

Even in its street trim, the Lusso performs in true Ferrari style. It is quick, agile and very reliable. Vintage racers have found the Lusso to be a potent weapon in the hands of a skilled driver. The car commands respect normally reserved for cars much more expensive.

Two years ago, then-Brooks, now Bonhams, sold a Lusso at its West Palm Beach Cavallino auction. The car was a top-flight example and went for $140,000, including buyer's premium, against an estimate of $130,000-$160,000. About that same time, a dealer friend of mine bought a nice driver for a little under $100,000 and flipped it to another dealer, who had a hard time reselling it for $115,000. What a difference two years makes—now Lussos are hot. The car here might have been a shade high in price, but you would be hard-pressed to find a premium example for under $200,000 today.

So who's Kurt Miska, and why does it matter that he owned this car? Miska did own a Lusso, but not this one. His was 4409GT. He did, however, write the definitive book on Lussos, The Berlinetta Lusso: A Ferrari of Unusual Elegance. *If you are interested in Lussos, it's a great resource, but it's unfortunately hard to come by. The original has been out of print for years and the company that was reprinting it recently dropped the title.—Steve Ahlgrim*

(Historic and descriptive information courtesy of Bonhams.)

From the October 2003 issue of *SCM*.◆

1970 365 GT 2+2

Chassis number: 12651

Back when they were under $10k, we didn't concern ourselves about cosmetic stuff

This "family Ferrari" was repainted in its original silver-blue from bare metal in 1997. There is new black leather on front seats, the brake system has been overhauled, and new rear self-leveling shocks fitted. A new clutch has been installed, along with fresh belts, hoses and motor mounts. The engine has never been opened and the carburetors are original. It is a three-owner car, with fully-documented history. It has never been stored, but regularly driven. It comes with the original tool kit and owner's manuals, and has covered just 59,800 miles. It is being offered at no reserve.

This imposing, but elegant, 2+2 sold for a reasonable $43,740, including buyer's premium, at Barrett-Jackson's Petersen Museum auction on June 22, 2003.

The 365 2+2 may be the best and least expensive way for an enthusiast on a budget to enjoy a traditional Ferrari V12. It's cheap and durable by Ferrari standards, and an ideal car for the person who wants a sports car that can haul the family or another couple. Just don't expect a lot of appreciation—or much depreciation, either.

The 365's air conditioning, power windows, power steering, power brakes, and electric vent-wings all added up, and it was dubbed the "Queen Mary" of Ferraris by Road & Track *in 1968, due to its two-ton weight. Still, it would reach 152 mph and went from 0-60 in 7.1 seconds. Succeeding the 250 and 330 2+2s, the 365 was the first 2+2 Ferrari to have independent rear suspension, giving the car fine handling despite its weight. It was as stable at 150 as most cars were at 70 and* R&T *concluded it was still a thoroughbred Ferrari.*

The conventional drivetrain featured a front-mounted 4.4-liter DOHC engine with three carbs and dual distributors. This basic engine design was over 15 years old; it would be the last of the two-cam Columbo engines from Modena. By this time, Ferrari had worked out most of the problems from the earlier 330's 4-liter engines. Although its head and block are similar, the 365's 4.4-liter engine has slightly different stud placement and sintered iron valve seats rather than bronze. These engines still used a multiple-row timing chain with well-developed tensioners (which rarely give trouble) rather than rubber belts. Despite the addition of some rudimentary emissions-control equipment, the 4.4-liter engines seem to be more trouble free than their predecessors.

The 365 2+2 was fitted with newly developed Koni hydraulic spring-ram load levelers that used suspension movement to pump up and maintain correct ride stance when the large trunk was full. While not nearly as trouble prone as many air-bag suspensions developed in the 1950s, they simply don't last 30 years. They can be rebuilt (at a cost of over $2,000), but many have been replaced with $150 Gabriel "HiJackers" air-adjustable shock absorbers. An owner of two 365s at January's Barrett-Jackson claimed his air-shock converted "driver" handled better than the rebuilt Konis on his "show" 2+2, at about a tenth of the cost, installed.

American 365 2+2s had air conditioning and extra cooling fans, which pulled more current than the 40-amp Marelli alternator provided. The factory installed a second alternator and a troublesome relay box, but details of how to rebuild and upgrade the box inexpensively have been available for 25 years. After the fix, it causes no problems.

In the mid-1970s, I took a delightful trip from Atlanta to Watkins Glen for the Ferrari Club Meeting with my wife and three kids in an 80,000-mile 365. We had bought the car over the phone; it had been described as "burgundy" with contrasting stripes. But when it arrived, it was more Cold Duck pink than Rothschild red. And the stripes? They were six-inch-wide, bright violet, fuzzy-edged accents in the best hot rod tradition. These days, an e-mailed photo would have prepared us for the weird paint. But back when 365s were under $10k, we didn't concern ourselves about cosmetic stuff. Did it pull to 8,000 rpm, get to 100 fast and have at least 11 of the 12 cylinders with decent compression? Yes. So we just bought it, but were careful to park around the corner at the next Ferrari club meeting.

After looking it over, I judged the silver-blue car here to be a 2-; another auction analyst said 3+. It had attractive, non-original five-star-type Cromodoras with good Michelins. The light metallic paint, a good color for these large 2+2s, had some minor bubbles. The car had a nice interior with some wear on the rear seat. The rear bumper chrome was thin, with pits in the pot metal taillight surrounds, a common problem. Trunk lid fit was way off, but there was no obvious rear-end collision damage inside. Other panel fits were up to original Pininfarina standards. The windows were tinted and a later stereo was installed, but the original was included. The chassis was clean, but not detailed.

The car started easily with no smoke and idled well, indicating no excessively worn shafts on the carbs. It picked up rpm smoothly, evidence that the distributors are still advancing and accelerator pumps still pumping. The owner said the A/C works but needs R12 refrigerant (likely at least a $1,000 problem). The car appeared to be well maintained, and never abused. This was a fair price if the mechanicals check out as well as claimed. If the new owner is a family man, this V12 will be a terrific and stylish way to transport his family to various car events around the country.—John Apen

(Historic and descriptive information courtesy of Barrett-Jackson.)

From the November 2003 issue of *SCM*.◆

Years produced	1968-71
Number produced	800
Original list price	$18,900, with A/C, radio, power windows and disc wheels
SCM Price Guide	$45,000-$60,000
Tune-up/major service	$2,500-$3,000
Distributor cap	$300+
Chassis #	Right front chassis rail, plate on right inner fender, DOT plate-driver's door jamb
Engine #	Right side, near starter motor, back of block
Club	Ferrari Club of America, PO Box 720597, Atlanta, GA 30358
Web site	www.ferrariclubofamerica.org
Alternatives	Mercedes-Benz 6.3, Lamborghini Espada, Ferrari 400, '63-'65 Buick Riviera
SCM Investment Grade	C

1978 400A 2+2 Coupe

Chassis number: F101CL24185

If there were a prize for the most undervalued Ferrari, it would have to go to the 400 Automatic

Christie's

From the onset, the intention of the 400 had been to challenge the finest luxury saloons available. It was anticipated that a large demand would come from the lucrative American market; sadly, the cost involved in meeting the stringent US regulations denied this option.

Introduced in 1976 at the Paris salon, it was available with either a five-speed manual gearbox or automatic three-speed transmission, sourced from General Motors. This option was targeted at those customers who wanted a long-distance GT without having to change gear; it was very much a boulevard cruiser in the modern idiom of the time. 502 examples of the standard, carbureted 400 models were built before fuel injection was introduced in 1979, mostly selling to the European market.

This 400 was purchased new by Alfred Heineken in France, as an update for a 308 model. The car was kept in France until 1983, when it was imported to Holland. It has the three-speed automatic option, 340-bhp V12 engine and four-wheel disc brakes.

This is the archetypal example of the model, right down to its period color. Throughout more than 20 years of ownership, its mileage has remained under 8,000 km (4,968 miles), and naturally its condition reflects its limited use. Furthermore, the benefit of its single ownership from new is that it retains its original tools, handbook, etc. A relatively small number of the model was built; they represent a tremendous value for the money in our opinion, with the glorious V12 engine and ample room to go long-distance touring. These aspects, combined with the uncomplicated history of this car, mean that we highly recommend this four-seat Ferrari.

Years produced	400 carbureted 1976-80
Number produced	502
Original list price	approx. $45,000
SCM Price Guide	$18,500-$24,000 (add $2,500 for five-speed)
Tune-up/major service	$4,000
Distributor cap	$450
Chassis #	On the inner fender well/frame area on the right passenger side of the engine.
Engine #	Middle of the V, toward the back of the engine. Does not match chassis number.
Club	Ferrari Club of America, P.O. Box 720597, Atlanta, GA 30358
Web site	www.FerrariClubofAmerica.com
Alternatives	Porsche 928S-4, Aston Martin DBS V8, BMW M6
SCM Investment Grade	D

This car sold for $32,994, including buyer's premium, at the Christie's Retromobile Paris auction, held February 8, 2003.

If there were a prize for the most undervalued Ferrari, it would have to go to the 400 Automatic. When a 4.8-liter, four-cam, 12-cylinder Ferrari—with a Pininfarina designed and built body—is the entry-level Ferrari, something's wrong.

The 400 is the best-known derivative of the longest-running Ferrari production series ever. Initially introduced in 1972 as a 365 GT4 2+2, the model metamorphosed into the 400 GT and Automatic, then the 400i and 400i Automatic, and finally, the 412 GT and Automatic. The series was finally discontinued in 1989, ending an unprecedented 17-year production run.

While four-seater Ferraris have never set sales records, they have always been steady sellers. They can be daily drivers and often show up with lots of miles and plenty of wear. Use equals depreciation, and four-place Ferraris quickly work their way to the bottom of Ferrari values. Since they contain very similar mechanical components to their two-seat siblings at a 30-60% discount in sales price, the four-place Ferraris can be an exceptional value. The most serious danger is underestimating restoration costs, as a paint job can run nearly half the value of the car and an engine job can cost more than the car itself. Normal maintenance is expensive, but it is less than newer Ferraris and required less frequently.

When choosing a 400, the five-speed is preferred and brings a 5-10% premium. The gearing of the three-speed automatic is not intuitive and kills the performance of the car. For instance, driven at any constant speed, the automatic shifts into top gear. At 30 mph, top gear equals 1,100 rpm, well out of the torque range needed for maneuverability. The flexibility of the five-speed allows you to choose a more appropriate gear and take advantage of the car's performance. The dual air-conditioning option is also desirable, as it makes the marginal output almost acceptable.

The single owner of 400 Automatic s/n 24185 was, indeed, a Heineken of the brewery fame. The car was presented with all the original books, tools and delivery items. It apparently suffered some neglect, and was reported as having stained seats.

There are legitimate reasons why low-mileage cars sell at a premium, but determining the amount is always a problem. The roughly 4,900 miles on this car is enough mileage to lessen the maintenance concerns of an ultra-low-mileage, rarely used car, but still low enough to make any new mileage a concern. The pride of ownership of a time-warp car is always contrasted with the knowledge that every new rock chip and every new mile moves it closer to just another used car.

This car had both low mileage and celebrity ownership. While the estimate was $16,000-$19,000, at least two people wanted it very badly. It sold for an unexpected $28,000, $33,000 after a stiff 17.5% commission. Was it a good purchase? I think so. A nearly new Ferrari with all the goodies for about 15% of the cost of its current replacement can't be all bad. My only reservation is the bronze color. The auction house noted it as a "period color," but I call it outdated.

400s will never have the respect or value of their two-passenger siblings, but the value of them today, when in decent condition like this, is just too low.—Steve Ahlgrim

(Historic and descriptive information courtesy of Christie's.)

From the June 2003 issue of *SCM*.◆

Elton John's 1986 Ferrari 412i

Chassis number: 63907
Engine number: 00145

Elton John may have thought it was a "classic Ferrari shape," but for most collectors it's a classic Fiat shape with more cylinders

Christie's

The 412 was the definitive version of the 2+2 coupe series that Ferrari introduced in 1972 as the 365 GT/4 2+2. Built to challenge the finest luxury saloons available, it was anticipated that large demand would come from the American market. Sadly, the costs involved in meeting US regulations denied it this market. Through updates, the model gained an automatic transmission, fuel injection, a larger engine and, with all these, improved performance and handling.

This Ferrari was purchased, used, by Elton John in 1992. Originally metallic brown, Elton had the car resprayed to the present black and toned down the interior, replacing the dash fascia with black to make the attractive combination it is today. It is offered with the original service folder, which confirms maintenance by leading Ferrari specialists and mileage slightly over 30,000 miles—with just 350 covered since 1997. The car was recently serviced in November of 2000 and is a well-preserved example. Of the 412, Elton John commented: "It's a beautiful car...I love the look. It's a classic Ferrari shape."

Sir Elton's fleet manager was somewhat less enthusiastic, however, remembering that when he first saw it, he had mistaken its identity. "It was a horrible bronzey color that you associate with a Datsun." His opinion, however, has gone up immeasurably since it was resprayed black, and he now says it's a lovely car to drive.

At Christie's London sale of 20 of Sir Elton John's cars, this 412, the first car to cross the block, brought an astounding $59,640. This exceeded Christie's high estimate by 65%, but then, every single car at this sale sold above Christie's high estimate—some reaching close to three times the amount predicted. Clearly, an astute auction house, in this case Christie's, can obtain results that bear almost no relation to current market values when celebrity ownership is a factor.

The catalog excelled in giving some nearly ordinary cars character. What royal-doting Englishman could resist the blue 1978 Aston Martin V8 Vantage coupe that was once painted bright yellow with black and red stripes—the Watford Football Club colors—and evoked Prince Philip to ask Sir Elton, "Oh, it's you that owns that ghastly car, is it?" Rated a condition #2+, it sold for $144,900, bringing $90,000 above market in the opinion of SCM *reporter Richard Hudson-Evans.*

As one perceptive auction observer put it, "These were buyers of memorabilia and collectibles who otherwise would be throwing away six-figure amounts for Fender Stratocaster guitars. Christie's cleverly positioned, marketed and promoted the sale as Sir Elton John's stuff that happens to be cars, not cars that happen to be Elton John's."

Years produced	1985-89
Number produced	576
Original price	$63,500 plus EPA DOT legalizing, $12,800–Amerispec 1981
SCM Price Guide	$35,000-$42,000
Major service	$3,500
Ignition ECU	$2,500
Chassis #	On top of steering column in driver's compartment
Engine #	Rear-center of engine block, non-matching
Club	Ferrari Club of America, Box 720597, Atlanta, GA 30358; Ferrari Owner's Club, 8642 Cleta St., Downey, CA 90241
Web site	www.ferrariclubofamerica.org; FerrariOwnersClub.org

Although he was in Atlanta at the time of the auction, Sir Elton followed the progress of the sale. "There's obviously a lot of money to be made from second-hand cars! It's great to know that the people who have bought my cars place such a high value on them, and that the care that has been put into looking after them over all the years has been well worth it. I hope that all of the new owners enjoy these cars as much as I did," he commented.

Driving them? These are objects bought to be talked about and to impress one's acquaintances. "Shall we take Sir Elton's Bentley tonight or would you prefer his Rolls?"

To step back into the real world for a moment, the 412, along with its predecessors, are at the bottom of the Ferrari pecking order, with perhaps only the lowly 308 GT4 or Mondial 8 selling for less money. Elton John may have thought it was a "classic Ferrari shape," but for most collectors it's a classic Fiat shape with more cylinders. The best US-spec 412 in the world can be had for $42,000, and that includes DOT/EPA paperwork. And when you go to sell it in five years, you're going to have to take a lot less.

So this particular 30,000-mile, repainted, two-owner 412i in condition #1-, with records and books, sold for $59,640. What does this say about the 412 market? Or the Ferrari market? Nothing. What it does say is that Sir Elton John's stuff is hot. No other London collector car auction has generated as much pre-sale publicity. And when his famous photography collection hits the block, that will really be a sale.—John Apen

(Historic data and photo courtesy of auction company.)

From the October 2001 issue of *SCM*.◆

1998 456 GTA

Chassis number: ZFFWP50A4W0109289

Owning a 456 may cause you to question your financial sanity, but if you can afford it, just do it and don't look back

Barrett-Jackson

When Ferrari released the 456 GT, it changed the perception of a high-performance 2+2. Refined, elegant comfort and performance were the orders of the day, and the Pininfarina-designed body is as intensely beautiful as the car is luxurious and fast.

Powered by a sporty 436-hp V12 engine, with a four- speed automatic (456 GTA), its aerodynamics and handling characteristics are unlike those of any other 2+2.

The 456 was the ultimate four-person conveyance, and some consider it to be the ultimate in practical super-car automotive design. This particular example is in excellent, like-new condition with less than 10,000 miles.

This 456 GTA sold for $108,000, including buyer's premium, at the Barrett-Jackson Scottsdale auction, held January 16-19, 2003.

The crash of the Ferrari market in 1990, combined with an uninspiring model lineup, just about wiped out all interest in new Ferraris during the first half of the 1990s. The flagship F40 dropped from $750,000 over its list price (approximately $389,000 plus taxes) to just sticker during this time. The Testarossa became terminally dated, and despite a race series and a warmed-over special edition, the 348 never caught on. The two- and three-year back orders of 1990 turned into warehouses full of cars by 1992.

The Ferrari line became so sale-proof by 1994 that Ferrari actually offered GM-style programs, with up to $30,000 combined in cash back and credit, to help sell cars. The program helped clean up the inventory problem, but Ferrari needed more than money to get people buying cars again.

The answer to Ferrari's problem came in a trilogy of new models. The luxurious 456 GT was first shown in 1993 and the sporty F355 Berlinetta followed shortly thereafter. They were an instant hit, earning rave reviews for performance and styling. When they finally hit the showrooms in 1994, so did a steady stream of customers. The recovery had begun.

The trilogy was completed with the introduction of the 550 Maranello. The 550 marked the return of the traditional front-engine Berlinetta, in the heritage of the Daytona, to Ferrari's line. It offered superb performance with aggressive yet understated styling.

Independently and together the new trio stimulated every nerve of the buyers' senses. The cars were fast, beautiful and fun to drive. They became immensely popular, and indisputably reaffirmed Ferrari as the king of the exotic car field.

The practical part of the equation was the 2+2 456, introduced to fill the void left when the 400/412 series was discontinued. Where the 400/412 was visually stodgy and technologically dated, the 456 was fresh and exciting. It was one of Pininfarina's best designs, a blend of elegance and performance in a package that is attractive from any angle.

Driving the 456 is a blast. Let the clutch out, get the car rolling, then floor it; the car quickly builds speed to about 3,500 rpm, then the rear tires begin to break loose. Modulate the throttle for traction, make a quick shift to second and the rubber will easily break loose again. Flick it left, flick it right, the power-assisted steering and excellent chassis follows your every move. Stand on the brakes and your cheeks will be pulled to the windshield. This is a driver's car in every sense.

Late-model Ferraris have become insanely expensive to maintain. The spectacular performance of the newer cars has come by way of exotic and expensive components. Routine maintenance will make you gasp and major repairs can be catastrophic. A fatally damaged automatic transaxle will set you back $52,000, while a new engine could run half again that much.

This blue with tan 456 GTA was sold new for $239,000 plus 20 large in taxes. First offered by RM at its Santa Monica auction on May 25, 2002, it was a no-sale at a $75,000 high bid. It was then reported sold for $120,000 a few weeks later at the 2002 Barrett-Jackson Petersen auction, reportedly to a principal of the auction company. When the owner decided he wanted a six-speed rather than an automatic, the car appeared at Barrett-Jackson.

2+2s have traditionally been the most expensive cars in Ferrari's production line. As new cars, the 330 2+2s were more expensive than the 275 four-cams, the 400 GTs were more expensive than the Boxers and the 456s were more expensive than the 550 Maranellos.

$108,000 might seem like a bargain for a 9,000-mile, quarter-of-a-million-dollar car, but it represents the high side of early GTA values. Even with incredibly good looks and truly impressive performance, the 456 suffers from the curse of all 2+2 Ferraris: Nobody cares. Despite the highest list price of the new Ferraris, 456s are always at the bottom of late-model used Ferrari prices.

Buy a 456 and you are certain to have steady depreciation. You will also have some serious maintenance expenses, and Lord help you if you break something big. On the other hand, you'll own one of the most beautiful cars ever built and you'll be rewarding yourself every time you get behind the wheel. Owning a 456 may cause you to question your financial sanity, but if you can afford it, just do it and don't look back. After all, no Ferrari owner would ever maintain that the best things in life are free.—Steve Ahlgrim (Historic and descriptive information courtesy of Barrett-Jackson.)

Years produced	456s 1995-98, GTAs 1996-98
Number produced	all 456s approx. 1,950; 456 GTA approx. 400
Original list price	approx. $239,000
SCM Price Guide	$85,000-$105,000
Tune-up/major service	$6,500 (incl. timing belts)
Distributor cap	N/A
Chassis #	Frame rail, passenger's side of engine compartment
Engine #	Passenger's side of engine in front, just under where head meets block
Club	Ferrari Club of America, P.O. Box 720597, Atlanta, GA 30358; Ferrari Owner's Club, 8642 Cleta St., Downey, CA 90241
Web site	www.FerrariClubofAmerica.com; www.FerrariOwnersClub.org
Alternatives	Ferrari 550 Maranello, Bentley Continental R, Aston Martin DB7
SCM Investment Grade	C

The Dollar is Falling! The Dollar is Falling!

Visions of container after container being filled in Long Beach with old cars, and destined for England, Holland or Germany fill their heads

More than a few self-proclaimed market gurus have been running around like the proverbial chickens with their heads removed, all aflutter because the Euro has appreciated by over 25% against the dollar in the past few months. Visions of container after container being filled in Long Beach with old cars, and destined for England, Holland or Germany fill their heads.

Well, it's always nice to have something to get excited about. But let's take a little closer look at the picture.

First, it is just a tiny segment, although a highly visible one, of the car market that is affected by any currency swing. Further, the economy in Europe is still in the toilet, far worse than the situation in the US, as their central banks have been slow to cut interest rates to get things moving again. Further, the endemic economic problems caused by the cradle-to-grave care offered by most European governments continue to bedevil their economic planning.

What this means is that even though prices of cars in America may be falling relative to the Euro, there still aren't a lot of Europeans out there buying cars, certainly nothing like the gold rush of 1988-91.

Of course, the rich are different. Especially the European car-collecting rich.

More than anything else, what sets European collectors apart is the way they use their cars. Unlike the American preoccupation with sanitized, beautified concours and tea-cup racing, where, when two cars enter a corner, each driver is expected to graciously say to the other, "After you," Europeans hammer their cars.

For instance, in the recently completed Modena Cento Ore, 275 GTB/C S/N 7271 GT fell off the road in the final special stage, and bounced off a few trees before coming to rest. The owner's reaction? "Where's the nearest carrozzeria? I need to get this thing fixed before the next event."

As events like the MCO, Tour Auto and Tour d'España become more popular, Europeans have begun to scour America for cars. And because so many of these cars were originally sold in the US, there are still barn-finds or unrestored original cars to be found. After the sprinkling of a few hundred thousand Benjamins, second-tier Ferraris such as Boanos, Lussos and 275 GTB/2s can be made competitive in their classes, with a total outlay of one-third that what an SWB or TdF would cost.

Project cars—such as alloy-bodied Boanos, Lussos and 275 GTB/2s—that can be converted into relatively low-dollar (in the Ferrari world) priced GT racers are the most sought-after model today, with project alloy-body Boanos and Lussos bringing as much as $150,000 and project 275 GTB/2s bringing as much as $175,000.

Restored alloy-body Boanos will bring $250,000-plus in the US, restored Lussos will bring $200,000-plus and restored 275 GTB/2s will bring as much as $300,000-plus. Today, these prices are cheap for Europeans, so these cars are going overseas.

As an example of the market swing, I sold 250 Lusso S/N 5859 GT to England in February for $195,000 US. The same 250 Lusso is now being offered, only four months later, by an English dealer for £195,000, which is €273,000 or $315,000.

I only know of one first-tier car that has gone to Europe recently, 250 LM S/N 6105, and I can only speculate at the buy and sell prices. I believe the buy was $2,200,000 and know the car was bought by an English dealer. We'll have to watch the adverts to see what he hopes to get for it.

After visiting a tree or two.

Short-nose GTB/2s are worth more in Europe than here.

I also sold 333 SP S/N 012 to Europe in May. With current exchange rates, it was simply cheaper than any of the 333 SPs on the market in Europe, even after adding in freight and import duty.

While I don't traffic in Jaguars, Austin-Healeys or Porsches, conversations with dealers who do sell these cars confirm the same trends. Anything that can be raced, from a Jaguar 120 to a Healey 3000 or a Porsche 356, has a better chance of selling, for higher dollars, to a European buyer than an American one. This is especially true for ratty cars, essentially sale-proof in the US, that can become good platforms for event cars.

While Lussos and 275 GTBs are crossing the Atlantic at a rapid rate, the American market for production cars such as Daytonas continues to show token appreciation, while 550 Maranellos, 456 GTs and even 360 coupes continue their predictable pattern of depreciation. Certainly the devaluation of the dollar has had a catastrophic effect on the gray market, as there's no way to buy a late-model serial-production Ferrari in Euros, pay for it to be legally imported into the US, and come out ahead.

So if you've got a nasty Lusso, or a very early 911, or a Jag 120 roadster with a decent body but a trashed engine, you might just have better luck getting good money for the car from a European buyer than from an American one. But if you are thinking of selling, I urge you to move fast. Currency swings are as much a matter of economic policy as they are of business realities, and if the world suddenly decides it wants a stronger dollar, it's a stronger dollar we'll see.—*Michael Sheehan*

From the July 2003 issue of *SCM.*◆

The Good and Bad of 456 GTs and 550 Maranellos

The user-friendly cockpit makes driving a pleasure and ten-year-old twins think the rear seats are great

The Ferrari 456 GT was introduced to the US market in 1994 and touted as a born-again replacement for the 365 GTB/4 Daytona. According to Ferrari North America then-president Gian-Luigi Buitoni, "We have clients today who don't want to give up the performance of a Testarossa, but they must have more room." Hence, the token 2+2 seating. The reality is that the 456 GT, with its less than-svelte styling and additional passenger capacity, was more accurately a replacement for the 365 GTC/4, the less sporty sister of the Daytona.

Fitted with a 48-valve, four-cam, 5.5-liter V12 that puts out 442 hp, the 456 offers staggering performance in the 2+2 class. The US version blasts through the quarter-mile in 13.4 seconds at 107.5 mph, and tops out at 186 mph. The user-friendly cockpit, luxurious seating, easily read gauges and six-speed shifter make driving a pleasure and, as a dad who knows, ten-year-old twins think the rear seats are great.

Unfortunately, like every other Ferrari 2+2 ever built, the 456 GT and the later 456 M have not fared well in the marketplace, depreciating like stones. Priced at $245,000 out-the-door when new, a prudent buyer should be able to find a nice 1995 456 GT with well under 30,000 miles and with the 30,000-mile service completed for about $85,000.

There were no 1996 models; add $5,000 plus a little per model year for a 1997 or 1998. While the asking prices for 1999-2002 456 Ms and GTAs run from $150,000 to $195,000, the real selling prices are in the $115,000 to $140,000 range. The 1995 456s should be considered nearly fully depreciated, and offer a lot of modern-day performance for a reasonable sum.

The 550 Maranello was introduced in 1996 and truly was the replacement for the 365 GTB/4. Like the Daytona, the 550 Maranello is an aggressively styled car with its cut-off tail and long-nosed good looks. Fitted with a 5.5-liter, 48-valve V12 that pushes out 485 horsepower at 7,000 rpm, the 550 has a top speed of 199 mph and will rip through the quarter-mile in 12.6 seconds. A total of 3,600 Maranellos were built for the world market during a model run from 1996 to 2002. Today a US-legal, European 1996 or 1997 550 Maranello is in the $115,000 to $125,000 range, while low-mileage 1997 or 1998 US cars are available in the $135,000 to $145,000 range. 1999-2002 models can be found for $160,000 to $185,000.

To get your new purchase to the US and legalized will require trucking to the docks in Europe (about $300); a European shipping agent who can coordinate containerizing the car and do the necessary export paperwork (about $500); shipping to the US (about $1,500 to the East Coast or $2,000 to the West Coast); customs entry fee ($300); US customs duty (2.5%, or about $2,250); a customs bond to guarantee the EPA and DOT will indeed be done (about $3,000); a bond application fee (about $250); and trucking from the dock in the US to the conversion shop that will do the work (about $100 to $200).

Then you've got the actual EPA and DOT conversion work (at least $12,500); the EPA and DOT warranty (at $350 each); and last but not least, the lab test processing fee ($900). The grand total ends up being about $22,300 to $22,900.

All-up cost is about $112,500 for a car that will have an

550 Maranello: the new Daytona?

"ask" price in the $125,000 range and an actual "sell" price of somewhat less.

As a moneymaking proposition, the math doesn't work well for a 550 (and even less well for a 456, which explains why there are very few Euro 456s in the US). Bluntly, the only reason to buy a Euro model 550 today is to use the car on a high-speed drive-it-like-Enzo-intended European dream vacation before bringing it home to our land of grand highways and pathetic speed limits. This assumes, of course, that while in Europe your 550 isn't stolen while parked in a supposedly secure spot in front of a hotel or restaurant.

As for the costs and pitfalls of ownership, the early 550s run much too much oil pressure and occasionally blow the oil filter apart, creating a major underhood mess. Should the oil filter start to leak as an inattentive owner cruises down the freeway, cheerfully chatting on his cell phone, a Ferrari dealer will be happy to install a new engine for a mere $75,000 or so.

If your 550 (or 456) pops out of reverse, truck it to your friendly local Ferrari service center and have the transaxle pulled and the circlip and reverse gear replaced at a cost of about $3,500. Choose to drive the car with the transaxle making ominous sounds and the repair bill will quickly will increase to about $7,500, after the reverse gear has bounced around in the transaxle like a ball in a squash court for a while.

As for factory recalls, the door windows sometimes don't seal well against the rear quarter windows. If you have a US car your authorized dealer should replace the electric window motors, door glass and seals—an $8,000 bill—at no cost. Be prepared, to throw a temper tantrum to get the work covered under warranty.

As for routine service, the cam and front seals tend to start leaking after about 10,000 miles, so most owners skip the 15,000-mile service and simply go straight to the 30,000-mile service, which includes cam seals, cam belts, valve adjustment and more at a cost of about $3,500.

At about $85,000 for a very good '95 456 or $125,000 for a '96 550, we are talking just over 365 GTC/4 or 365 GTB/4 prices for much more modern and user-friendly cars. Yes, they are expensive to maintain, but as the saying goes: premium product, premium price. And, no offense to VW, don't you think you'll get more respect at the car wash when you pull up in your V12 456 Ferrari than in your new similarly priced VW W12 Phaeton, even if you start bragging that it's the "most expensive Volkswagen in the world?"—*Michael Sheehan*

From the December 2003 issue of *SCM*.◆

The Valve Job Wars: Alfa vs. Ferrari

No one is more persistent in his questions about how to have an affordable Ferrari than our Editor, who seems to believe it is his destiny to discover the "Northwest Passage" to the land of cheap Ferrari valve jobs

No one is more persistent in his questions about how to have an affordable Ferrari than our editor, who seems to believe it is his destiny to discover the "Northwest Passage" to the land of cheap Ferrari valve jobs.

Here's today's plaintive and misguided inquiry: "Cindy's '78 Alfa Spider has gone in for a head gasket and valve job and it will probably be around $1,500. Since a four-cylinder Alfa is one-third of a 330 Ferrari V12, and there should be some economies of scale here, shouldn't a valve job on my 1963 330 America be $4,500?" There are many reasons why our editor is hopelessly adrift in fantasy-land.

First, there is no economy of scale. The Alfa is a smaller, more compact engine, and the overall labor is much less. The single distributor and fuel-injectors on the Alfa can be removed and pushed aside while the head is removed. The cylinder head is easily accessible from either side and can be removed by a single mechanic. Most shops will quote 12 to 14 hours for the job at a labor rate of $60 per hour or $720 to $840.

As for parts and machining, the Alfa has four intake valves at $22 each for $88, four exhaust valves at $38 each for $152, eight guides at $8 each for $64, eight valve seats at $13 each for $104, a gasket set at $125 and machining the new valves, guides and seats at about $160 for a total of $693.

Parts, labor and machining for a valve job on Cindy's 25-year-old Spider should indeed be in the $1,500 range. Since the car is worth, being kind, around $7,500, this investment, which represents about 20% of its value and will make the car much more pleasurable to drive, makes a lot of sense.

With the Ferrari, a car that is 15 years older, the equation disintegrates quickly. Labor will be much higher. The Ferrari's cylinder head studs are almost always corroded solidly onto the head studs and a one-half-inch thick steel puller plate must be used to apply massive pressure to slowly and evenly pull the cylinder heads off the block. This can't effectively be done by a single person. Head removal is really best accomplished by taking out the whole engine—in fact, every shop I spoke with explained that in the end it is generally cost effective to pull the engine out of an old V12, even for a valve job. It makes dealing with any other eventualities, and there will be several, much easier.

Before the 330 cylinder heads can be removed, the Weber carbs and linkage, both distributors, the cam covers, the 24 rocker arms and their pedestals all must be removed for access. Assuming the heads come off without difficulty, the head studs don't have to be removed by a hack saw and the cut-off head studs don't have to be laser cut from the block, the total time to remove and refit the heads, install the cams, retime the distributors, remove and install the engine, etc., is 60 hours at $75 per hour, or $4,500.

Our very parts-intensive Ferrari has 12 intake valves at $102 each for $1,224, 12 exhaust valves at $110 each for $1,320, 24 valve guides at $11 each for $264, 24 valve adjustment screws at $14.75 each for $354, 24 cam roller pins at $30 each for $720, 24 valve seats at $32 each for $768, 24 valve guide seals at $1.50 each for $36 and a cylinder head gasket kit at a staggering $450, for a total of $5,136 for parts alone.

Alfa engine: one-third the valves, one-sixth the cost.

Machining the new valves, seats and guides is a modest $480, bringing the total for parts and machining for our Ferrari to $5,616.

Total parts, labor and machining on our 35-year-old Ferrari is just over $10,000, or more than six times the cost of the Alfa job, even though the engine has only three times as many cylinders.

Last but not least, the maximum time estimate on the Alfa is about a week while the minimum time estimate for the Ferrari is a month.

With an estimated value, being kind again, of $35,000 for ED.'s Ferrari, this valve job is nearing one-third the value of the overall car. That doesn't sound too bad, but there's really more to this dismal picture.

With an old engine, the chances are that a valve job, with its resultant increased compression, will simply exacerbate the problems in the lower end of the engine. Rings, pistons and liners really should be replaced, and, in words well-known to anyone with an old car, "while you're in there," the bearings should probably be renewed as well. How do you spell $25,000?

Now you're approaching two-thirds of the value of the car, and begin to understand the ultimate pitfall of doing anything to a 2+2 Ferrari. The cost of a valve job or rebuilding an engine to stock specs on a Daytona, a 330 GTC, or even an SWB won't be much different than on Editor Martin's 330. But when a car is worth $1.2m, spending $25,000 is really chump change. For a $35,000 car, it's the end of the world.

For three years, now, each time our Editor comes up with a new scheme, my response is the same. I send him a case of ultra-cheap, straight 40-weight oil (since it's not going to stay in the engine very long, what's the point of buying something expensive?) with a label attached that says, "Oil is cheap and motors are expensive."—*Michael Sheehan*

From the September 2001 issue of *SCM.*◆

The Grinch Who Almost Sold the GTO

The automotive equivalent of a Cezanne or Van Gogh, the 250 GTO S/N 4293 was well presented and glorious to behold

If it weren't for the GTO that failed to sell, the Bonhams & Brooks auction at Gstaad, Switzerland, would have been called a great success. By raising their own bar and trying to sell a car for $10 million, B&B created a kind of "all or nothing" scenario. In the eyes of the collector car world, if they sold the GTO, nothing else that crossed the block would have mattered. Conversely, if they failed to sell the car, no matter how the rest of the auction went, B&B would have failed.

Gstaad is a terrific place to have a high-end auction, and Switzerland is a pretty nice place to be just a few days before Christmas. I was surprised at how few Americans were there—aside from Chris Renwick, recently departed from Symbolic, Rick Anderson, curator of the Chinetti collection, and myself, it looked like the rest of the audience was completely European. A large number of dealers were in attendance, looking to snap up undervalued cars for their inventory.

Forgetting the GTO, this was a great auction if you were selling a Daytona Spyder, and a terrible one if you hoped to get big bucks for your Boxer. B&B got all the money for the 1971 365 GTS/4 Daytona Spyder S/N 14761, magnificently restored, when the hammer fell at $450,291. To put this price in perspective, the 365 GTS/4 S/N 14395, in similar condition, sold for $100,000 less just sixty days earlier.

Additionally, the 250 SWB California Spyder S/N 3007 brought a strong price at $1,319,945, showing once again that the prices of these cars continue to march upwards.

Conversely, the buy of the auction was the 1965 Ferrari 500 Superfast, S/N 6043, which sold for a mere $265,741. Bought new by Lord Hanson, it came with its original delivery papers and virtually every piece of paperwork documenting its entire life with Lord Hanson.

This LHD car had only 12,000 original miles, and was extremely handsome in its original color, a British Racing Green variation so dark it almost looked black. Set off with a black interior, the car was a real head-turner, and it was a nice change to see a V12 Ferrari in something other than red. By way of market comparison, a very similar 500 SF, S/N 6039, recently sold for over $365,000.

Many of the lesser, serial production Ferraris at the event, such as the 246 GT S/N 2224, sold cheap. It went for $45,479 to a dealer from Marseille, who told me he believes it will sell quickly in the $75,000 range. The 365 BB S/N 17641 sold for just $53,508, presumably to the trade, and we'll most likely see it advertised soon in the $70,000 range. The Mondial, 208 and the pairs of 308s and Testarossas all went away at wholesale prices, again, generally to the trade, and will all be shortly gracing various showrooms around Europe at higher prices.

The automotive equivalent of a Cezanne or Van Gogh at a top-rank art auction, the 250 GTO S/N 4293 was well presented and glorious to behold. I am told that one of the bidders was willing to go very close to the announced $10m reserve, but there were no other bidders there to force the price. Where's that aggressive chandelier when you need it? The bid price of $7.7m was, in my opinion, just not enough for this sterling car, and I expect we'll hear of it selling nearer to the estimate over the next few months.

"B&B's Christmas attempt to be the Grinch and steal the title of 'seller of the year's most expensive car' came close, but not close enough."

Consigning the GTO and publicizing it heavily was a risky move on the part of B&B, but necessary as they continue to compete at the highest levels against RM and Christie's. When Dermot Chichester hammered down the 330 P3 at Pebble for $5.6m, it gave Christie's bragging rights for the year. B&B's Christmas attempt to be the Grinch and steal the title of "seller of the year's most expensive car" came close, but not close enough.
—*Michael Sheehan*

From the February 2001 issue of *SCM*.◆

A Hot Rod Lusso

All Ferraris have a racing heritage, and you will be amazed at what they will deliver when properly piloted

Dear Mr. Sheehan: *I've got a 250 Lusso I'd like to hot-rod. At Ferrari track days, I'm tired of watching ungainly, four-headlight 330 GTs pull away from me. Can you tell me your thoughts on the cost/benefit ratio of a) installing a 6-carb setup, b) hotter cams, and/or c) a more efficient exhaust system? Are there other things I could do that would bring a decent performance return for the money spent?—**G.E.R., Long Beach, CA.***

You want to go faster, right? Then let's start by talking about the easiest way to get better lap times. I quote from Carroll Smith, the author of *Tune to Win,* the racer's bible, who wisely says, "Tune your suspension, gain 50 horsepower." Your engine options, which we will address shortly, will cost you over $20,000. Suspension work will give bigger results, and will cost much less.

"A funky little FIA Historic license or a letter from Steve Earle with three gold stars for not hitting anybody at the Monterey Historics doesn't mean you can drive your way out of a paper bag, in real competition terms."

The Lusso and the 250 GTO were the last evolution of the Ferrari 250 GT series and share many components, like the Watts-link rear suspension. However, the Lusso front suspension is lacking. It probably has positive camber, causing excessive understeer and increasing lap-times. A good race prep shop can make offset suspension bushings to kick the bottoms of the A arms out and bring the top A arms in. Go for about one degree negative front camber. Add a stout front sway bar along with stiff polyurethane bushings and the front suspension will be transformed. Send the Koni shocks out to be rebuilt to street-track specifications, or replace the old-style Konis with newer shocks, then add a set of carbon-metallic brake pads and switch to high- temperature brake fluid.

You'll be amazed how much quicker your Lusso will go around a race track. Convert to the bigger 330 2+2 calipers and brake pads and have even better brakes. You will carry far more speed through the corners and will therefore be faster down the straights. These improvements will result in a gain of nearly three to five seconds per lap at most tracks, at the very modest cost of $5,000 to $7,500.

As for the engine, while the Lusso V12 may have been rated at 280 hp, the reality is about 240 hp. Yes, you can add six carbs, but to optimize the improved airflow you should also have your engine builder send the heads to a good porting service, match the intake manifold ports to the cylinder head ports, and add the usual improved cams, modern pistons and rods. Then you'll easily have 290 hp, better torque and much better driveability. You will also have found another three to five seconds per lap, but the cost will range from $20,000 to $30,000.

But here's the real issue. Unless you have an FIA grade A or B competition license, go to a driver's school like Skip Barber's. A funky little FIA Historic license or a letter from Steve Earle with three gold stars for not hitting anybody at the Monterey Historics doesn't mean you can drive your way out of a paper bag, in real competition terms. All Ferraris have a racing heritage, and you will be amazed at what they will deliver when properly piloted.

—*Michael Sheehan*

From the January 2001 issue of *SCM.*◆

The 275 GTB/2—Sorry Guys, The Cheap Ones Are All Gone

Barely adequate brakes, a sexy squared-off nose that caused aerodynamic front-end lift, and vague steering over 100 mph combined for high-speed driving that kept a driver busy, to say the least

Last year it was Lussos that were in the Prancing Horse flavor-of-the-month club. Their values languished in the "why-would-you-want-one-of-those" $125,000-$150,000 range. Today, there are folks standing in line to buy great ones at $250,000 plus, and cars with period race history have cracked the $400,000 barrier.

Now it's the 275 GTB/2s that are making their run.

But before we talk prices, a short history lesson. These cars are properly called just 275 GTBs. That makes sense, because when they were built, there were no longnose or four-cam models being produced. It's just like with Jaguar E-types: The pre-1968 cars were never called "first series," not until the second series was introduced.

The 275, with its sensuous Pininfarina designed and Scaglietti-built body, is a study in mechanical evolution. The four variations are the original 275 GTB (referred to hereafter as the 275 GTB/2 shortnose), the 275 GTB/2 longnose, the 275 GTB/2 longnose torque tube, and the 275 GTB/4.

The 275 GTB/2 shortnose entered series production in 1964 with S/N 6003. It was Ferrari's first attempt at incorporating four-wheel independent suspension and a rear-mounted transaxle into a production car. It was also one of the final cars built by Ferrari that made a real attempt at being a true dual-purpose car, as capable of winning races as cruising down to St. Tropez in the summer.

The 275 was and continues to be visually breathtaking. In addition to its classic and sensual bodylines, it offered more-than-adequate performance, nimble handling, and the sounds of a screaming V12 rated at 280 hp (but actually producing about 260). But cockpit comfort and ventilation, rustproofing and the driver's rear vision were not high on the design committee's agenda.

Add in brakes that were described, in period, as "adequate" and a sexy squared-off nose that caused aerodynamic front-end lift and vague steering over 100 mph, and the end result was high-speed driving that was exciting and kept a driver busy, to say the least.

The 275 also had a solid-mounted driveshaft, with no U-joints, but instead a center-mounted bearing that required the crankshaft centerline, the driveshaft, the center support bearing, and the gearbox input shaft to be in perfect alignment or your teeth would be vibrated loose.

The 275 GTB longnose entered production in early-mid 1966, starting with S/Ns in the 7800 range. Its longer, lower front-end shape cured the aerodynamic lift problems, and a new driveshaft with constant-velocity joints solved the driveshaft vibration. A larger back window improved rear visibility, and dual side-mounted fuel tanks allowed the spare to be lowered, which coupled with external trunk hinges, provided more trunk room.

At the same time, the cylinder heads were fitted with improved valve guide seals, helping to reduce the typical early Ferrari exhaust smoke problem. About 102 longnose, CV-joint 275s left the factory.

In mid-1966, at S/N 8305, the "interim" driveshaft was replaced with a torque tube between the engine and gearbox, eliminating all driveshaft vibrations. About the same period, the brake system was updated with a much-improved master cylinder and power booster, improving the braking from "adequate" to "acceptable." About 108 of the 275 GTB longnoses were delivered with torque tubes.

Barrett-Jackson

European buyers are snapping these up.

The final iteration was the four-cam. Beginning with the prototype, S/N 8769, the new-and-improved 275 GTB/4 featured a dry-sump engine, with six dual-throat Webers standard (they were optional on some earlier models). Breathing and performance from the four-cam heads was much improved, with 300 claimed horsepower. Production ended with S/N 11069 for a total of 330 cars.

Shortnose 275 GTBs have jumped from the $200,000 range to the $275,000 range in only the last year, with almost all cars sold staying in or going to Europe.

There are two factors at work here. The first, although surprisingly not the most important, is the continuing devaluation of the American dollar against the euro. Cars with asking prices in cheap American "pesos" are simply 30 to 40 percent less expensive to a German, Swiss, English or French buyer than they were 18 months ago.

Second, and most important, is the continued rise in interest in events such as the Tour Auto, the Modena Cento Ore and the Tour d'Espagna. The cut-off date to be eligible for an overall win is generally 1965 or 1966, the final build years of the 275 GTB/2, although later cars can enter. European collectors are known for being less risk-averse than their often-timid American counterparts, and these "balls-out" events give them a chance to run their cars hard on hill-climbs and racetracks.

But as the numbers of applications continue to climb, event organizers look for cars that are increasingly exotic. They could easily fill their entire fields with 1965 Porsche 911S's, but instead try to have as many rare high-performance cars as possible. Hence the appeal of the 275/GTB2, as it was built in the right period, has a great look, and, of course, is a vintage V12 Ferrari.

Is it too late to get a great buy on a 275 GTB/2? If you mean in relation to last year's prices, yes. But Ferrari isn't building any more, and the number of rich guys who want to play hard with their toys continues to increase. Assuming the global economy continues to march along, there is no reason to expect that prices won't continue to rise to the tune of 10 to 15 percent per year.

If you're in the game for the long haul, I believe this is a model that hasn't yet hit the redline on its value curve.—*Michael Sheehan*

From the January 2004 issue of *SCM*.◆

C/4 or 456—No Shortage of Opinions

The C/4's sound is much better, and old sports cars are just plain cool... and cool counts for a lot

Last month we discussed Editor Martin's desire to have another four-seat, four-cam V12 Ferrari. After narrowing the choices to a 365 GTC/4 or a 456, we asked SCM'ers for their opinions. Veritably, the floodgate was thrown open, and my mailbox was overfilled with passionate responses. Here are some excerpts:

Dear Keith: Asking which car is for you is puzzling. You value the vintage ones, and the 456 sure ain't that. The 456 looks like a glorified Accord or Prelude. What's the question again?

The C/4 will only go up in price, while the 456 will only go down. Plus, the C/4's sound is much better, and 30-year-old sports cars are just plain cool. And cool counts for a lot.—***Tom Bush, Mauston, WI***

Dear Keith: As you know, I wasn't thrilled with your first two Ferrari purchases. I thought the 330 America needed too much work. And Mondials aren't my favorite for several reasons. Now you're thinking about a C/4 or a 456.

My advice? Get the C/4 or step up to a 330 GTC (financing is cheap these days, if you need it to make the step). The C/4 is a great driving car. I think they look better in person than photos, and are a good buy at today's prices for what they are.

The market disagrees—there are always a bunch for sale and few buyers, so when the time comes it will probably take far longer to sell than most other classic Ferrari models. I guess the looks and two back seats hold down their value. The 330 GTC is a great car all around—period.—***Randy Simon, via e-mail***

Dear Keith: Like Sheehan, I have owned a bunch of C/4s. When they were still new—and by that I mean less than 15 years old—they were considered on the same plane as a Daytona, but this was the car for the more mature enthusiast. It certainly made sense, with power steering, the extra room that is jokingly called rear seats, the nice upright seating position, etc.

However, once these cars started to acquire mileage their faults became obvious, not least of which was the extreme cost of the major service. As Mike noted, to do said service required the removal of all the carburetors, lines, etc. That's when the "while we're at it" comment comes from the mechanic, referring to doing new needles and seats, rebushing the throttle shafts, new fuel lines, etc.

Additionally, the C/4's water pump design, dead in the middle of the motor, requires a motor-out, timing case-off, chains-off labor bill of $5,000 minimum when the $20 bearing fails.

There's more: The A/C blows from the top of the dash, right onto the hot windshield. Nice, warm, wet air by the time it gets to you. That "mouse fur" dash material starts to lose its color on day one. Apparently Pininfarina never thought the cars would see sun.

Yep, these were fun cars, but once the services became due, it was *arrivederci.* So, unless you can verify that a major rebuild was done by a competent shop within the last few thousand miles, Pasadena on this model. (P.S. The Euro model has a single distributor with four sets of points. Try setting that sucker on the side of the road.)

As awful as these comments seem, an early 456 is worse. Much worse. It certainly is a lovely looking car, but I have been advised off them by my mechanic, who will be pleased to regale you with the stories about the poor quality and expensive repairs. For example, the auto trans (I appreciate that you'd get the stick) is a Ferrrari-built unit, which is sold only as a unit—no parts—and lists for $52,000!

Forget those four-seat toads, step up to a 330 GTC.

Now, I wouldn't be such an aggressive critic if I didn't have something good to say about a model that will fill the bill. I have owned five or six of these, and I find them to be delightful, irrespective of the initial ballyhoo about size when they first came out. If you are looking for a true four-seater, with easy service, a powerful and foolproof motor and well-designed accessories—the A/C actually blows from the face of the dash, onto the passengers, rather than off the top—you should seriously consider the 365 2+2.

Mistakenly called the Queen Mother, this car's wheelbase is the same as the C/4, it has modern four-wheel disc brakes, four-wheel coil-over-shock suspension—just like the C/4 and Daytona—has the same front-mounted five-speed ZF transmission as the C/4, power steering, power windows, a beautiful wood-fascia dash, a wood wheel in most cases (the late ones had leather), available wire wheels (same as Daytona), and in the right color—not red—like silver or grey metallic, black or navy, looks quite handsome.

On the road, the car never feels big, handles neutrally and is extremely comfortable to drive. The two-cam, three-carb, 320-hp motor has gobs of torque and a fabulous sound. It is the best of both Ferrari worlds, combining old handcrafted PF touches, like the wood, with modern Ferrari in the independent suspension and four-wheel discs. I would prefer that you get a Euro version for a lot of reasons, including the single rather than dual alternators, which I would discuss with you if you should like.—***Barry Russinof, via e-mail***

Dear Keith: In searching for a Ferrari, I researched these same two models. Having owned, maintained and driven 1960s Ferraris, Maseratis, Ford Mustangs and others, I remember the good and the bad. But now that I am in my 50s I have arrived at the conclusion that nostalgia sure ain't all that it is promoted to be. For my money I will wait for the price of 456Ms to come down a bit and then make my purchase.—***Jon F. Gasper, via e-mail***

From the April 2003 Issue of *SCM.*◆

What $200,000 Buys Today

You can buy a great 250 SWB or GTO rebody for vintage racing, but be prepared to watch $30,000 Corvettes pass you on the track

"I've always wanted to own a Ferrari." That's something I hear every day. It's usually accompanied with, "I've worked hard and my business is doing great. My kids are in college, and I just want to have some fun."

Okay so far. But then it gets a little more confusing. Some of these Prancing-Horse newbies are determined to only buy a Ferrari that's a good investment. Others want a daily driver. Some want to have a guaranteed entry in the Mille Miglia. Others want to go on the New England 1000. In one e-mail, I was asked to compare a 360 Spyder, a Daytona, a 288 GTO and a 246 Dino. Well... they all have wheels.

A number that seems to keep cropping up in these requests is $200,000. There seems to be some swagger to saying, "I've got 200 large to spend for a toy." Only a few years ago, this money would buy a Ferrari suitable for vintage rallies, vintage racing or the concours circuit. But rising prices have made your choices more limited today.

What follows is a quick survey of the $200,000 Ferrari market, starting with current production cars.

In the world of newer Ferraris, $200,000 will buy you a 2001 U.S.-market 360 spyder, a new 360 coupe with change left over, or a year-old, mid-miles 575. Using the 575 as an example, the "as-new" cost, out the door with tax and license was $250,000 to $275,000. Today's asking price, according to the most recent *Ferrari Market Letter*, runs from $207,500 to $218,900 for a 2002, but real money is around $200,000. The first owner took a $50,000 to $75,000 hit to get to drive his car. As the second owner, your depreciation will be less, but not by much if you keep the car for very long. If you want a 550 Barchetta, $200,000 is getting close for a Euro car that has been DOT-ed, but you'll need $250,000 to $275,000 for a U.S. model. However, if you wait until the snowdrifts get deep, you'll save. With its ridiculous top, the 550 Barchetta is a fair-weather-only car. By January you'll be able to by a Euro car for $200,000, and be $25,000 closer on a U.S. model.

In the older Ferrari market, only two years ago $200,000 would have given you your pick of 275 GTB short-noses, Lussos, or a pair of not-so-nice Daytonas. However, recent sales have seen short-nose 275s at a stunning $275,000, good Lussos over $200,000, and very nice Daytonas selling quickly for as much as $150,000. Most Ferrari "experts" have always maintained that these cars have been undervalued for a decade—it's nice to be right once in a while!

Want to go racing? While $200,000 might buy you a non-factory competition Daytona conversion or a steel-bodied Boano, they are only eligible for the U.S. Historic Challenge, not in Europe. The same amount will get you a great 250 SWB or GTO rebody, but forget the top-flight events. You had better be happy racing in VARA or HSR events where you will have a great seat to watch $30,000 Corvettes pass you by. As for the Mille Miglia, Tour Auto or other top European events, $200,000 will no longer get you a car that will be accepted.

Club racing your passion? 360 Challenge cars start at $100,000, 355 Challenge cars at $60,000 and 348 Challenge cars at just $50,000. They are all Cavallino and FCA national meet eligible, and SCCA eligible. This is your chance to be a real Ferrari race driver on the cheap—if you don't stuff your toy into the tire barriers. Alas, few seem to care about this series here in the U.S. Unlike Europe, where Challenge grids are always chock full, risk-averse Americans don't seem eager to flog their cars every weekend, leading to thin fields and consequently low resale values on these cars.

Determining exactly how you are going to use your car will significantly narrow your selection.

Concours your thing? If you want to be on the lawn at the Greater Syracuse Italian Exotic Car Show and Barbecue, your $200,000 will get you a Daytona or a pair of Dinos and a VIP pass. (As an aside, some concours seem to make a point of giving some sort of an award to every Enzo, which I find exceedingly odd—isn't it just a new car?) In any event, $200,000 will no longer get you within shouting distance of a car eligble for Pebble Beach or the Bagatelle. Time and the market have passed you by.

Finally, what about American vintage tours? Well, there's good news and bad news. The good: There are still a number of Ferraris in this price range that will be acceptable to most of these events. The bad: Given American driving styles and our often-exuberant state troopers, you're usually better off with a cheaper car that you can flog harder without winding up in jail.

The premier American event is the Colorado Grand, where all the big boys show off their pre-1961 cars. While $200,000 will still buy a 250 PF Cabriolet series II or a steel Boano, both acceptable, a Maserati Vignale Spyder will get you in even faster and be as much fun to drive, this at half the price. For the California Mille, with all its twisting back roads, I suggest an Alfa Giulietta Spyder. Pay $30,000 for a great one and put the rest of your money into a perfect Daytona to use as a support car. For the New England 1000, how about a nice 365 GTC 2+2 for $50,000? You'll have a better time than the guys in the Barchettas, and have room in the back seat for all the outfits your significant other will want to wear to the great dinners at all the tony resorts.

In most automotive circles, $200,000 is still a lot of money. It will buy a pair of Porsche Cayenne Turbos, three E-Classes and who cares how many Kia Rios. But when it comes to new or high-end-vintage-event eligible Ferraris, two hundred large is just a starting point.—*Michael Sheehan*

From the December 2003 issue of *SCM*.◆

Please Stand Back While We Smash Your Hood

As you might expect from people new to the world of bureaucracy, their knee-jerk reaction to anything in the least bit unusual is to "Just Say No"

If you're thinking of bringing a Ferrari into the US, I have some simple advice that might save you months of aggravation and thousands of dollars. Simply put, under no circumstances should you bring your car in through Los Angeles or Miami.

Chicago, San Francisco, Seattle and even, strangely enough, New York have proven to be "import friendly." But dealing with Customs in LA or Miami is a completely different situation. I speak from experience.

Strangely enough, '57 TRC won't meet 1968 EPA regulations.

Some background: When forced to bring a car from overseas in through LA, I generally use Martin Button at Cosdel International to do the forwarding. To physically clear Customs, a car is brought to Price Transfer, a secure facility the size of four football fields. Ferraris, containers of tires and piles of foodstuffs from Pakistan all sit in the same warehouses, waiting to be cleared.

In fact, Price is so large that it has a US Customs office inside of its warehouse.

I have learned the hard way that Customs agents are generally rotated every 90 to 120 days, each time going to an area that is often completely new to them. Further, since the Homeland Security program was instituted, the experienced Customs agents have generally been promoted, and those assigned to low-priority jobs like clearing cars tend to be new to the job. And as you might expect from people new to the world of bureaucracy, their knee-jerk reaction to anything in the least bit unusual is to "just say no."

I recently imported 500 TRC S/N 0708 MDTR from Japan, with the car ultimately bound for a Canadian client. The Ferrari arrived at Long Beach harbor and was taken to Price Transfer for de-containerization and Customs clearance on Dec. 19, 2002.

I provided paperwork to Cosdel, which sent it to Price, which furnished it to Customs. A few days later, Customs gave Price, which forwarded to Cosdel, which sent to me, a rejection of the importation.

The reason? We had not provided proof that the 1957 TRC was exempt from EPA and DOT regulations. Customs wanted to know why there was not an EPA or DOT exemption plate attached to the car. As nicely as I could, I replied (through Cosdel to Price to Customs), that it seemed unreasonable for Ferrari, in 1957, to have guessed that 11 years later, in 1968, the US would implement DOT and EPA regulations, and to have "forward-fitted" an exemption plate.

Finally, a month later, on Jan 19, 2002, the 500 TRC was cleared through Customs. As the car had originally been scheduled to appear at the Cavallino Classic—which started on January 21 in West Palm Beach, Florida—and unveiled there as a surprise to the owner's wife, the owner was not a very happy camper. Of course, neither explanation nor apology for the delay and inconvenience was provided by Customs.

While this was going on, I imported 1962 250 SWB S/N 3409 (with engine #3441, from a 1962 250 GTE) from Japan, also through Long Beach Customs. It arrived at Price Transfer on January 7 for de-containerization and Customs clearance. Since this time the Customs officials had been briefed on the non-applicability of the EPA and DOT regulations, bringing in 250 SWB S/N 3409 should have been a walk-through.

But Customs decided that since S/N 3409 was fitted with a different engine than it was born with, they wanted proof that this "different engine" didn't need to be EPA and DOT approved.

More trees died in our effort to prove that engines built prior to the not-yet-thought-of DOT and EPA regulations were indeed exempt from those not-yet-thought-of regulations. Finally, Customs decided that an engine built in 1962 was exempt from the 1968 and later regulations, and that S/N 3409 would be released.

Wait, not so fast. At the last minute, the ever-vigilant folks at Customs decided they should inspect this newer engine, just to make sure it was okay and eligible for importation.

Getting to the engine required opening the hood. It would have been easy to ask any of the staff at Price Transfer to open the hood for inspection, but they had all been banished from the room so that they wouldn't "interfere" with the process. Using the standard "we-can-beat-it-into-submission" approach, the agents literally pried one side of the hood open, destroying the hood hinges and buckling the hood.

But even with the hinges destroyed, the hood still refused to open. So the agents used a large piece of wood, inserted through the opening of the now partially pried-open hood, to beat the hood latch into oblivion, releasing the hood. After careful inspection of whatever it was they wanted to inspect, the car was released by US customs and dutifully picked up. Total time in custody: 60 days. Once again, there was neither an explanation nor an apology given for the time delay, the extra storage charges or the obvious damage to the hood of the 250 SWB.

In the official Customs evaluation of the incident, when answering the question of, "How do we prevent this incident from happening again," the agent responsible wrote, "Learn how to open hoods of cars we are examining."

Unless we want to hire an attorney and sue Customs, we have no recourse for the damages. I spoke with some of the folks at the Customs office about reporting the damage to the director of the office there, and their advice to me was to just keep quiet—unless I wanted to be guaranteed that every car I brought into Long Beach for the next 20 years would take slightly longer than forever to clear Customs.

During this period, I also imported 1955 Ferrari 857 Monza S/N 0578 in February of 2003. Coming in through Chicago, it cleared Customs in just two days.

I'm all in favor of doing everything necessary to help keep our country safe. I just can't help but wonder how destroying the hood on an SWB makes things any better for any of us. And a little politeness, courtesy and explanation of various delays from Customs might make us feel much better about the whole process.—*Michael Sheehan*

From the June 2003 issue of *SCM.*◆

Clone Wars

The creative (and sometimes lucrative) end result of a single crashed or otherwise destroyed car becoming two or more re-created cars, each claiming remnants of the original

Of the 33 250 TRs originally built by Ferrari, there are at least 46 in existence today. As with Alfa Monzas, Bugatti Grand Prix cars and Jaguar D-types, this TR population explosion is often the creative (and sometimes lucrative) end result of a single crashed or otherwise destroyed car becoming two or more re-created cars, each claiming remnants of the original. One example of this automotive cloning is 250 TR S/N 0720TR, a version of which was offered at the recent Bonhams Auction at Gstaad.

The original 250 TR S/N 0720TR, a standard left-hand drive, pontoon-fender car, sold new to Luigi Chinetti Motors and then to amateur racer Jim Johnston of Cincinnati, Ohio. It was raced by Johnson in 1958 and '59, and then sold to Dave Biggs of Clarksville, Missouri, who raced it in the early 1960s. In 1965 this Ferrari was virtually destroyed when lightening struck Biggs's barn, starting a fire that destroyed the building, an adjoining garage and workshop, and the other cars, including an Alfa 8C 2900, inside.

Now the plot thickens. Some claim that Biggs decided to bulldoze the burned ruins, and buried the debris in a ravine, with the frame eventually ending up under the Forest Park Highway.

Others claim that the remnants of the frame, along with a front suspension, steering and a crankshaft of the Biggs 250 TR were dug up by *SCM* subscriber Henry Wessels on April 23 and 24, 1987, as he went about finding the chassis and other bits from which the 8C 2900, S/N 412021, could be reborn.

In any case, the Wessels-found Biggs frame and bits were sold to English collector Rodney Felton, who had a complete car recreated by Rod Jolley Coachwork in England. This 250 TR eventually went to Harald and Ingeborg Mergard, a German couple with a substantial Ferrari collection who also sponsor the Barchetta website (http://www.barchetta.cc/All.Ferraris/), a favorite of many Ferrari enthusiasts. For photos of the frame and parts, as recovered, and the Mergard's version of this saga, the reader is invited to visit www.barchetta.cc/All.Ferraris/250-tr-0720tr/index.html.

But our excitement is just beginning. A second chassis, allegedly also carrying S/N 0720TR, turned up in Italy in 1980. In 1981 the frame, now restored, was sold to Dutch collector Paul Schouwenburg, who spent the 1980s collecting an impressive array of original TR parts for this project. Dutch panel builder Alwin Hietbrink later built a duplicate pontoon-fender body. The car was completed in early 1996 and in December of last year was offered at the Bonhams & Brooks Gstaad sale, carefully described as a "1958-type Ferrari 250 Testa Rossa Reproduction Incorporating Many Original Components, with Coachwork After Carrozzeria Scaglietti."

TRs are too easily duplicated.

"As so often happens when big dollars and big egos are on the line, lawyers soon appeared and the Schouwenburg 250 TR was slammed with an injunction initiated by the Mergards, removed from the sale, and Bonhams was ordered to render pages 124 through 129 of their catalog unreadable."

As so often happens when big dollars and big egos are on the line, lawyers soon appeared and the Schouwenburg 250 TR was slammed with an injunction initiated by the Mergards, removed from the sale, and Bonhams was ordered to "render pages 124 through 129 of their catalog unreadable." (Personally, I consider most pages of auction catalogs unreadable anyway.) But now 0720TR, or the replica thereof, is embroiled in yet another exotic car court action, in which only the lawyers will be the victors.

To add further excitement, there are rumors of a third "duplicato" existing in Italy, also carrying S/N 0720TR. A hearing on the Bonhams car is scheduled for the near future, so stay tuned for future developments.

For more information about S/N 0720TR, see Cavallino *magazine, #79 (February/March 1994) for Jerry McDermott's "The Phoenix Testa Rossa," a detailed and thorough history of the car until that time.—Michael Sheehan*

From the February 2002 issue of *SCM*.◆

Which Ferrari for the Mille Miglia?

First, ask yourself if you want to be dry, relatively warm and comfortable, or if you want to go fast, be wet, cold and dazzle the crowds

The Mille Miglia is the ultimate vintage car event, and a Ferrari is the ultimate car to drive in it. Which Ferrari to pilot, however, depends on your checkbook and tolerance for pain.

First, ask yourself if you want to be dry, relatively warm and comfortable, or if you want to go fast, be wet, cold and dazzle the crowds.

My "luxury" choice would be any of the 250 coupes or Berlinettas that qualify for acceptance.

250 TdF, the luxurious way to go.

The best 250 TdF will cost over $1,000,000 today, and a properly sorted one (i.e., not Rodeo-Drive puffed but road-race ready) will offer prodigious power, light weight, nimble steering, adequate brakes and predictable handling wrapped in a package that represents landmark styling. A TdF is one of those friendly race cars that makes a bad driver look good.

If your budget is a little more modest, for $150,000 a 250 Boano with period race history has nearly everything that the TdF does, except for the styling. Under the skin, a Boano and a TdF are really the same. And, with the magic of today's technology, a good mechanic can make a Boano go faster than its creators ever dreamed it could.

By comparison, masochists can choose a very early 166, 195, 212 or 225 coupe, any of which will immerse the driver in total automotive agony. For starters, you get inadequate brakes, a recalcitrant and noisy gearbox, a weak differential and gearing best suited for a garden tractor. Add a hamster-sized powerplant, extraordinary oil consumption and seats crafted for a deformed Italian midget, and you've got the total picture.

The primitive coupes do have a roof, windows that will keep out some rain, defrosters guaranteed to drive you mad and token wipers usable until moisture appears. Your car will always be surrounded by fawning Italians while you are stopped by the side of the road, hood-up, desperately trying to locate that strange whining or grinding sound or find the source of all the oil and water that is leaking onto the rich, Italian soil.

If you opt for an early open car, get ready for a stylish but slow boat ride. You'll find yourself in the rain, dripping wet, freezing and sloshing in a leaky but very expensive (and soon to be rusting) Italian bath tub, all while fighting off terminal exhaustion with fading headlights.

> **"The Italian crowds went mad at the sight of our pontoon-fendered Testarossa...the teeming masses parted as if I were Caesar entering Rome, returning victorious from protecting the Empire ..."**

The ultimate car for the MM is a 250 TR. Driving one requires only chutzpah and an unlimited checkbook. They are blindingly fast, so you can get through the rainstorm a little faster. And the heat coming off the engine will keep your toes warm even if your nose, cheeks and fingertips are freezing.

I drove the MM in 250 TR S/N 0732, white with a blue stripe. On a rare warm and sunny afternoon, the Italian crowds went mad at the sight of our pontoon-fendered Testarossa. In the towns, the teeming masses parted as if I were Caesar entering Rome, returning victorious from protecting the Empire.

Hearing Italians of all ages shout, "*bella macchina*" as you speed by, engine shrieking at 8,000 rpm, is an experience that simply can't be replicated. Suddenly, you forget about all the discomforts and revel in the extraordinary experience of driving a legendary race car on the very roads it was born to compete on.—*Michael Sheehan*

From the November 2001 issue of *SCM*.◆

Pay to Play - Restoring a 250 SWB

As the former owner of a restoration shop, I can provide blow-by-blow details of the financial misery

"This 250 SWB has been the object of a $200,000 restoration," is an oft-seen phrase in auction catalog descriptions. Just how can you spend that much on a car? As the former owner of a restoration shop, I can provide a blow-by-blow detailing of the financial misery.

Any "total" restoration begins by taking the car completely apart. In this case, we'll assume it's a steel-bodied 250 SWB, but it would be nearly the same for almost any vintage V12. All chrome, glass, doors and body trim are removed; the engine, transmission and differential come out; the suspension and brakes removed; and the complete interior, dash and wiring harness are removed. Each component must be properly (and painstakingly) organized, labeled and stored. Estimated time for a single mechanic is about two weeks for a total of 80 hours at $75 per hour ($6,000).

The next step is stripping 40 years of accumulated paint and filler. Total time is about 80 hours at $50 an hour ($4,000), plus another $1,000 in stripping materials, masking paper and the disposal of hazardous waste. Total: $5,000.

While procedures vary from shop to shop, most shops next sandblast the frame and subframes to remove decades of rust. Estimated cost for frame and subframe blasting: $2,500.

Next it's time to zinc chromate, epoxy coat and paint the frame and floor to rust proofing standards never dreamed of when these cars were new. Total time is 20 hours at $50 per hour, plus materials of $500. Total: $1,500.

With our subject car in bare metal, it's now time to face the realities of 40 years of previous accidents, bad repairs, rust, poor factory panel fit and other evils that surface when you take a Ferrari apart. While in theory it's possible the car could be undamaged, the reality is that the owner would be very lucky to get by with only several long weeks of panel repair. Best case, I would figure about 100 hours at $75 an hour, or $7,500.

A much more likely scenario, however, is that our subject 250 SWB will have been hit in the front and require substantial repairs to the nose, new door skins, two new rocker panels and a complete trunk floor. Assume that new floors will be needed, which will take 400 hours of metal work at $75 an hour, or $30,000 for all the necessary body work.

A good paint job will take 300 hours, but factor in another 100 hours at $60 an hour, plus another $3,000 for materials (a total of $27,000) if you are aiming for that Platinum Award at Pebble Beach.

A top-quality leather interior with new carpets and headliner will add $7,500, show-quality chrome will add $5,000, and rebuilding the wire wheels and knock-offs will add $5,000. Accessories such as the correct radiator cap, decals and trim, a replica tar-top battery, and new lenses will consume another $5,000. We have just added at least $22,500 to the bill.

An engine rebuild will start at $25,000, a gearbox rebuild at $5,000, a differential rebuild at $5,000 and a new exhaust will add $4,000. Re-plating the suspension, all new suspension bushings and shocks will add another $5,000 and a complete brake system rebuild will add $5,000. Subtotal for mechanical work, before we talk about updated pistons, bigger valves, short ratio gear sets and other improvements? $49,000.

Should the owner want big cams, higher-compression pistons, cylinder head porting work, suspension sorting and other "wish list" items, add a minimum of $10,000.

Another $35,000 to make sure wipers wipe and switches switch.

But there's more. The car has to be put back together without the slightest scratch. The wiring, steering, engine, gearbox, differential, fuel system and all-new brake lines must all be properly remounted. In my experience, the real time killers are things like door trim that has to fit perfectly, door glass that has to go up and down, a heater and wipers that are actually supposed to heat and wipe, and switches that are supposed to switch. To accomplish the re-assembly, add another 400 hours at $75 an hour, or $30,000.

The total for all the above? Close to $200,000, and there's still more.

We need to disassemble the grille, have it polished and refitted (at $2,500), get all new hoses ($1,000), new tires ($1,500) and a mass of other things that could continue for several pages. Of course we also have to test drive the car to find the many minor oil and water leaks that will develop, door latches that won't shut, and electrical systems that mysteriously will not cooperate. It is virtually impossible to give an estimate for these extras.

The sum for most "total" restorations done to the highest standard? About 2,000 hours, or an entire man-year. Then you have to add in parts, sublet and materials. Suddenly, $200,000 makes sense. There is no Wal-Mart option when it comes to a top-flight restoration.

And, last but not least, the kicker. It costs more to do the same thing on a lowly 250 PF coupe than on a 250 SWB, as the Pininfarina bodies are more complicated to work on, have many more trim and detail parts, more luxurious interiors, and simply require more hours, parts and materials. Which, of course, is what makes a perfectly and correctly done PF coupe at $125,000 a relative bargain, even if a market-value risk.

Of course, you don't have to go this route, and can simply take your 330 GT that runs well and doesn't smoke too much, have it sanded down and smoothed out, and throw a $3,000 paint job on it. Add a couple of sheepskin seat covers from Costco and get ready to enjoy that snazzy Neahkahnie Beach Cruise In trophy you'll surely win. And who's to say that the SWB owner at Pebble, should he fail to get his Platinum, is any happier after spending his $200,000 and coming up just a bit short.—*Michael Sheehan*

From the October 2002 issue of *SCM*.◆

Four Cams and Four Seats, 456 Meets 365 GTC/4

In many ways, the C/4 and the 456 GT are interchangeable... the difference is over 20 years of evolution

SCM readers are aware that our esteemed editor, Keith Martin, is once again on the hunt for a V12 Ferrari. Reading that he was looking for a 365 GTC/4, subscriber John Weinberger of Continental Motors, an authorized Ferrari dealer in the Chicago area, called him immediately. "Do yourself a favor," he said. "Get a manual 1995 456 GT that's just had a recent major service. It's a better car in every way, you'll have much less grief, and it is really a more pleasurable ownership experience for not much more money."

Limited production translates to possible appreciation.

Not as rare, but easier to live with.

And so Martin called your faithful scribe and asked his opinion.

In many ways, the 365 GTC/4 (the "C/4") and the 456 GT are interchangeable. When new, both were built for the affluent buyer who wanted a top-of-the-line Ferrari with two occasional rear seats. What sets them apart is over 20 years of evolution in terms of creature comfort and mechanical sophistication.

The 365 GTC/4 is an affordable front-engine 1970s V12 classic with, in my opinion, the best exhaust sound of any street Ferrari ever built. Its 24-valve, four-cam, 320-horsepower 4.4-liter V12 propels the C/4 through the quarter-mile in 15.7 seconds. With a 152-mph top end, it has enough performance to put the owner in jail in all 50 states. Power steering makes the C/4 user-friendly and the heater and air conditioning are adequate. The cockpit personifies the '70s look with a large steering wheel, big gauges, a prominent shift lever and rear seats acceptable to human beings under 12 years of age. The C/4 is mechanically simple and can be tuned by a Weber-fluent technician. Best of all, you don't need a laptop computer to diagnose anything.

Unfortunately the C/4 is now 30 years old, with mechanical, body and trim parts that have far outlived their original planned duty cycle. This makes the C/4 the Ferrari poster child for a very detailed pre-purchase inspection. A major service, should you need one, starts at about $5,000, and the "while-you're-at-its" of new clutches, cam chains, water hoses, air conditioning reseals, new synchros, suspension bushings and shock rebuilds can quickly double or triple that amount.

The much-newer 456 GT is a technological showcase, and offers an ownership experience just eight years removed from what is currently available on the Ferrari dealer's showroom floor. Like the C/4, it has diminutive rear seats. For $75,000 to $85,000, you get a 48-valve, four-cam, 5.5-liter V12 engine that puts out 436 hp and 398 pounds-feet of torque. The 456 offers staggering performance, blasting through the quarter-mile in 13.4 seconds and 107.5 mph, and tops out at 186 mph.

The user-friendly cockpit, luxurious seating, easy-to-read gauges and six-speed shifter make driving a pleasure. The air conditioning and heating are nearly up to world-class (i.e., Honda Accord) standards. And while the 456 may lack the wonderful exhaust sound of the C/4, its comfortable and quiet cockpit will make a 200-mile drive to your vacation home a memorable experience rather than a reason to get out the aspirin or visit your chiropractor.

A major service on a 456 starts at about $5,000 but can go up if you add a new clutch, shocks, etc. Because the 456 is more than 20 years further down the road of Ferrari evolution than the C/4, the potential mechanical and electrical problem list is shorter, and the dependability and parts availability are much improved. As with all Ferraris, a pre-purchase inspection is still mandatory, and with the 456 must include a leak-down and compression test, no matter how few miles the car may have. There have been more than a few disturbing reports of otherwise pristine 456s (and 550s and 355s) having serious compression problems due to valve seats poorly machined by the factory.

1995 456 GTs have dropped from their original MSRP of $225,000 to $75,000 to $85,000. An updated 456 variant is scheduled for 2004, which is guaranteed to hurt the market value of all current 456s.

With 1,548 456 GTs, 403 GTAs and more than 2,000 GTMs built (and still being built)—an 8:1 ratio when compared with the C/4—the newer 456 will never have the same exclusivity as the vintage four-seater.

Almost all the same "old versus new" arguments can be made for those choosing between the classic lines of a 365 GTB/4 Daytona (1,279 built) versus a 550 Maranello (3,600 built) or, for those with a few more dollars to spend, choosing between a 365 GTS/4 Daytona Spyder (121 built) versus a 550 Barchetta (448 built). I would guess that in 20 years the value of a C/4, Daytona or Daytona Spyder will probably be more, perhaps double, that of the much more common 456, 550 Maranello and 550 Barchetta.

Since both the 365 GTC/4 and the 456 GT were built for the same potential buyer profile (albeit three decades apart), and both are very close in price today and nearly interchangeable in use, the bottom-line question is simple. Does our editor want to revisit his long-lost youth and experience the sounds and sensations of the classic Ferrari he couldn't afford when it was new in the early 1970s, or does he prefer to move up to the world of the 1990s, with all of its technological and creature-comfort advances?—*Michael Sheehan*

From the February 2003 issue of *SCM*.◆

Russian Roulette, Ferrari Style

When the car arrived, it was beautiful in its fresh, high-dollar paint job, the redone chrome sparkled in the Southern California sunlight, and the immaculate Connolly leather interior looked as if it had never been sat in

I have a client who has purchased many modern Ferraris over the phone with no inspection, including an F50, a pair of F40s, a 550 Maranello and numerous 360 coupes and Spyders. All of the cars arrived exactly as described, that is, "essentially a new car with no stories."

Lulled into a sense of complacency by the ease of these transactions, he recently purchased an early V12 2+2, which was described as "restored to new-car standards with no stories." No pre-purchase inspection, no test drive, nothing. When the car arrived, it was beautiful in its fresh, high-dollar paint job, the redone chrome sparkled in the Southern California sunlight, and the immaculate Connolly leather interior looked as if it had never been sat in.

Beauty may only be skin deep.

The new owner drove the car around the block, commented on how "vintage" it felt (that being Ferrarese for clunky and heavy) and put it into his warehouse. A few weeks later, when he drove the car on the freeway, he smelled raw gas. It appeared the carburetors were leaking so he had the car shipped to FAI, an independent Ferrari specialist in Orange County. The estimate to repair the leaks was $300. At the same time, he asked for a detailed mechanical inspection and evaluation.

The initial inspection filled a full page, including radiator leaks ($300); a lower radiator hose leak ($50); a much-needed water pump rebuild ($400); carburetor fuel log leaks ($300); fuel filter leaks ($300); fuel leaks at the mechanical pump ($400); missing bolts on the header flanges (no charge); a rear main seal leak (yikes!); cam cover leaks (two yikes!); and warped brake rotors and worn front spindles.

"The owner, of course, didn't have a clue how bad the car was until it was inspected. He had simply assumed that 'all old Ferraris drove like that.' If he had had the car evaluated before he bought it, he would have walked away."

I was called to confirm the inspection report and, unfortunately, found all of the above to be painfully accurate. $300 had quickly grown to an all-too-necessary $2,000 plus.

A few days later, after the many fuel leaks were repaired, it was back to FAI for a very short test drive. Within two city blocks the list grew to include an overdrive that didn't work (three yikes!); a rotten driveshaft rubber coupling; a differential that leaked and had that very expensive bucket-of-rocks death rattle (a $3,000 to $5,000 yikes); worn-out shocks ($1,500); and a thoroughly worn-out front suspension ($2,500 to $4,000). In FAI's estimation, all of the above work was desperately needed, and the car was better off not being driven until these things were fixed. (Well, I suppose they could wait on the overdrive and he could buzz down the freeway in fourth.)

The owner, of course, didn't have a clue how bad the car was until it was inspected. He had simply assumed that "all old Ferraris drove like that." If he had had the car evaluated before he bought it, he would have walked away.

There are three lessons here. First of all, when buying an old Ferrari, be skeptical of anything a seller says that isn't backed up by independent verification. With this car, it appears that the "total restoration to new car standards" went only as far as the cosmetics. The visual presentation was stunning, but everything mechanical was apparently not overhauled, just cleaned and detailed. To me, this indicates a restoration done to a budget. When choices between mechanical functionality and visual beauty came up, the owner and restorer opted to put their limited resources towards the pretty things instead of the hidden, and perhaps more important, things.

Second, although we at *SCM* often preach about the fiscal propriety of buying a restored car ("buy the restoration, get the car for free"), in fact, there are some real advantages to having a car restored yourself. Most important, you get to make all the decisions about the type and quality of work done. Yes, it will cost more, yes, it will take longer, and yes, there will be numerous frustrations encountered. But in the end, you will know exactly what you have under the metal skin.

Finally, old cars are old cars. Buying a new Ferrari, or even a 10- or 15-year-old one that has a perfect ownership history and service records, is really not very complicated. However, with a 40-year-old V12, chances are that at some point every single part on the car has worn out and been touched. From paint to wheel bearings to exhaust tips, they've all been serviced, repaired or replaced. And for many years, when these Ferraris had little real value, they rarely received the best of care.

Consequently, you can't be too careful when you buy an old car, even if it is claimed to be "as new." In fact, it will never be "as new," at best it can only be completely restored. To what standard, and to what budget, are the questions you will have to try to find answers to.

If you must buy cars over the phone without an inspection, for your own fiscal sanity, please stick to late-model cars that have never been touched. Buying vintage V12s without an inspection is like playing financial Russian Roulette with a bullet in every chamber of a Desert Eagle handgun.—*Michael Sheehan*

From the April 2002 issue of *SCM*.◆

456s and 550s: Just Used Cars

The good news is that if your reasons for owning a 456 or 550 extend beyond impressing the parking lot attendant at Spago, these cars are becoming really good buys

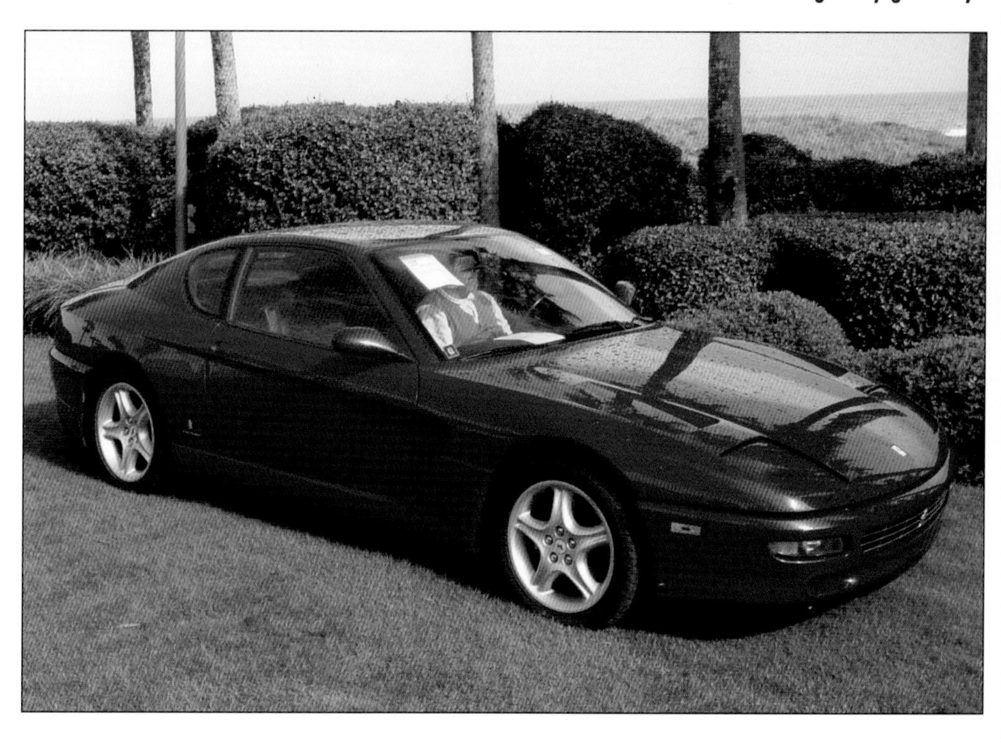

The 550 Maranello and 456 GT and GTA are today's state-of-the-art grand touring Ferraris, offering supercar performance in a luxurious and very stylish package. Yet in the past year these cars have dropped drastically in value. Today, real money for a 1995 456 GT with low miles, good colors and full service is about $95,000 while a 1997 550 with the same features will sell for about $150,000, both down about $40,000 in the last year.

Further, less-than-perfect cars are taking a real hit. At the eBay/Kruse auction in Scottsdale, a yellow, partial respray, non-mileage-verified, lease-return (how's that for a list of attributes) 1997 456 GT (S/N 100270) sold on Saturday for $88,250, and was resold on Sunday for $94,350 (page 33). I wouldn't want to be the one trying to resell it again.

Of course, all new cars, even Ferraris, depreciate. But this recent drop has been hastened by a recession centered on the high-tech industries and the drop in the NASDAQ. The consensus among dealers is that high-tech whiz-kids in their 20s, 30s and early 40s made up a solid 25 percent of the recent new Ferrari buyers. Many have left the market until their businesses recover.

Additionally, both the 550 and the 456 are near the end of their production run and will be replaced soon. This means many of those who can afford to play are waiting for the latest new toy and have already had, and often sold, their 456 or 550, adding more cars to the secondary market.

Remember that few people use their new Ferraris on a daily basis. They are more often purchased as a statement of success. And somehow, bragging about "getting a good deal on a used, lease-return 456" doesn't carry the same panache as saying, "I cashed in a few options and went down to Ferrari of Seattle to pick up my new 360 Modena Spyder."

While Ferrari now builds world cars, with identical emissions and safety equipment wherever they are sold, the cost of a new 550 or 456 is much more in the US than in Europe. Many enthusiasts and entrepreneurs have taken advantage of this Ferrari arbitrage and bought, converted and imported Euro cars, making that many more cars available in our market.

"The consensus among dealers is that high-tech whiz-kids in their 20s, 30s and early 40s made up a solid 25 percent of the recent new Ferrari buyers. Many have left the market until their businesses recover."

The good news, of course, is that if your reasons for owning a 456 or 550 extend beyond impressing the parking lot attendant at Spago, these cars are becoming really good buys. Furthermore, with a 550 at $150,000 approaching the value of a good Daytona (about $125,000) and a 456 GT at $95,000 (not too much over the price of a good 365 GTC/4 at $60,000). I believe that both the 550 and the 456 are nearing the bottom of their depreciation cycles. Post-1970s serial-production Ferraris seem to find a level and just stay there, like 308 GTSs at $25,000-$30,000 or first-generation Testarossas in the $40,000-$60,000 range.

It is my prediction that within a year a 1997 US-model 550 Maranello will bottom out at about $125,000 while a similar 456 will stabilize at about $75,000. For the user, both offer one hell of a lot of performance for not a lot of money—and if properly taken care of, will suffer very little from further depreciation. *—Michael Sheehan*

From the March 2002 issue of *SCM*.◆

The Cost of a Dream

I just want to have the experience of owning the car for a while... hopefully I can get the damn thing out of my system without losing my house

Dear Mr. Sheehan: *Over 25 years ago I nearly bought a '67 Ferrari 330 GT 2+2 and have kicked myself ever since for not doing so. Now, being richer but not necessarily wiser, I would still like to own this car. I realize it's not a "collector," but it is a V12 Ferrari.*

If one could find a reasonably good example for $50,000 to $60,000, with the idea of driving it for a year or two (weekends, nice days, etc.), what kind of routine operating expenses might be expected? I'm not expecting to sell at a profit. I just want to have the experience of owning the car for a while. Hopefully I can get the damn thing out of my system without losing my house.—***H. N., Redwood Shores, CA.***

In the early 1970s, *Road & Track* chose Ferrari owners for their first owner's survey, and in that survey was the fateful sentence that inspired my first Ferrari purchase, "It's the nicest thing I ever did for me." Since you only live once, you should get the car of your dreams.

"'It's the nicest thing I ever did for me.' Since you only live once, you should get the car of your dreams."

While lacking the voluptuous good looks of their cousins, the 275 GTBs, the 330 2+2s offer the same performance at less than one quarter the cost. Choose the later two-headlight version and you have an attractive mount with a bulletproof five-speed, perfunctory air conditioning, power windows and even power steering—all in all a very user-friendly package.

Since no one wants to have their dreams turn to nightmares, your first mission is to look at every 330 2+2 that comes up for sale within a reasonable distance, as well as 250 GTEs, 365 GT 2+2s and 400s. Try to go to a couple of the larger auctions where there are usually a few affordable V12s on offer. The more cars you look at, the better.

Fortunately for you, many Ferraris were restored or over-restored in the crazy late 1980s. Your goal is to find a 330 2+2 that once had a $100,000 restoration but is now priced under $50,000.

When you find the right car, have it inspected by a Ferrari shop and get their estimate of recommended repairs in writing. As well as the usual bad ball joints, loose tie-rod ends, rubber hoses as hard as hockey pucks and the seemingly standard issue oil leaks, the car will probably also need a minimal mechanical service, a wheel alignment, an oil and filter change and a flush of the hydroscopic brake fluid. Also, make sure the body is inspected by a qualified body shop for rust and previous damage or repairs, an area many overlook.

1966 330 GT 2+2

Don't be surprised if the best car you find needs $5,000 to $10,000 in recommended repairs and deferred maintenance. Use the shop's estimate as a negotiating tool to drive the best deal possible.

If you do your homework, have patience and negotiate well, you'll find the right car. Then you can write the checks for the car and the recommended repairs, and drive off a happy first-time Ferrari owner. Since you will probably be driving the car 3,000 miles a year, you should only need to change the oil in the first year and possibly repair frozen heater valves or cables, replace dead window switches or any of the other minor gremlins that seem to appear in all 30-plus-year-old exotic Italian cars.

The only substantial maintenance you can count on in the first 10,000 miles of ownership is a $3,000 minor service, including a plug change, carb synchronization, valve adjustment and distributor setup. In the end, you will not only keep your house, but you will finally have that Ferrari you've dreamed of, while doing "the best thing you ever did, just for you."
—*Michael Sheehan*

From the May 2001 issue of *SCM.*◆

A Salvage-Title 456 and Other Oddities

Ask yourself why an insurance company would total a car if it could be economically repaired

Our esteemed Editor is always quick to pass Ferrari related questions on to me. A sample of this month's questions, from the sublime to the silly, follows:

Dear Mr. Sheehan: *I saw a salvage-title 456 GT on eBay, item #544964159. It is black with a gray interior, and shows 44,422 miles. From what I can see, it's been in a light accident. It appears to need a front and rear bumper, and possibly a right quarter panel and radiator. Bidding is currently at $58,000. I see 456 GTs advertised in the* Ferrari Market Letter *for $130,000-$150,000, which makes me think this might be my chance to get a contemporary Ferrari for cheap. Do you agree?*—**R. Y., Birmingham, AL**

Yikes! Ask yourself why an insurance company would total a car if it could be economically repaired? Insurance companies know the body business better than most body shop owners, and they have obviously decided the car doesn't make sense to repair. If not convinced, call your local Ferrari dealer and ask for a few parts prices, but sit down before they answer, or be prepared to hit the floor. The front bumper is $3,205.38, the rear bumper is $3,172.36, the rear fender is $1,368.81 and the radiator is $2,084. Add in the myriad inner and trim panels that will have to be replaced (but aren't listed), a paint job at $10,000, and all the necessary labor to put the whole thing back together and you're past $30,000 in a heartbeat. That's assuming there aren't even any bad surprises, and we all know there are always bad surprises when you buy a collision-damaged used car that has a salvage title.

With bidding up to $58,000 and a minimum of $30,000 in repairs, you're past $88,000 for a 456 with 44,422 miles, and a 456 with 44,000 plus miles is a very hard sell. If undamaged it would be a $75,000 wholesale car, retailing well back of $100,000. The cars listed have mileage that ranges from 4,800 to 23,000, which is less than half of the car you are looking at. Add in a salvage title, which knocks 30% to 50% off the value of a late model Ferrari, and once repaired you will have nearly $90,000 into a car worth $50,000 to $60,000.

Need more convincing? A very nice 456, with only 16,556 miles, and needing nothing but a new home, sold at the Barrett-Jackson auction in January for $97,200. Bluntly, with 44,000-plus miles *and* a salvage title, run away from the damaged car!

Dear Mr. Sheehan: *Has the vintage Ferrari world gone crazy? At the recent Barrett-Jackson auction, I saw a 246 GTS sell for $46k, a C/4 for $49k, and a 330 GT 2+2 for $55k? More money for a 2+2 than a Dino? Does that mean we should all run out and sell our Dinos and C/4s to buy 2+2s?*—**G. B., Sacramento, CA**

Nope, the 246 GTS and C/4 were, at best, just used cars. The 330 2+2 was nicely restored and in good colors (dark blue over gray). It had made the rounds of the auction circuit (Kruse Auburn and Scottsdale) and the owner had given up trying to get his restoration costs back, finally deciding to sell it for what it would bring (which was, in my mind, all the money and more). The bad news for the 330 2+2 buyer is that he paid too much, the good news is that he probably bought the car for less than the cost of the restoration, with the restored car thrown in "gratis."

A "just-a-car" 246 GTS can quickly consume $25,000 and more in paint, an interior, synchros, a suspension overhaul, ad infinitum in deferred maintenance and all you'll have is a prettier example of deferred maintenance. In this instance, a wise buyer chose quality over flash, opting for a handsome but pedestrian 2+2 that appears to have few needs, over two sexier cars, the Dino and the C/4, that might have sucked his bank account dry.

Dear Mr. Sheehan: *I'm offered a 1990 Testarossa with 68,000 miles for $50,000. The car is red/tan (of course), and had the 60,000 mile service, according to the owner (a broker), although he can't find any paperwork. Is this a deal? What would you pay for the car, and should I just believe him that the service has been done?*—**W.O., San Diego, CA**

Another Yikes! To quote myself, "The whole secret is low mileage. It's very Freudian. Everyone wants a virgin car" (May, 1991 *SCM*). A 60,000-mile Testarossa is sale-proof, and if the 60,000 service isn't done, it will cost you a cool $5,000 plus for the service. This is a $35,000 car, or, sadly, a parts car. Don't believe me? Pay $50,000 and find out for yourself. Run away. Run far away.

Dear Mr. Sheehan: *Do you think 348s will soon be cheaper than 328s? If so, why? Isn't the 348 a much more technologically advanced, not to mention newer, car.*—**J.G., from Omaha, NE**

Yep, newer technology, but service is a killer on the 348s, and they are now ten-year-old cars that need lots of service. The 348 uses a single long cam belt, so timing the car is a nightmare, and the cam belt tensioner bearings are about $400 each. They eat clutches like a refugee reaching a UN feeding station, at $1,500 a pop. Should you need a water pump, there are no parts available, and a complete pump is $1,700. So, if you really want a 348, it's your choice, but, as in all used Ferrari purchases, have the car inspected by a very qualified Ferrari mechanic, get an evaluation in writing (and yes, there will be recommended work), and use the list as leverage to negotiate the price.

I don't think they will sink below the value of 328s, but will probably be worth the same amount, in equal condition, a year or two from now.

From the March 2001 issue of *SCM*.◆

Front-Engine V12

"On-site auction reporting is the trademark of *SCM*. When an *SCM* expert attends an auction, his job is to personally evaluate the cars crossing the block, taking note of everything from the chassis number to the originality of the seat stitching. They analyze each car as if they were going to buy it for themselves. As you'll see in the Ferrari reports below, *SCM* experts

don't hesitate to call a prince a prince and a toad a toad.

Their reports are always honest, sometimes witty, and always make you feel as if you were there looking at the car with them."

—Keith Martin

Modern V12s

#168-**1963 FERRARI 400 SUPERAMERICA Coupe**. S/N 3949. Eng. #3949. Red/black. LHD. Odo: 46,196 miles. Exhibited at '62 Turin Auto Show. Nice Borrani wires, original luggage, radio. Paint, retrimmed interior still acceptable. Like-new engine bay. Chassis could use detailing. Looks like a great driver and decent concours entrant, if not a trophy-winner. Cond: 3+. **SOLD AT $432,000.** *Very strong price, indicative of a climbing market. Many SAs have gone across the block in the last three years, most selling close to $350k. The most expensive one, for $391k at Christie's Pebble Beach 2001, was a completely original, unrestored car.* ***Barrett-Jackson, Los Angeles, CA, 6/03.***

#274-**1964 FERRARI 500 SUPERFAST Speciale Coupe**. S/N 6267. Pine Green/tan. LHD. Odo: 14,273 km. Uniquely fitted with 4.0 motor for first owner Prince Bernhard of Holland (other 36 500 Superfasts 4.9). Ordered with bench front seat. Never fully restored. Full chain of ownership, including sold by Ron Tonkin in Portland in 1985. Paint marked and splitting, rear lamp chrome pitted. Driver's side leather slightly grubby, passenger side unused. Air filter box marked. Cond: 2-. **SOLD AT $336,203.** *Odd to think of ordering a Ferrari with a smaller motor than stock. Price was in line with current market— Superfasts are superb road machines, and are perfect for many touring style vintage events.* ***Bonhams Europe, Gstaad, CH, 12/03.***

#279-**1964 FERRARI 330 AMERICA Coupe**. S/N 5061. Purplish-blue metallic/black leather. LHD. Odo: 44,739 km. Just 50 built, 250 GTE with 4-liter 330 motor. Polished Borranis. Crepaldi Auto of Milan restored 1991. Driver's door edge chipped, brightwork poor, retrim fair. Period Nardi wood rim. Wheels dull and marked, engine bay dirty. Just a car. Cond: 3. **SOLD AT $60,385.** *A good 330 is probably worth $10,000 more than a smaller-engined 250 GTE. This car, in what seems to be unremarkable condition, brought a surprisingly high price.* ***Bonhams Europe, Gstaad, CH, 12/03.***

#254-**1965 FERRARI 275 GTB Shortnose Coupe**. S/N 6827. Gold/black. LHD. Odo: 25,516 km. Originally gray. Tool kit and books. Small rear window and concealed hood hinges. Believed original mileage. One owner since 1974. Earlier repaint cracked and lifting along passenger side door top, evidence of filler. Wheels marked, slight scuffs to original leather. Engine bay in need of TLC. Cond: 2-. **SOLD AT $239,631.** *Despite being in the shadow of the better performing and handling longnose GTBs, prices of shortnoses have been rising. They are extraordinarily attractive, and always attract attention. A bit on the high side, but no harm done given the trend in the market.* ***Bonhams Europe, Gstaad, CH, 12/03.***

#262-**1965 FERRARI 275 GTS Convertible**. S/N 07841. Red/black. LHD. Odo: 79,022 km. Factory hardtop. Repainted from original white to current red pre-1982. Paint now marked and scratched, hood bubbling. Chrome marked by enthusiastic polishers. Leather very dull. Wheels could stand refinishing. Aside from respray, appears essentially unrestored and appears honest. Cond: 2-. **SOLD AT $151,838.** *While within the estimate, should be considered a small bargain. The 275 GTS, for those who consider the Daytona a bit crass, is the ultimate open V12 bodystyle (the 330 motor would make it even better, of course).* ***Bonhams Europe, Gstaad, CH, 12/03.***

#547-**1965 FERRARI 275 GTS Convertible**. Body by Pininfarina. S/N 275GTS07337. Red/tan leather. LHD. Odo: 91,629 km. Reported restored in the 1990s, with extensive service records. Paint and panel fit appear good overall, yet heavy taped-off edges in doorjambs and a few bubbles raise questions. Right side inner fenderwell wrinkled. Interior nice, engine detailed. Cond: 2-. **SOLD AT $157,500.** *1 of 200 built. Sale price in line with market and condition. Ex-Oregon car.* ***Bonhams, Carmel, CA, 8/03.***

#246-**1965 FERRARI 275 GTB Aluminum Longnose Berlinetta**. Body by Pininfarina. S/N 8123. Red/black. LHD. Odo: 46,880 miles. US-based 1970s, vendor acquired at 2000 Geneva auction for $242,122. Windshield sealing rubber split, brightwork good, wheels and engine bay dull. Previously thought 1966-made, but found to have been built Dec. 1965, therefore major FIA event eligible. Cond: 1-. **SOLD AT $269,040.** *Price hardly surprising in view of historic race potential. Just over top estimate paid by major UK marque specialist. What a difference a 1965 vs. 1966 build date can make.* ***Bonhams, Monte Carlo, Monaco, 5/03.***

#256-**1965 FERRARI 275 GTB/6C Berlinetta**. Body by Pininfarina. S/N 06639. Red/tan, dark brown inserts. LHD. Odo: 68,711 km. Factory-fit six-carb option from new, major US resto pre-1976. Changed hands at auction Paris 1992 and Geneva 1997 in Mimran Collection disposal. French refurb 1993. Touched-in chips to paint, brightwork surface corroded, wheels shabby, interior grubby. Cond: 2. **SOLD AT $226,560.** *$24,000 below over-optimistic estimate price paid for only average example.* ***Bonhams, Monte Carlo, Monaco, 5/03.***

#293-**1966 FERRARI 275 GTS Convertible**. S/N 07359. Blue/black. LHD. Odo: 83,945 miles. Trunk, hood and right door gaps off. Most chrome good, some pitted. Paint weak, cracking and pitting. Interior a bit dirty with faded rear tray carpet and Motorola tape player. Engine looks rough. Possible older front-end damage. Cond: 3-. **SOLD AT $124,950.** *Seen before at the Mecum Elkhart Lake sale in July where it was passed on at $130,000. Said to have been owned by Raquel Welch. Looks uncared for and unloved now (I meant the car). Cheap if it can be cleaned up for $10,000.* ***Mecum Auctioneers, St. Charles, IL, 10/03.***

#5500-S151-**1967 FERRARI 330 GTC Coupe**. S/N 11340. Silver/black. LHD. Odo: 58,282 miles. Wires. Excellent paint and panel fit, only flaw a loose right side vent window. Very nice interior as well. Shifter chrome poor. Cond: -1. **SOLD AT $124,200.** *A well-presented 12-cylinder Ferrari that brought over-the-top money. I would have expected more like $100k. Was it just the Scottsdale weekend or have GTC prices jumped when I wasn't looking?* ***Russo and Steele, Scottsdale, AZ, 1/04.***

#5353-S148-**1967 FERRARI 330 GTS Convertible**. S/N 9781. Yellow/black. LHD. Odo: 54,735 miles. Minor paint chips to front and windshield. Scratches on deck-lid where top folds back. Glovebox door doesn't fit tight. Car appears excellent everywhere else. Cond: -1. **SOLD AT $260,000.** *A magnificent car. Six first place awards in 1985-2000, including the Ferrari Nationals. 1997 Meadow Brook First Place Overall. Records, books and tools. This car also recently completed the Copperstate 1000 and Gauthier Road Rallies. The dead bugs on the front spoiler attest to use. The original cost was $16,426. A good healthy price for what some think is the very best of the open, vintage Ferraris.* ***Russo and Steele, Scottsdale, AZ, 1/04.***

#482-**1967 FERRARI 330 GT Michelotti Coupe**. S/N 9083. Eng. #9083. Maroon/tan. LHD. Odo: 30,632 miles. Nice-condition engine and chassis restored to original specifications. But just a rebody, albeit by established Italian designer. Not one of Michelotti's best designs, appears especially awkward from rear. Frame-up resto '87-'89. Pebble Beach 2nd in '89. Cond: 2+. **SOLD AT $143,000.** *Could have looked better if done on shorter, more modern two-seater 330 GTC chassis instead of 330 2+2. Sold at just under low estimate.* ***RM Auctions, Monterey, CA, 8/03.***

#457-**1967 FERRARI 275 GTB/4 Berlinetta**. S/N 9609. Eng. #9609. Red/black, blue cloth. LHD. Odo: 2,427 miles. Probably nicer than when delivered new, now equipped with Borrani wires and proper knock-offs. Restored in early '80s with new nose from Italy. Certified Platinum, 95 points or better, in 2003 at Cavallino Classic and Amelia Island. Tools and manuals. Cond: 1. **SOLD AT $621,500.** *Only 9 of these alloy-bodied four-cams exist out of 14 made. The 275 series is the most collectible '60s Ferrari, and the alloy-body four-cams are in a class by themselves. Another record-beating price, but if you want the ultimate four-cam, this is it.* ***RM Auctions, Monterey, CA, 8/03.***

#259-**1967 FERRARI 275 GTB/4 Coupe**. S/N 10011. Silver/black. LHD. Odo: 74,952 km. Special ordered with electric windows. One owner since 1972, paint excellent apart from some chips. Chrome, including nose-protecting nerf-bar, very good. Engine bay sharp. Wiper scratches to windshield. Curiously, one alloy crackle-finished. Cond: 1-. **SOLD AT $402,048.** *Sold to an Italian bidder. Worth nearly twice a short-nose two-cam? Market says yes, and we agree. Considered by many to be the ultimate Ferrari, with timeless styling and terrific performance.* ***Bonhams Europe, Gstaad, CH, 12/03.***

#750-**1967 FERRARI 330 GTC Coupe**. S/N 10555. Red/black. RHD. Odo: 59,424 miles. Medium quality respray, very good chrome. Interior is quite nice, seats and carpets appear quite fresh. Clean Nardi wood wheel, good wood on dash. No radio fitted. Chrome on wire wheels has seen better days, has Viracon replacement windshield. Michelin XWX radials quite good. Cond: 3. **SOLD AT $117,173.** *Color sanding the paint would help, but only to a point. RHD Ferraris from the 1960s are few and far between. As an original right-hand-drive car, this example will remain more valuable in right-hand drive markets. Price for condition was about $20,000 more than stateside.* ***Coys, London, UK, 12/03.***

#18-**1967 FERRARI 330 GTC Coupe**. Body by Pininfarina. S/N 11517. Eng. #11517. Fly yellow/black. LHD. Odo: 60,660 miles. Restored in 1997 in CA, no mileage since. Nothing specific about mechanical restoration work was stated. Winner of many first place awards since restoration, nothing to fault. Paint, interior and chassis to original, like-new condition. Cond: 1-. **SOLD AT $156,000.** *Someone paid a lot to avoid the pangs of restoration. Even if the mechanicals had been done competently and documentation were available, this is still a very strong price for a GTC, especially in the none-too-flattering bright yellow.* ***Christie's, Pebble Beach, CA, 8/03.***

#233-**1968 FERRARI 275 GTB/4 Berlinetta**. Body by Pininfarina. S/N 10715. Yellow/black. LHD. Odo: 11,711 km. Egidio Brandoli of Modena restored within last few years, repaint from then still super, mint and not too thick. Brightwork excellent, seats apparently only slightly sat-in, woodrim steering wheel unmarked. Cond: 1. **SOLD AT $472,826.** *$68,000 over estimate price forthcoming from Scottish collector for truly drop-dead gorgeous four-cam in Giallo Fly.* ***Bonhams, Monte Carlo, Monaco, 5/03.***

#263-**1969 FERRARI 365 GTB/4 Daytona Coupe**. S/N 12705. Red/black. LHD. Odo: 77,874 km. Originally dark blue with beige. Early Plexiglass headlamps car, 38th production Daytona. Repainted pre-1977, optional 9-inch wide rear alloys. Factory-fit radio cassette and air-conditioning. Paint very good apart from bumpy trunk lid edge. Very nice wheels. Original interior good. Cond: 2+. **SOLD AT $121,110.** *Near top estimate paid for Daytona which cost Lepeltier $51,587 in 1977. Four-cams were good value then, even better today. Prices of Daytonas seem stronger in the US than in Europe; this car might have brought a bit more stateside. According to Sergio Pininfarina, it was nearly impossible to see at night with the Plexi covers once they aged a bit.* ***Bonhams Europe, Gstaad, CH, 12/03.***

#718-**1970 FERRARI 365 GTB Daytona Coupe**. S/N 13479. Dark blue/red. RHD. Odo: 61,576 miles. Early car with Plexi headlight covers. Said to be owned for majority of its life by Bob Roberts, founder of Midland Motor Museum. Paintwork shows plenty of flaws, of so-so quality overall. Lots of patina, i.e. wear, to the interior—would have been replaced by now if it were in the US. Just a used car. **SOLD AT $110,980.** *Everyone loves the Daytona, one of the prettiest cars built with the classic front engine V12. With the value of the Euro and pound increasing and the dollar heading downwards, look for lots of Daytonas to leave our shores in the next few years. This car sold at what could have been expected in the US—no more and no less.* ***Coys, London, UK, 12/03.***

#275-**1971 FERRARI 365 GTB/4 Daytona Convertible Conversion**. S/N 14425. Black/tan. LHD. Odo: 58,626 km. Given chop early 1980s by Straman. Power steering fitted. Paint scratched by polishers. Chrome excellent, 1994 Luppi interior retrim. Driver's seat slightly used. New Nardi wood rim. Engine bay dull around edges. Striking in black. Cond: 2+. **SOLD AT $195,734.** *Strong price for clearly well-fettled example. If you cannot get hold of one of the 123 factory-opened Daytonas, then a conversion—as long as well executed like this one—will make a decent and apparently appreciating substitute.* ***Bonhams Europe, Gstaad, CH, 12/03.***

#169-**1971 FERRARI 365 GTB/4 Daytona Coupe**. S/N 14819. Yellow/black. LHD. Odo: 22,947 miles. Borranis, Becker Mexico stereo. Nice paint, vent windows converted to bolt-on latches. Interior nice but pedal pads badly worn. Dash material original, showing typical loss of nap. Engine clean, not concours. Mark X ignition subbed for Marelli. Cond: 3+. **SOLD AT $145,800.** *Original hood struts unable to hold hood open, chassis clean but not detailed, fabricated "hot rod" exhaust system. A surprisingly high price, given how many Daytonas are for sale. Maybe they are finally bouncing back.* ***Barrett-Jackson, Los Angeles, CA, 6/03.***

#572-**1971 FERRARI 365 GTB/4 Daytona Berlinetta**. Body by Pininfarina. S/N 14513. Dino blue metallic/beige, black with herringbone inserts. RHD. Odo: 2,893 miles. Genuine mileage since driven off 2002 London Motor Show stand. Ex-factory paint and brightwork still like new, squab leather only slightly age-crazed. Wheel paint thickness original. All tools and glovebox paperwork intact. Cond: 1+. **SOLD AT $166,374.** *Even clock-operating instruction tie-on label still dangling! Just over estimate forthcoming*

for what must be unique time warp in really super and unspoiled condition. Good Daytonas are now at least $150k and climbing, with pigs stuck in the $110k mud. ***Bonhams, Goodwood, UK, 7/11.***

#253-**1972 FERRARI 365GTB/4A Daytona Coupe**. S/N 15069. Yellow/black. LHD. Odo: 37,499 km. Another former Geneva Show car, one owner, claimed still to be largely original. Flaking paint on driver's door edge, bubbling on rear passenger side. Original interior good, brightwork very good, optional chromed nudge-bar. Cond: 2-. **SOLD AT $151,838.** *Originality and low mileage responsible for $16,400 over top estimate result. Lepeltier paid $50,000 for it 31 years ago. Good looking in yellow, a nice departure from the more usual red or black.* ***Bonhams Europe, Gstaad, CH, 12/03.***

#66-**1972 FERRARI 365 GTS/4 Daytona Spyder**. Body by Pininfarina. S/N 15845. Eng. #B1576. Red LHD. Odo: 51,316 km. Ripples down side of body, some minor repainting (nose, passenger door edge). Carpets replaced, original leather, dash and soft top all very good. Slight split on driver's seat, original Becker Mexico radio/cassette. Tidy engine bay, not run for some time. Cond: 2-. **SOLD AT $365,500.** *Ferrari spotters were in a frenzy over the never-seen-before German side indicators. This car is 1 of just 25 spyders built to European specifications and 1 of just 2 for Germany. Sold by original owner. Fair price.* ***Bonhams, Nurburgring, DE, 8/03.***

#284-**1972 FERRARI 365 GTC/4 Coupe**. S/N 15853. Red/tan. LHD. Odo: 16,030 km. Acquired by seller at Gstaad 1998 auction. Older repaint now only fair with some shrinkage, door handle chrome pitted, alloys marked, original leather good. Cond: 2-. **SOLD AT $46,663.** *Fair market price. Still great value with lots of Ferrari quad-cam for your dollar. Perfect ones are in the $60,000 range (asking, anyway) so this one with a few cosmetic needs was on the money.* ***Bonhams Europe, Gstaad, CH, 12/03.***

#815-**1972 FERRARI 365 GTB/4 Daytona Coupe**. S/N 14899. Red/beige/black leather. LHD. Odo: 72,191 miles. Good doors and panels. Straight body, very clean interior. A/C and electric windows. Appeared to be an honest, well-maintained car ready to hit the road and enjoy. Cond: 2+. **SOLD AT $104,500.** *On the low end of* SCM *Price Guide, but that's the 2003 Guide, and it needs to be revised upwards. A small bargain here, but the real action in the Daytona market is for very, very nice cars. They are now hitting $150k with some regularity.* ***Bonhams, Hummelstown, PA, 10/03.***

#270-**1973 FERRARI 365 GTC/4 Coupe**. S/N 16057. Anthracite/black. LHD. Odo: 8,095 km. In receipt of nine-year restoration (costing $158,730!) by Pebble Beach entrant Bruno Wyss. All mint—apart from shrinkage crack to one hood aperture corner. Modern radio/CD multi-player. Spectacular; great color too. Cond: 1-. **SOLD AT $103,552.** *Buyer thought it worth paying $7,900 above high estimate for really super (possibly best-in-world) example. Better to spend this much for a perfect C/4 than a ratty Daytona. Too bad that Wyss never got to enjoy his car.* ***Bonhams Europe, Gstaad, CH, 12/03.***

#742-**1973 FERRARI 365 GTS/4 Daytona Spyder**. S/N 15917. Red/tan. RHD. Odo: 55,371 miles. The real thing, not a conversion. Dirty and fully used interior shows plenty of scuff marks, wear to edges of seats and dry marks. Mouse fur on dash has some stains but is too good to change out. Paint is quite good. Some light scratching but no harm done. Good chrome and glass, very good Michelin XWX tires. A very honest appearing car. Cond: 3+. **SOLD AT $483,300.** *Imagine how rare this car is in the U.K. market, as one of just 7 RHD Spyders built. Demand will almost always exceed supply here. Close to a half a million dollars for a Spyder with needs? Overpriced by $150,000 by US standards, mostly exchange rate at work here.* ***Coys, London, UK, 12/03.***

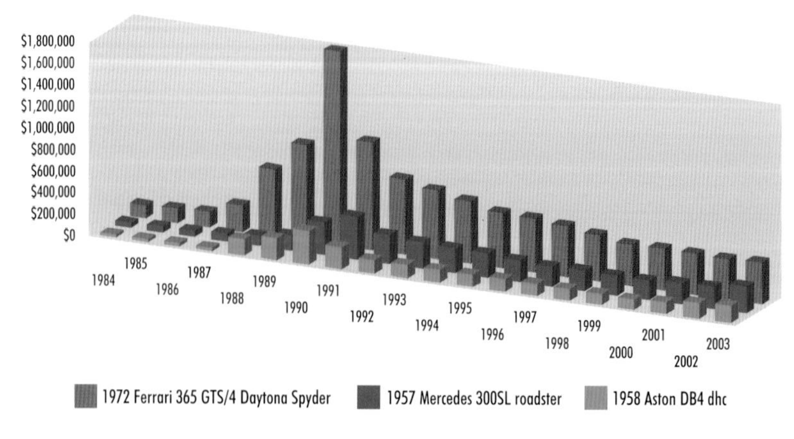

Prices are for cars in excellent condition. This information is provided courtesy of the Black Book and Cars of Particular Interest Value Guide. CPI is the guide most often used by credit unions to determine loan values of collectible domestic and imported cars. www.blackbookusa.com From the April 2004 issue of *SCM.*

#224-**1974 FERRARI 365 GTB/4 Daytona Berlinetta**. Body by Pininfarina. S/N 17029. Red/black. LHD. Odo: 79,769 km. Likely to be correct kilometers from new. Optional 9"-wide rear wheels, air conditioning, period radio. Ex-Hans Durst Collection, acquired at 2000 Gstaad auction. 17-year-old part repaint, original interior and engine bay presentation all still good. Cond: 1-. **SOLD AT $126,260.** *Super example from final batch of Daytonas in fine, slightly used-looking condition, hence $9,400 over estimate result.* ***Bonhams, Monte Carlo, Monaco, 5/03.***

#244-**2001 FERRARI 550 Fiorano Barchetta**. Body by Pininfarina. S/N ZFFZR52B000124234. Silver/tan. LHD. Odo: 104 km. Delivery mileage, all still as-new. Leather trimmed high-back big-ear buckets, red brake calipers, matching crash hats, Schedoni fitted luggage. 48-valve, 5.5-liter V12. Cond: 1. **SOLD AT $200,600.** *Unsold at Geneva for $196,100 earlier this year, near estimate price wisely accepted here. 256th of 448 produced. Must be what it's worth. A Ferrari "instant collectible" that continues to slide in value. No racing heritage, no reason to collect these.* ***Bonhams, Monte Carlo, Monaco, 5/03.***

Vintage V12s

#453-**1956 FERRARI 860 MONZA Race Car**. Body by Pininfarina, Scaglietti. S/N 0604M. Eng. #0604M. Red/black. LHD. One of the great 3.5-liter, four-cylinder engines pivotal in Ferrari winning the 1956 Make Championship. Restored 10 years ago in France, still appears perfect. Tremendous race history, with original engine, body panels, chassis and most mechanical parts. Cond: 1-. **SOLD AT $2,057,001.** *Recently run in the Colorado Grand; a usable race car with impeccable provenance. Top sale of the weekend for an outstanding, usable piece of Ferrari history. World record for a 4-cylinder Ferrari, but deserved here. (4-cyl incl. W/12-cyl cars)* ***RM Auctions, Monterey, CA, 8/03. (Monza included with 12-cylinder cars.)***

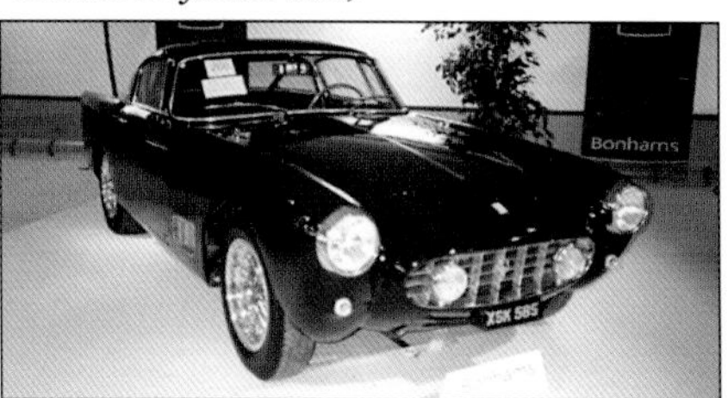

#265-**1956 FERRARI 250GT Boano Prototype Coupe**. S/N 0521GT. Dark blue/black leather. LHD. Odo: 13,207 km. Restored from dismantled project by UK marque specialist Terry Hoyle 1989-94. Road evented since. Paint and wheels still excellent. No bumpers, large Monza outside filler cap. Pair of very long twin exhausts. Interior very nice. Half roll cage. Non-Ferrari low-back buckets with full racing harnesses. Wood rim steering wheel. Some unique original features, some added during restoration. Cond: 2+. **Sold At $171,248.** *Unsold at $142,857 under hammer. Well prepped and event-ready Boano was much admired during viewing and deservedly sold immediately afterwards for more. Although not completely authentic, it was attractive and changes were documented, so price was fair enough.* ***Bonhams Europe, Gstaad, CH, 12/03.***

#206-**1958 FERRARI 250 GT Coupe**. Body by Pininfarina. S/N 1157. White/tan. LHD. Odo: 87,314 km. First supplied to pre-Castro Cuban dictator's son in Switzerland, acquired by vendor at 1998 Geneva auction for $50,157. Mechanics overhauled 1990, more recent thick repaint and still too-new-looking retrim, brightwork fair. Cond: 2+. **SOLD AT $63,720.** *Correctly valued at $8,000 under estimate paid. Bump in price since '98 is an indicator that the market has improved for these handsome, but lorry-like to drive, two-seaters.* ***Bonhams, Monte Carlo, Monaco, 5/03.***

#266-**1960 FERRARI 250GT Series II PF Cabriolet**. S/N 2091GT. Red/black leather. LHD. Odo: 56,819 miles. Smoke gray when supplied new to California. Paint mainly good, although poor around windshield base. Chrome scratched by careless polishing. Wheel rims marked. Driver's side seat leather crumpled. Engine bay in need of TLC, visually at least. Recent eventing, said to be roadworthy. Cond: 2-. **Sold At $165,006.** *A fair price, maybe even a small bargain. These are the cheapest open V12 Ferraris, and their prices have been steadily creeping upwards. Perfect ones can bring over $200,000, so the new owner has room to make some improvements here without going underwater.* ***Bonhams Europe, Gstaad, CH, 12/03.***

#264-**1961 FERRARI 250 GT SWB Coupe**. S/N 2469GT. Red/black leather. LHD. Odo: 56,819 km. Many factory-fit extras (such as leather-covered dash, central console, electric windows, different door handles, all four wing vents chromed). Modified front fender and headlamp treatment from 1970. Repaint very good. A-post to passenger door fit poor, rear fender dimpled. Originally gray, numbers match, some vintage eventing this year. No stated competition history. Cond: 2-. **Sold At $836,621.** *Just under high estimate forthcoming from Italian bidder for SWB with unique spec, to much applause. Lack of racing provenance and oddball modifications caused Ferrari marketers to spank this car. If all correct, and with some good historical tales to tell, could have easily broken $1m.* ***Bonhams Europe, Gstaad, CH, 12/03.***

#568-**1962 FERRARI 250 GT Series II Cabriolet**. Body by Pininfarina. S/N 3311. Red/tan leather.

LHD. Odo: 35,139 km. Older repaint, highly deteriorated, chips, bubbles, cracks, fading. Except for right door, does not appear Bondo-laden. Gaps okay. Chrome slightly pitting. Stone shot in windshield. Borranis peeling. Chassis and engine dirty but appear sound. Cond: 4. **SOLD AT $135,000.** *Reported past ownership for 29 years, mostly original, engine rebuilt during ownership. Restoration candidate or maybe cosmetic upgrade to driver; mechanicals a question. Decent buy if no big-dollar surprises. PF Cabs have doubled in four years.* ***Bonhams, Carmel, CA, 8/03.***

#489-**1962 FERRARI 250 GT Series II Cabriolet**. Body by Pininfarina. S/N 3407. Eng. #3407. Black/red. LHD. Odo: 35,458 miles. Recently restored to very nice and original standard, not shown yet in National FCA competition but should score mid-90s. No visible flaws. Owner says it drives as good as it looks, no smoke on start-up. New paint, chrome, rebuilt Borranis, Koni shocks. Cond: 1-. **SOLD AT $258,501.** *202 Series II open-headlight cabriolets were made. A quarter of a million dollars must be a new 21st century record price for this model.* ***RM Auctions, Monterey, CA, 8/03.***

#711-**1962 FERRARI 250 GTE 2+2**. Red/white. LHD. Odo: 20,864 km. A true barn-find fright pig. Exceptionally bad red respray over blue original paint, side vents missing left and right, leather discolored and moldy, front turn signal lenses missing. Door panels in back seat, no carpet. 15 years ago, this would have been the discarded car found behind a Ferrari shop. Cond: 5. **Sold At $46,322.** *Many a 250 GTE has given its original bodyshell to become a faux 250 GT. Will this sad case be next? At some point when they have all become replicas of Ferrari racers, will the last few original survivors trade in a stratospheric market? I doubt it, but it would be nice to think so. No one in their right mind in the US would pay more than $20,000 for this car; perhaps this is exchange rate at work.* ***Coys, London, UK, 12/03.***

#255-**1963 FERRARI 250 GT LUSSO Coupe**. S/N 4509. Burgundy/beige. LHD. Odo: 67,307 km. One owner (Lepeltier) since 1964. Accident including frame damage repaired by factory when nearly new. Many blemishes to 1963 factory repaired paint. Rear fender chrome flaking, still original front seat leather slightly dry-cracked with stitching pulled. Original wood rim steering wheel still good. Wheels have some road-rash. Cond: 3+. **Sold At $191,822.** *Time-warp Lusso with original interior and near 40-year-old paint. Find another like that! Given how Lussos have been climbing in value, the buyer did just fine.* ***Bonhams Europe, Gstaad, CH, 12/03.***

#279-**1964 FERRARI 330 AMERICA Coupe**. S/N 5061. Purplish-blue metallic/black leather. LHD. Odo: 44,739 km. Just 50 built, 250 GTE with 4-liter 330 motor. Polished Borranis. Crepaldi Auto of Milan restored 1991. Driver's door edge chipped, brightwork poor, retrim fair. Period Nardi wood rim. Wheels dull and marked, engine bay dirty. Just a car. Cond: 3. **Sold At $60,385.** *A good 330 is probably worth $10,000 more than a smaller-engined 250 GTE. This car, in what seems to be unremarkable condition, brought a surprisingly high price.*

#249-**1964 FERRARI 250 GT LUSSO Berlinetta**. Body by Pininfarina. S/N 5883GT. Metallic silver/black. LHD. Odo: 16,695 km. Supplied new to US; Atlanta and NY resident. Resto by Sauro of Bologna 1989, re-paint from then still very good. Minor dents to nose, both windshield surrounds slightly corroded, brightwork poor, particularly rear bumper. Leather nicely worn. Cond: 2. **SOLD AT $223,610.** *Such is current strength of Lusso prices; mid-estimate money was forthcoming for this one. It's invigorating for the market to see prices soar on any model—it proves that there is still room for romance and irrationality in collecting!* ***Bonhams, Monte Carlo, Monaco, 5/03.***

The Twenty Year Picture
Entry-Level Exotics

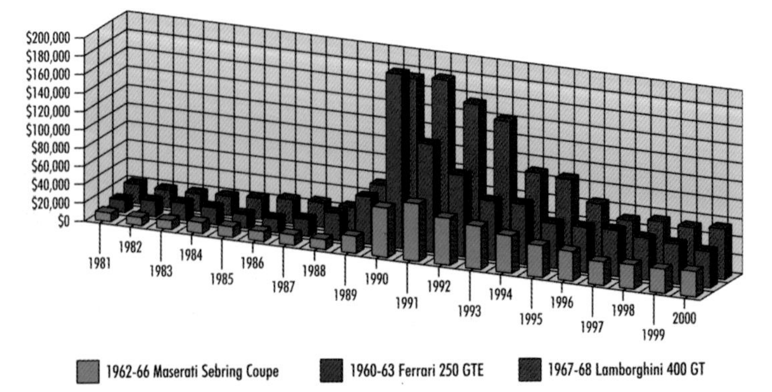

(Prices are for cars in excellent condition. Data provided courtesy of CPI. Additional data compiled from SCM archives.)

This month value guide is courtesy of Cars of Particular Interest. CPI is the pocket guide most often used by credit unions and banks when dealing with loan values of collectible domestic and imported cars. From the September 2004 issue of *SCM*.

2+2 V12s

#133-**1966 FERRARI 330 GT 2+2 Coupe**. S/N 8485. Eng. #8485. Blue/crème leather, blue piping. LHD. Odo: 25,269 miles. Hard to tell what this car is—seems to have had competent cosmetic restoration, although blue piping was not factory option and looks a bit gaudy. Hood gap off. No mention of mechanical work or significance of low odometer. Factory A/C. Cond: 2-. **SOLD AT $51,500.** *If the mechanicals check out, not a bad price for a nice-looking car.* ***RM Auctions, Monterey, CA, 8/03.***

#5330-S164-**1968 FERRARI 365 GT 2+2 Coupe**. S/N 12065. Red/black. LHD. Odo: 81,359 miles. Paint very nice and all panels fit well. Some trim scratches and dents visible with pitting to both vent window chrome trims. The leather handbrake boot is worn through in one spot, seats distressed. Inside driver's door handle broken. Aluminum-painted components underhood. Nice paint, chrome, air-conditioning blows cold. Not too much smoke on start-up. Cond: 2. **SOLD AT $55,080.** *All the money here for a car that is less than perfect. All 2+2 Ferraris are a tough sell for big bucks, so the seller should be smiling.* ***Russo and Steele, Scottsdale, AZ, 1/04.***

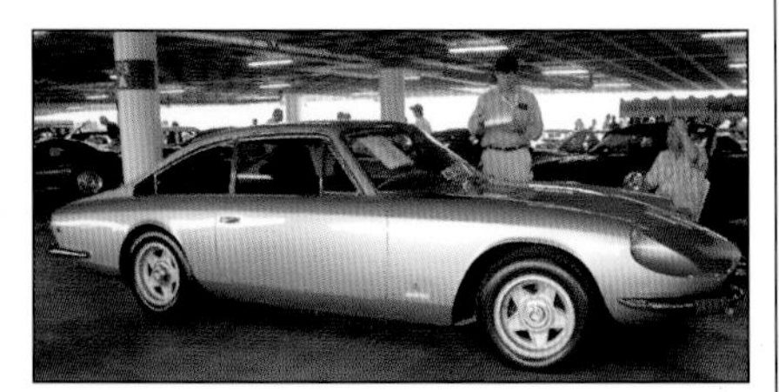

#149-**1970 FERRARI 365 GT 2+2 Coupe**. S/N 12651. Light blue/black. LHD. Odo: 59,909 miles. Attractive five-star style Cromodoras with XWXs. Minor bubbles to re-paint. Good color, attractive car. Nice interior, some wear to rear. Rear chrome thin, pits to pot-metal taillight surrounds. Surprisingly, trunk lid fit way off. Started, idled well. Cond: 2-. **SOLD AT $43,740.** *Appears to be well maintained. Fair price if mechanicals check out as well as they appear. Could be a really neat first Ferrari for a family man.* ***Barrett-Jackson, Los Angeles, CA, 6/03.***

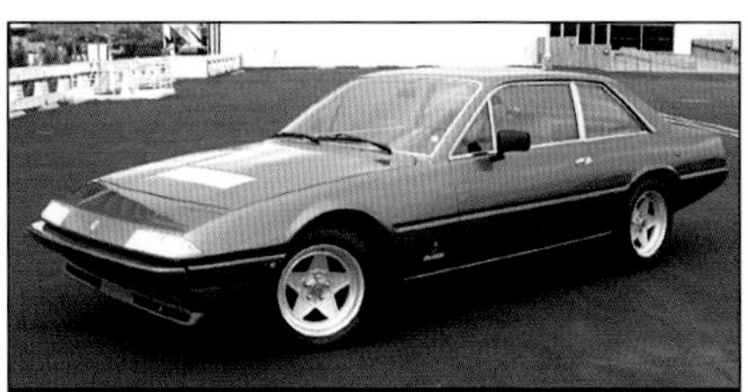

#143-**1981 FERRARI 400i Coupe**. S/N 35097. Light brown/light tan. LHD. Odo: 59,378 miles. Very good looking from 20 feet. Paint okay, panel fit about normal, glass good. Seats and armrests show wear, dash leather shrunk and hard. No detailing to chassis, engine has replacement MSD box. Five-speed. Power steering and windows. Cond: 3. **SOLD AT $21,600.** *A decent average used car with a V12 and four seats. At $21,000, with 5-speed, seems like a real deal. Oh, everyone forgot to mention that it has a California salvage title. Still, if it drives out well, a small bargain.* ***Barrett-Jackson, Los Angeles, CA, 6/03.***

#167-**1986 FERRARI 412i Coupe**. S/N ZFFYD25B000062895. Silver/tan leather. LHD. Odo: 59,599 miles. 5-speed. Looks to have been driven hard, and now in need of cosmetic attention. Lots of bodywork evident on left rear, nose has a ding next to the badge. Rust bubbles evident in numerous places. Good dash binnacle, original leather is tired but might come back with treatment. Clarion AM/FM, trunk shows evidence of mold. Cond: 4-. **SOLD AT $14,904.** *Sold to an astute SCM subscriber who happened to be in the right place at the right time. My prescription is just drive it until you sell it or until something breaks. Probably worth more in parts; the best way for the new owner to get hurt would be starting a restoration.* ***Kruse, Ft. Lauderdale, FL, 1/04.***

The Twenty Year Picture

More Seats Than Doors

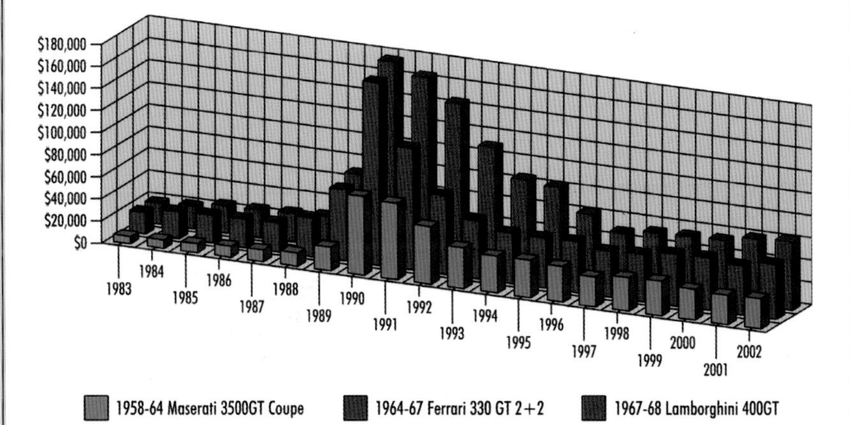

(Prices are for cars in excellent condition. Data provided courtesy of CPI. Additional data compiled from SCM archives.)

This month value grade is provided courtesy of Cars of Particular Interest. CPI is the pocket guide most often used by credit unions and banks when dealing with loan values of collectable domestic and imported cars. From the November 2002 issue of *SCM*.

PART II
Mid-Engine Ferraris

I was just 19 when I drove my first mid-engined Ferrari, a 1973 246 GT "Dino" coupe that a trusting friend gave me for the day. I recall that it was bronze metallic with a black leather interior, and that it was simply the most incredible car I had ever been behind the wheel of.

I was still living in my hometown of San Francisco, so the first thing I did was to zoom across the Golden Gate Bridge and head up 101 to my all-time favorite automotive playground, Lucas Valley Road.

The road just seemed to unwind between the two sensuous fender tops that filled either side of the windshield. The engine revved willingly to redline, and the gearbox ratios seemed to always put me right in the powerband. And after all these years, I can reveal that in a fit of Jimmy Clark-like exuberance, I came into a corner too hot, did a 360-degree spin and nearly slid off the road, down a cliff and into a ravine. Figuring out just how long it would take at my busboy's wages of $2/hr to pay my friend back for his car caused me to exercise a little more caution afterwards.

Since then, we've owned a variety of 308 GT4s, 308s and 328s. While no one would ever accuse the Bertone-styled GT4 of being attractive ("cheese wedge on wheels" is how one of our writers described it), it has the best driving position of all the little Ferraris, and with its space behind the seats was by far the most practical. And due to their exposure on the television show "Magnum P.I.," the 308/328 series has become the most recognized Ferrari of all time.

As the sales manager at Ron Tonkin Gran Turismo in the late 1980s, I had the opportunity to drive a number of Testarossas and Boxers. While their styling is dated now, at the time both cars were simply the most reliable, best-engineered exotics you could buy, and the flat-twelve engines just poured out horsepower.

And then there are the current "Bad Boys" of the Ferrari world, the F40, F50 and the Enzo. They stand as proof that when it comes to translating racing technology to the street, Ferrari takes a back seat to no one.

This is a great section of the book, covering everything from baby Ferraris to fire-breathing monsters. Above all, the cars we look at here stand as a reminder of the breadth of brilliant mid-engined designs that Ferrari has produced over the years.
—Keith Martin◆

1973 246 GTS Dino

Chassis number: 3652
Engine number: 3652

So beautiful they almost looked feminine, yet so powerful they were unmistakably masculine

This European-registered car has a 2,418-cc V6, double overhead camshaft, cast iron block and light alloy heads, and produces 178 bhp at 7,000 rpm. It has a five-speed manual gearbox with front and rear independent suspension with unequal-length A arms, coil springs, tubular shock absorbers and four-wheel disc brakes.

Christie's

The forerunner to the hugely popular Ferrari 246 GT and GTS was the 206 S Speciale, a styling exercise that Pininfarina exhibited at the 1965 Paris Motor Show. This car evolved into reality when a working prototype appeared at the Turin Motor show in 1966, and by 1969 the first 246 GT Dino was shown. The V6, four overhead camshaft engine was mounted transversely behind the driver and in front of the rear axle, while the gearbox was in unit with the differential and sump. The Pininfarina-styled body was an instant success, and the fact that the car performed brilliantly ensured it sold well.

There were a few detail changes during the production run, such as center-lock wheels changing to five-bolt types, and then a GTS version with removable roof panel. Just 1,274 GTSs, compared to 2,609 GTs, were built between 1969 and 1974, and they have always remained popular sports cars with classic car enthusiasts.

The early history of this car is unknown. It underwent a comprehensive restoration before being imported to Europe in the late '80s.

This well-presented Dino is finished in the desirable classic color combination for the marque of red with black leather and has period six-branch alloy wheels. Regularly used by the vendor, it's ready for enjoyable open-top spring and summer motoring, and is currently EU registered and tax paid.

This car sold for $86,292, including buyer's premium, at Christie's Retromobile Paris auction, held February 8, 2003.

$86,292 is all of the money for most Dinos. Eighty-six grand for a US model in Europe that was restored over two decades ago and has been regularly driven since then is well over the top. The same car in the States would be lucky to break into the $70,000s. It would need the coveted "chairs and flares option" or unrealistically low mileage to break into the $80,000s, and it would have to be in top condition at that.

There's something universally appealing about a Dino. The sensual body follows the design theme of the Pininfarina race cars and show cars of the era. The theme was a response to the introduction of mid-engine cars. These new cars required new expressions of automobile design, and Pininfarina met the challenge with this masterpiece of compound curves.

It was as modern, bold and perhaps as purely artistic as any automotive design theme before or after. Pininfarina respected function but strived for beauty. The shapes were so beautiful that they almost looked feminine, yet they were so powerful they were unmistakably masculine.

Driving a Dino was as exciting as looking at one. The Ferrari-designed, Fiat-built V6 is an impressive piece of work with a distinctive sound and reasonable performance. Its 195 horsepower moved the 2,300-pound Dino to 60 mph in a respectable 6.8 seconds. The power was found high in the rpm range and spirited driving required lots of gas and lots of shifting.

The need for driver's input was a contrast from the big-engine Ferraris, and it made the Dino a sports car rather than a GT car. The mid-engine design with its low center of gravity raised the bar on handling and added confidence to both novice and experienced drivers. Owners found themselves going deeper and faster through corners and looking for new twisty roads.

While the best examples can be a pleasure to drive, good ones are few and far between. New Dinos sold for around two-thirds the price of a contemporary Daytona, and while the missing six cylinders caused some of the disparity, there was a marked difference in the component and build quality of the Dino. Everything on the Dino looked, felt and was cheaper than the 12-cylinder Ferraris. While that meant a lower price, it also meant more maintenance.

The Ferrari for the masses cost more than the Daytona to keep up, and these cars were being sold to people who, for the most part, were less prepared to pay for the maintenance. They were quite often ridden hard and put away wet. Worn components weren't repaired until they broke and quality wasn't goal one when making repairs.

A nice-looking car could have thousands of dollars of problems hiding under its skin and often did. Rust, soft cams and weak synchros are a few of the problems affecting Dinos, and any Ferrari shop can give you a list of more. A good look-over by a professional is essential for any Dino purchase.

Dinos often do well at auctions; perhaps their sexy lines are a siren's song for the Benjamins in the billfold. Maybe it's because there's no pre-purchase inspection on auction cars to dispel a buyer's fantasy, or maybe it's just because Dinos look like everyone's idea of what a classic sports car should look like.

Perhaps this particular car did well because Spyders are scarce in Europe. Whatever the reason, the auction fairy sprinkled magic dust on this car and the seller should be very happy.—Steve Ahlgrim

(Historic and descriptive information courtesy of Christie's.)

From the May 2003 issue of *SCM*.◆

Years produced:	coupes 1969-74, Spyders 1972-74
Number produced	2,609 coupes, 1,274 Spyders
Original list price	approx $15,000
SCM Price Guide	$70,000 $95,000 (add $7,500 for "chairs and flares")
Tune up/major service	$3,000-$5,000
Distributor cap	$160
Chassis #	Top frame rail, driver's side in engine compartment
Engine #	Side of block directly inside and in front of oil filter
Clubs	Ferrari Club of America, P.O. Box 720597, Atlanta, GA 30358; Ferrari Owner's Club, 8642 Cleta St., Downey, CA 90241
Web sites	www.FerrariClubofAmerica.com, www.FerrariOwnersClub.org
Alternatives	Ferrari 348 Spyder, Jaguar XKE convertible, Porsche 2.2L 911S coupe
SCM Investment Grade	B

1974 Ferrari 246 GTS Dino

The beauty of these cars lies in the thrill of the glorious roaring engine noise, the voluptuous view from the driver's seat and the amazing go-kart feel

Chassis number: 06470

This left-hand drive Ferrari was delivered new to main agents Tayre Ferrari in Madrid in October 1974 and sold to an American citizen, William Kemmerer, its first owner. The latter was then serving with the USAF, and brought the Dino back to the US from Spain when his tour of duty was completed. *Ferrari Market Letter* records that the car was serviced by Algar Ferrari in Philadelphia in the late 1970s and early 1980s.

Bonhams & Brooks

The Motorcar Gallery of Fort Lauderdale, Florida, subsequently advertised the Dino for sale, describing it as "a one-owner car since October 1974." Its next recorded owner, H. Levy, of Gwynedd, Pennsylvania and Boca Raton, Florida, prepared the car to the concours standards of the Ferrari Club of America and regularly exhibited it on the concours circuit between 1993 and 1995. The car was featured at the Cavallino Classic and the FCA Nationals, consistently placing in class at both venues. In August 1998, it passed to its next owner, a New York enthusiast, and was purchased from him by the vendor.

Thoroughly serviced in the spring of 2000 by Spott Autos, of Gaylordsville, Connecticut, the car is described as in excellent mechanical condition. Its unusual Pino Verde metallic green color scheme is most attractive, while the interior features air conditioning, electric window lifts and the "Daytona" black ribbed squab panels set in brown leather upholstery. The wheel arches have been flared to accommodate larger than standard 7" x 14" alloy wheels. The indicated mileage of 55,500 is believed to be genuine, and this well-presented example of a most desirable Ferrari Dino comes with its original owner's manual, warranty card and tool kit.

On January 20, 2001, this handsome 246 GTS brought $85,000 at the Bonhams & Brooks Cavallino auction, including buyer's premium.

The 246 GTS Dino has to be one of the most well-rounded classics of all time. The beauty of these cars lay in the thrill of the glorious roaring engine noise, the voluptuous view from the driver's seat and the amazing go-kart feel. (I have never met anyone who, on pure aesthetics alone, loved those miserably flared wheel arches.) It's understood that faster, stronger and better-built cars have been produced before and after the Dino, but as my friend, Lisa Stone, once proclaimed, "The 246 is the prince of all sports cars." I think Ms. Stone was on to something; that may be as succinct and correct a description as I've ever heard.

I was under the false assumption that Pino Verde (metallic green) must have been a damn popular color for 1974 Dinos, as I have seen three of them for sale in the last four years at auction. Upon closer inspection, it has been the same car offered on all three occasions. It was a no-sale at Christie's/Tarrytown on April 29, 2000, at $70K, and a no-sale at RM/Monterey on August 14, 1998, at $85K. What the...? Let's unravel this a bit.

Occasionally, you may observe the same car being offered over and over again for sale at auctions. Perhaps a buyer can't be found and the seller tries again at a different venue. Perhaps the reserve is too high. Or, perhaps the car simply isn't desirable enough to anyone other than the chandelier in the back of the room. (Pity the poor chandelier, always bidding, usually on great cars, but never having quite enough money to get the job done.)

Back to Pino Grigio, I mean Verde. What I find particularly odd about this frequent-auction Dino is that it seems to be a very nice car with an unblemished traceable history and excellent service/maintenance records. Many Dinos have been run into the ground, abused or wrecked over time. Not terribly robust to begin with, they were "just cars" that weren't even accepted as true Ferraris for an unfairly long period. This is not one of those mistreated cars.

(Note: For those of you who add Ferrari emblems to your Dino, stop it, or we'll send Enzo's ghost to your house and he'll wreak havoc with your Dinoplexes. I own one (1969 246 GT), and seeing a Dino festooned with Prancing Horse badges and stickers that scream "I'm really a Ferrari even if Enzo never called me one" just bothers me.)

Dinos have risen steadily in value over the past 36 months while their bigger, faster, 12-cylinder siblings, the Boxer and Testarossa, have fallen. Dinos are fun and easy to drive in real-life situations and look like sex on wheels in your driveway. Running costs are not absurd and parts are not terribly difficult to find. Denny Shue runs the helpful Dino Registry and there are several good books to educate the new buyer.

Kudos to the new owner. You paid near top dollar, but got a great car. I only hope I don't see your Pino Verde exotic for sale any time soon under yet another tent.—Steve Serio

(Historical data and photo courtesy of auction company.)

From the April 2001 issue of *SCM*.◆

Years produced	1972-74
Number produced	1,274 (VIN 02174 through 08518)
Original list price	$15,225 (1974)
SCM Price Guide	$65,000-$90,000 (Add $7,500 for "chairs and flares")
Tune-up/major service	$350-$1,500; 30K-mile major service with cam belts $2,500-$3,500
Distributor cap	$140 cap/$70 rotor
Chassis 06470	Stamped on driver's side rail in engine compartment; chassis plate in engine bay on firewall
Engine #	Above timing cover below cylinder head on block
Club	Ferrari Club of America, Box 720597, Atlanta, GA 30358; Ferrari Owner's Club, 8642 Cleta St. Downey, CA 90241
Web site	www.ferrariclubofamerica.org; 222.FerrariOwnersClub.org
Alternatives	Porsche 911S, Maserati Merak SS, Lamborghini Urraco P300, Lotus Esprit S2

1981 308 GTBi

Chassis number: ZFFAA01A9B0037187

Following on the heels of the mechanically inspired but visually challenged 308 GT4, the new 308 was drop-dead gorgeous

RM Auctions

The advent of the new Pininfarina-designed 308 GTB was hailed as one of the best Ferraris of modern times. And it is no wonder—following on the heels of the mechanically inspired but visually challenged 308 GT4, the new 308 was drop-dead gorgeous.

As Sergio Pininfarina himself pointed out, "Every Ferrari car previously designed by us was a great success in the market." From a styling point of view, the 308 owes more to the legendary 246 Dino than to any previous road-going Ferrari. Perhaps equally important, the 308 GTB was the first non-12-cylinder road car to carry the Ferrari badge.

The car was quite sophisticated, particularly for the time, with a transverse-mounted all-alloy four-cam V8 engine, initially producing 205 hp—a remarkable figure. With four-wheel independent suspension and four-wheel disc brakes, the car was extremely well-balanced, and offered taut handling along with a compliant ride.

Originally sold in 1982, this 308 was immediately treated to sympathetic ownership and care. Showing less than 15,000 miles on the odometer—believed to be correct from new—this original example is in excellent overall condition. It is complete with its original manuals, as well as with the original and correct Campagnolo alloy wheels.

This car sold at RM's Monterey auction, August 16, 2002, for $26,400, including buyer's premium.

Even the best manufacturers make mistakes. Porsche made a series of 911s with chain tensioner problems, Mercedes had the single-row timing chain fiasco and Ferrari has the 1980-82 Ferrari 308s.

1980 marked the beginning of some rather draconian federal emissions regulations. Ferrari, recognizing its carbureted 308 engines would not meet the 1980 standards, set out to solve the problem. The result was the 308 GTBi and 308 GTSi.

These new "i" cars became the second generation of 308 GTB/GTS cars. The i indicated the introduction of fuel injection and the Marelli Digiplex Ignition system as a solution to emissions problems. The i might also be seen as meaning "improved," as these cars benefited from a host of changes. A new interior appeared in the all-new 1980 308 with Michelin TRX tires, high-tech enamel paint, a lighter clutch and a longer shift lever phased in as the year progressed. The changes were not free—1980 models cost 17% more than their 1979 counterparts.

The carbureted 308s pumped out a reasonable 205 hp in US trim. The new i model was still rated at 205 hp but actually produced somewhere around a lackluster 180 hp. The new car was further demeaned by the loss of the Weber's crisp response and wonderful induction noise.

The loss of power was a significant blow, but the real problem was far more sinister. A design or manufacturing problem—one that was never identified—caused many i cars to develop serious oil consumption issues. Problem cars drank a quart of oil in less than 200 miles.

To Ferrari's credit, they stood behind their mistake. Problem cars were treated to an engine transplant. Unfortunately many of the afflicted cars were never diagnosed as having a problem, and there was neither rhyme nor reason as to when the problem would surface. One car might have a problem from new, one at 20,000 miles, and many never developed a problem at all. The cars did not drip oil and did not smoke. Often owners never realized they had a problem until their car was years out of warranty.

Many afflicted cars became hot potatoes, passing from owner to owner as soon as a problem was noticed. Dealers quickly awoke to the problems and became wary of offering used i models. Even a repaired car was suspicious as the replacement engine could be susceptible to the same problem. Bad examples exhibited some telltale signs (such as stained paint behind the license plate), but without performing an elaborate test the problem was—and still is—difficult to recognize.

"Many afflicted cars became hot potatoes, passing from owner to owner as soon as a problem was noticed."

The car pictured here was a risky buy. With only 15,000 miles, it could very easily harbor a bad engine or one that just hasn't gone bad yet. With no mention of a major service, chances are good a $3,000 service is due immediately, with the potential for more expensive fixes to follow soon thereafter. That's also the upper mileage allowable for the TRX tires that are currently obtainable only through Coker Tires for around $1,000 a set. And for that amount, you get 20-year-old tire technology.

On the other hand, if everything is good and performance is not an issue, $26,400 is on the money. Sharp, low-mileage 308s are becoming extinct. Finding another one with this low mileage and in this un-abused condition would be difficult.

Nonetheless, while the price is market-correct, I would hesitate to recommend this car, or a similar 308i, to a client. The downside of an i is an engine rebuild, and there is no upside. The next generation 308 Quattrovalvoles only cost a few thousand more and were virtually trouble-free. If you're looking for a 308, my advice would be to find a good carbureted car or spend a little more for a Q.
—Steve Ahlgrim
(Historical and descriptive information courtesy of RM Auctions.)
From the January 2003 issue of *SCM*.◆

1989 328 GTS

Chassis number: ZFFXA20AXK0081058

The 328 is the best built, most reliable Ferrari ever... period

Bonhams

Ferrari's line of highly successful V8-engined road cars began when the 308 GT4 of 1973 took over from the preceding 246 Dino V6. The newcomer's wedged-shaped styling, by Bertone, was not universally well received, but the performance of the 3-liter V8 certainly was. A new two-seater car using the same power unit, the 308 GTB, debuted at the Paris Salon in 1975. Built on a shorter wheelbase, the stunningly beautiful GTB marked a welcome return to Pininfarina styling.

The 308 was superseded by the mechanically similar but larger-engined 328 in 1986. By increasing both bore and stroke, the engine's capacity was raised to 3186 cc, which, together with a higher compression ratio, lifted maximum power to 270 horsepower at 7,000 rpm.

Top speed was raised to 160 miles per hour with 0 to 60 mph covered in 5.5 seconds. The elegant simplicity of Pininfarina's original 308 had been updated by the addition of molded bumpers and an unobtrusive roof spoiler. *Motor* magazine observed: "In our book, this is still the most beautiful of all contemporary exotics—a gorgeous looking car."

Possibly the lowest mileage 328 in the world, and one of the last built, the exceptional "time warp" example shown here has covered a mere 87 miles from new. Finished in Rosso Corsa with beige leather, the car comes with the original certificate of origin. FAF Motorcars, Inc., of Tucker, Georgia, supplied the car new to the current owner and it has never been registered. Both factory tool kits are in place and the unused owners' manuals are in their wallet. The overall appearance is as if the car were delivered just days ago. The 87 miles covered over the past 13 years have only been accumulated through routine start-ups, done to avoid any ill effects from prolonged inactivity.

This car sold for $59,455, including buyer's premium, at the Bonhams Geneva sale, held March 11, 2002.

I was sales manager at FAF Motorcars in 1989, a wild time to be in the Ferrari business. Virtually any Ferrari was hot property and the 328 was no exception. There was a waiting list for new cars and people were buying used 328s for more than the list price of a new one. Many Ferrari dealerships were selling new cars at MSRP knowing that buyers were immediately reselling for a profit.

To help combat this rampant speculation, FAF didn't generally sell cars to people we didn't know well, and we tried to avoid selling any cars for export. However, a check of old records revealed that this car had been sold, by regular SCM *contributor and FAF co-owner, John Apen, to a Swiss national with a textile business who also had a home in the Carolinas, thus getting around our export concerns.*

We never saw the buyer again so he probably returned to Switzerland with the car, and left it in storage for years.

Years produced	1986-89
Number produced	6,068
Original list price	$84,780
SCM Price Guide	$37,500-$45,000
Tune-up/major service	$3,000
Distributor cap	$387.09 (two required)
Chassis number	On plate on top of steering column, in driver's door jamb and on top right frame rail next to engine in engine compartment
Engine number	Top of block on passenger side
Club	Ferrari Club of America, P.O. Box 720597, Atlanta, GA 30358; Ferrari Owner's Club, 8642 Cleta St., Downey, CA 90241
Web site	www.FerrariClubofAmerica.org, www.FerrariOwnersClub.org
Alternatives	Dodge Viper GTS, Ferrari Testarossa, Porsche 996
SCM Investment Grade	B

In my opinion the 328 is the best built, most reliable Ferrari ever. Period. It is the product of a dozen years of 308 experience. It was solidly constructed, with a steel body welded to an oval tube frame. It featured simple Bosch fuel injection, a go/no-go electronic ignition system and an engine you serviced without removing from the car.

Most important, it was the last Ferrari that could be repaired by a good import shop. The following generation of V8 Ferraris evolved into temples to high-tech gadgetry. When something goes wrong with one of these technological marvels, you have to truck your car to an authorized Ferrari dealer—they're the only place that has the computer necessary to fix your car.

Cars don't like prolonged storage. Rubber seals become hard, shock absorbers seize, brake calipers start to stick and tires get flat spots. On the other hand, it only takes a minimum amount of attention to keep things from going bad. If this car was started and moved as little as once a year, it may be fine.

Assuming there were no storage-related surprises (and perhaps pigs can fly as well), this car was very well bought. 1989 was the last year for the 328s and they've become the darling of 308/328 collectors. Examples with less than 10,000 miles will sell for over $60,000. 328s with fewer miles can approach $70,000. A Ferrari dealer recently paid $63,000 for a 1,000-mile example and still had to pay shipping and a broker's commission before he could bring it home. And he expects to be able to resell for a profit.

Here, the new owner's biggest problem may be figuring out what to do with his new toy. Does he keep it as the lowest mile example in existence or drive it?

If he chooses the latter course of action, common sense dictates a complete $3,000 service before heading out onto the highway. If he does that, and then demonstrates the car's solid condition by driving it for a few hundred miles, he may actually increase *its value. Furthermore, he could probably enjoy his time-warp car to the tune of 9,000 miles (three years at the standard collector car usage rate of 3,000 miles per year), and then sell the car for what he paid for it, or more.—Steve Ahlgrim*

(Historic data and photo courtesy of auction company.)

From the August 2002 issue of *SCM*.◆

1991 348 tb Berlinetta

Chassis number: ZFFRG35A2M0088479

As the lowly kid brother to the Testarossa, it was expected to look pretty but performance was not top priority

The 348 tb was a dramatic departure for Ferrari. Its 3,405-cc dual overhead-camshaft engine is mounted longitudinally in the chassis like the 288 GTO. However the 348's chassis is only four inches longer than the transverse-engined 328 GT that preceded it. To accomplish this magic, Ferrari applied lessons learned in its Formula One racing program, developing a transversely mounted gearbox in unit with the differential to minimize the drivetrain's length and contain the masses of the drivetrain for optimum handling. The 348 tb also utilized a monocoque chassis, further reducing its mass and containing it within the extended wheelbase for quicker response.

Like other manufacturers, by the time the 348 was introduced in 1990, Ferrari was learning to live with emissions restrictions. Bosch Motronic port fuel injection and electronic engine management delivered 300 horsepower at 7,200 rpm from the 348's four-valve-per-cylinder engine. Luxuriously equipped with air conditioning, sound-deadening insulation and a multitude of power assists, the 348 has one horsepower per 10.6 pounds of weight, a figure that even today ranks it among the top street performance GTs.

The 348's engine was lowered some five inches from the 328, complementing a track that was much wider at the front (1.2") than the rear (4.4"). This made the 348 both more stable and more responsive.

The 11-year-old 1991 348 tb Berlinetta shown here is an extraordinary time capsule, with barely 100 miles from new.

This car sold for $66,000, including buyer's premium, at RM's New York auction, held September 21, 2002.

"...the 348 will do 0 to 60 in 5.4 seconds and will top out at 171 mph. Put in perspective, this is as fast as a Boxer."

So goes a promotional piece I wrote about the 348 for the FAF Motorcars Buyers Guide back in 1991. This proclamation was controversial at the time, but concisely captured the essence of this new generation of V8 Ferrari.

The macho 512 Boxer was one of the premier supercars of its time. Its looks made high school boys drool, and its performance impressed people even after a $10,000 EPA emasculation. The 348, on the other hand, was just the replacement for the 328. As the lowly kid brother to the Testarossa, it was expected to look pretty but performance was not top priority.

However, instead of being just another small Ferrari, the 348 was the precursor to a line of new Ferraris destined to revitalize and invigorate the proud firm. The 348s, and the 355s and 360s that followed, not only looked good, but packed kick-butt performance. They were no longer little brothers to the 12-cylinder and turbocharged 8-cylinder supercars, they were full-fledged alternatives.

The 348 was new from the ground up. It started as a fresh sheet of paper and changed Ferrari's thoughts on how automobiles should be built. Virtually every component of the 348 was new, the only holdover from the 328 being the basic V8, mid-engined sports car layout. Where the 328 had a separate chassis and body, the 348 was built with unitized construction. Where the 328 had a transverse engine, the 348 had a longitudinal one. And where the 328 transaxle sat under its engine, the 348's was attached behind its V8 and mounted in a transverse position.

RM Auctions

Ferrari has traditionally been a follower when it comes to technology. Enzo Ferrari was legendary for his resistance to disc brakes and mid-engined cars. The 348 finally featured up-to-date components, and its innovative use of manufacturing technology set it far ahead of the supercar competition. The 348 was designed to be built faster, cheaper and less labor-intensive than any previous Ferrari.

So was this 100-mile 348 coupe a good buy? It depends on if you want a 100-mile 348 coupe. Despite the significance the 348 may have played in Ferrari's manufacturing history, it was a dud in the marketplace. Its design was uninspiring and the impressive drivetrain performance was compromised by a far-less-impressive chassis. The electronics, perhaps in an unintended homage to the notoriously finicky Mondials, were plagued with gremlins that caused warning lights to illuminate erroneously, and control computers to fail prematurely. There weren't enough problems to call the 348 a bad car, but there were too many to call it a good one.

Further, the 355 and the 360 that followed were better cars in every way, including that all-important aspect of visual appeal. Without question, you'll get more attention showing up at a club meet in a Modena Spyder than you will in a 348 coupe.

At the right price a good 348 offers an enormous amount of performance for not much money, but you get no prancing horse swagger. Furthermore, it will never appreciate. $66,000 is a heck of a good price for a "new" Ferrari (the MSRP on a 360 coupe is $154,550) but all the money for an 11-year-old coupe from an unloved model. Best bet for the new owner is to put 3,000 miles on it a year, sell it in 2005 for about the same amount paid here, and just enjoy the ride. —Steve Ahlgrim

From the February 2003 issue of *SCM*.◆

Years produced	1989-94
Number produced	2,895
Original list price	$105,500
SCM Price Guide	$45,000-$55,000
Tune up/major service	$4,000 (with cam belts)
Distributor cap	N/A
Chassis #	Top right frame rail, just above right shock
Engine #	Passenger's side of engine in the V, just in front of the oil filter
Club	Ferrari Club of America, P.O. Box 720597, Atlanta, GA 30358; Ferrari Owner's Club, 8642 Cleta St., Downey, CA 90241
Web site	www.FerrariClubofAmerica.org; www.FerrariOwnersClub.org
Alternatives	Lotus Esprit S4, Porsche Boxster S, Acura NSX, Aston Martin Virage
SCM Investment Grade	C

1991 Ferrari Mondial T Cabriolet

Chassis number: ZSSKC33B000085478

The virtues do not outweigh the vices, and the vices usually come calling with large and expensive repair orders

Brooks

The Ferrari Mondial Cabriolet occupied a unique niche in the luxury car market: a four-seat mid-engine Cabriolet with pedigree. The improved Mondial T received a 296-hp, 3405 cc V8 engine mounted longitudinally in the frame. Along with a new engine came a completely new five-speed transmission, electronically controlled variable suspension, and a three-position manual suspension selector. Top speed was 158 mph and the 0 to 100 km/h sprint could be covered in 6.3 seconds.

The French-registered Mondial T pictured here has been cherished throughout its life, having covered just 36,700 km. The 40,000-km service was carried out by French importer Charles Pozzi last April at a cost of $7,500. Finished in Rosso Corsa with a black leather interior, the car is fitted with new tires and also has ABS and power steering. The vendor described it as "excellent" in every aspect.

The above-described Ferrari was recently sold by the Brooks auction house at Nürburgring, Germany for $25,603, which included buyer's premium.

It seems our fellow European Ferraristi care less about the Mondial Cabriolet market than we Americans do; is that possible? Low mileage, late model, just serviced, traditional colors—why the lukewarm interest generating a low hammer price, at least $20,000 below what we'd expect to retail a Mondial Cab for over here?

For VW Passat money, was this a deal or correct fair market value? Let's talk.

In my humble, and admittedly biased opinion, being fair to the Mondial Cabriolet is sort of like trying to understand how a White House intern with the mental power of a Crosley Hot Shot could seduce the President of the United States. Well, as they say, there is a bottom for every seat.

Before you Prancing Horse owners start cringing and calling for me to be burned in effigy at the next Mondial owners club meeting (assuming the electrical systems don't bug out and they are actually able to get there), I'll point out the practical positive attributes of a Mondial. In a bigger effort to be fair, I'll even go ahead and admit that the buyer at the 'Ring seems to have gotten an okay deal.

With nicely balanced brakes and suspension, a pedal box suited for perfect heel-and-toeing, a cab-forward design and reasonably decent power, these mid-engine rides can be fun with the top down and the bugs in your teeth. If you're in luck, you'll never have to raise the top (note the subtle hint about the top mechanism). You can stuff lil' Biff and cutesy Mandy in the back and travel with luggage for an extended period—option boxes rarely found on an exotic car order form. And the exhaust note of the Mondial Cabriolet demonstrates perfectly how a Ferrari should sound. However, from my perspective, that's it. That's all you get.

The virtues do not outweigh the vices, and the vices usually come calling with large and expensive repair orders.

Miserable convertible top design, temperamental electronics, interior ergonomics from the Bert and Ernie school of engineering, expensive servicing and overall mediocre build quality do not make for an easy car to sell. I haven't even begun to hammer on the boring exterior design.

Two franchised Ferrari dealers (who shall remain nameless) refuse to stock these cars under any conditions because of the fear of what they will have to warranty. Give these cars five more years and, like the owner of a Land Rover Discovery, you may need to start carrying a canvas bag to collect all the pieces the car constantly sheds. That may seem harsh and somewhat unfair, but I take the franchised dealer comments as a clear warning about this road-going Andrea Doria.

If you're truly interested in buying a Mondial, you would be well-advised to read Winston Goodfellow's article in the November 1999 issue of Forza, *the quintessential puff magazine for Ferrari owners and wannabes. Read between the lines of his well-researched faint praise and muse about your decision.*

Here's the point: If you take the Ferrari badge off, you possess a very forgettable car.—Steve Serio

Years produced	1989-93
Numbers produced	1,010
Original list price	$117,000
SCM Price Guide	$42,500-$50,000
Tune-up/major service (30k miles):	$4,200-$4,900 w/cam belts
Distributor cap	$175 (two required)
Chassis #	On engine compartment upper right chassis tube and plate on right bulkhead of front compartment; in windshield on DOT tag; on steering column
Engine #	Affixed to center of the block vee beneath the injection casting at the rear of the casting
Clubs	Ferrari Club of America, Box 720597, Atlanta, GA 30358; Ferrari Owners Club, 8642 Cleta St., Downey, CA 90241
Web sites	www.ferrariclubofamerica.org; www.FerrariOwnersClub.org
Alternatives	Porsche 911 Cabriolet, Porsche 968 Cabriolet, Jaguar XJS Cabriolet

Counterpoint: *All Ferraris have their quixotic moments. If you want to have a true high-performance, open, affordable exotic with room for a couple of small kids, your list will have only one car on it, the Mondial Cabriolet. So what if you have an electrical gremlin now and then? So what if the top is hard to put up? If you want a stupid, boring car that never gives you problems, buy a Chevy Cavalier rag top. If I were presented with a nicely kept, low-mileage Mondial Cabriolet for $25,000, I'd buy it in a heartbeat. I suspect Mr. Serio would as well, if only to resell it for a $10,000 profit.—Keith Martin*

(Historical data and photo courtesy of auction company.)

From the February 2002 issue of *SCM*.◆

1997 F355 Spyder

Chassis number: ZFFXR48AA8V01107072

The press loved the car, the people loved the car and customers had to get on a waiting list to buy it

This is truly a beauty, in iconic Ferrari red with camel leather interior and matching boot, and a black automatic convertible top. The legendary engine is a 3.5-liter V8 producing 375 horsepower, with 11:1 compression ratio, twin overhead camshafts per cylinder bank and five valves per cylinder. A CD changer is located in the trunk. A two-owner vehicle, it has been maintained as an exotic car should be. Fully serviced and documented, the 30,000-mile service was done at the cost of $7,000. Your Ferrari dream can come true today, especially as this car is offered with a very low reserve.

This car sold for $99,360, including buyer's premium, at the Barrett-Jackson West Palm Beach auction, held April 10-13, 2003.

The collapse of the collector car hypermarket of the late '80s brought on a nuclear winter that virtually froze Ferrari sales for the next several years. Riding the crest of the speculation wave, Ferrari had bumped production from 3,119 cars in 1985 to a record high of 4,594 cars in 1991. When the crash came, new Ferrari sales dried up, and units began quickly piling up in showrooms and warehouses. Ferrari responded by slashing production: A 25% cut in 1992 still left supply exceeding demand, and another 20% cut in 1993 brought production down to a scant 2,325 units. Ferrari needed some magic, and it needed it fast.

Ferrari President Luca di Montezemolo pulled a rabbit out of his hat when he decided to update the uninspiring 348 for 1994. Normally, this would mean adding a few more horses and sticking on some body trim, but di Montezemolo challenged everyone at Ferrari, from design to marketing, to create something special, something far more dramatic to bring buyers back to the showrooms.

It's said that a picture is worth a thousand words, and one photo in the 355 press kit told the story. In the midst of some glamour shots was the image of the underside of a 355, seemingly floating on air. The bottom of the car was completely covered in sculpted panels of fiberglass. This under-tray of air diffusers and venturis produced the sort of racecar aerodynamics that had never before graced a street car. The statement was made: The 355 was a serious performance car.

The engine was all new and bumped horsepower up a whopping 25 percent. Ferrari engineers redesigned the chassis to accommodate the power of the new motor and improved grip from new 18-inch wheels. Then they went to work on the body and smoothed it to be more aggressive and more distinctive. The transmission got another gear to make it a six-speed and in 1997, a Formula One-style paddle-shift transmission became available. The interior was likewise spiffed up and—ta da!—the rabbit appeared, and Ferrari sales were about to get back on track.

The marketplace acceptance of the 355 was nothing short of magical in its own right. The press loved the car, the people loved the car and soon customers had to get on a waiting list to buy the car. Ferrari had a hit, and rightly so. The 355 had the looks, performance and cachet that made it worthy of the marque. In 1997, the introduction of a 355 Spyder and the new 550 Maranello model pushed Ferrari production up to 3,518, well on the way to the current 4,200-car level.

Years produced	1994-99
Number produced	2,664 six-speeds, 1,053 F1s
Original list price	approx. $137,075
SCM Price Guide	$95,000-$115,000
Tune-up/major service	$5,500 with cam belt
Distributor cap	N/A
Chassis #	Stamped on the frame directly above the passenger side rear shock absorber
Engine #:	Top of engine on the passenger side in the rear. The number does not match the chassis number.
Club	Ferrari Club of America, P.O. Box 720597, Atlanta, GA 30358
Web site	www.FerrariClubofAmerica.com
Alternatives	Porsche 993 twin turbo, BMW Z8, Ferrari Daytona, Lamborghini Diablo

If you're going to buy a car like this—or any car—it's best to do a little homework first. Auction catalogs and objective information don't always go hand-in-hand. I pulled a Carfax report (www.carfax.com) on this 355 Spyder, which indicated it should have around 31,000 miles, as it did. Carfax also told me the car sold new to an owner in Virginia before it was transferred to a second owner in Maryland. The car made its way to Florida by way of an East Coast dealers' auction. Yearly emission inspections showed a believable progression of mileage and no damage history was recorded.

With nothing in this car's history to arouse suspicions and an expensive major service documented, a further look at the car is warranted. Ferrari 355s have a couple interior defects to watch for: Plastic in the interior can melt, dissolve or otherwise turn into a sticky mess, and the dash leather is prone to shrinkage, looking unsightly and often distorting the dash frame. On the mechanical side, headers and ECUs on early cars sometimes go bad and the power tops on Spyders are notably fragile.

Assuming this car passed a visual inspection with no major issues, this was a fair buy. A low-mile, top-notch '97 Spyder can bring up to $110,000, while rough cars with checkered histories go through dealer auctions in the $70,000s. The 30,000 miles on this car is high for a Ferrari and was reflected in the price. While I might have expected a low-to-mid $90,000s price, the fact that the service was done, and the car presented itself well, accounted for the slight premium.

355s are wonderful cars, and the new owner should get miles of enjoyment out of his new toy.—Steve Ahlgrim

(Historic and descriptive information courtesy of Barrett-Jackson.)

From the August 2003 issue of *SCM*.◆

2000 360 Modena Coupe

Breathtaking is the only word to describe the 360, introduced in 1999. From its sculpted looks, crafted over a superbly fabricated aluminum chassis, the Modena exudes Ferrari at its best

Chassis number: ZFFYU51A0Y0121894

The line of Ferrari Berlinettas has been a long and distinguished one. From the first 166 Barchetta through the 195, the 212, and then the highly collectible 250 GTs of the 1960s, the cars have always been designed for just two passengers; light, nimble and equipped with a powerful and reliable V12 engine.

In the 1970s, with the 308 series, the Ferrari two-seater Berlinetta changed from a front-engine V12-powered car to a mid-engine V8. The resultant models included the iconic 308/328, the 348, the 355 and now the 360 Modena.

Breathtaking is the only word to describe the 360, introduced in 1999. From its sculpted looks, crafted over a superbly fabricated aluminum chassis, the Modena exudes Ferrari at its best. The engine is turbine-like in its power delivery through a six-speed gearbox, rocketing the driver to a top speed of 190 mph, with 0-60 mph coming in just 4.3 seconds. From a standstill, 100 mph takes just 10.2 seconds, accompanied by extraordinary handling and braking.

The car pictured here is in superb condition, having covered just 1,837 miles from new. It has been regularly serviced and maintained since being purchased in 2001. Finished in Ferrari red with a tan interior, this low mileage 360 Modena is, as one would expect, simply stunning—and virtually new. A perfect modern Ferrari for the most discerning buyer, this example offers no disappointments.

The SCM *analysis: This car sold for $159,500, including buyer's commission, at the RM Monterey auction, Aug. 16-17, 2003.*

Traditionally, Ferrari was a refiner, rather than an innovator. Advancements like disc brakes, mid-engine design and serious aerodynamics were in common use elsewhere long before Ferrari picked them up. Indeed, Ferrari's reliance on powerful engines kept it competitive during onslaughts of new technology, but seldom did it answer the competition with its own advancements. That is, until Luca Cordero di Montezemolo seized the reins of the company in 1992.

Di Montezemolo's vision is that Ferrari make history, not just be a part of it. He doesn't just talk the talk, he make things happen. His marketing expertise has included installing a Ferrari dealership in a major casino, as well as leveraging the Ferrari brand with myriad lucrative licensing agreements. His influence is found everywhere in the company, from the champion Formula One team to the new state-of-the-art manufacturing facilities.

While the new Enzo may, in time, prove to be di Montezemolo's finest accomplishment, it could not exist if not for the 360 paying the rent. It follows the 308, 328, 348 and 355 as the standard-bearer eight-cylinder, cars that now account for nearly two-thirds of Ferrari's production. Under di Montezemolo's watch, these have evolved from lower-cost siblings into serious alternatives to the traditional twelve-cylinder Ferraris.

RM Auctions

The Modena had specific design targets: superior performance and reduced weight over the 355, with a larger cabin and more luggage space. A bigger interior takes just the strike of an engineer's pencil, yet it's usually antithetical to reduced weight, requiring that the Modena be designed from a clean slate. The major innovation was an entirely aluminum spaceframe, a first for a Ferrari street car, co-developed by Alcoa and made of both castings and extrusions.

The suspension was also aluminum—the whole package was wrapped in gorgeous aluminum skin designed by Pininfarina. The styling house looked back into Ferrari's history, and took styling cues from the 250 LM and the Dino. These were blended with modern aerodynamics to produce the most aggressive looking, high performing eight-cylinder Ferrari ever.

The 360 is 10 percent larger than the 355, but 28 percent lighter and 40 percent more rigid. Lighter weight obviously helps performance, but not as much as its new 3.6-liter, 400-horsepower engine. That, along with a new braking system and improved aerodynamics, helped the car to circulate Ferrari's Fiorano test track almost three seconds faster than its predecessor.

But value-wise, the 360 Modena is starting to show the first signs of getting a little long in the tooth. After all, it's been available for nearly five years now, and seeing one on the street no longer stops you in your tracks as it once did. The base MSRP on a 2004 Modena is $153,182, and sources tell me that if you're willing to pay sticker, you can have one today, in your choice of colors. You might even be able to wrangle a small discount. Used coupes are now available from $130,000, depending on miles. (The Spyder still commands a premium; its MSRP is $175,750, but it will take $200,000-$225,000 to put one in your driveway without a wait.)

Coupe prices will stay relatively flat until the successor to the 360 Modena is announced, which should happen sometime in the next 12 months. At that point, everyone will rush to be first on the block with the newest toy, and the former newest toy, the 360, will become yesterday's hot item and values will plummet.

The seller of this car was wise to market it when and where he did, and the result achieved last August in Monterey would be hard to replicate today. If you're in a 360 coupe for the short term, selling it sooner is better than later. If you're a potential buyer, just be patient. Time is on your side; prices will only come down.—Steve Ahlgrim

Years produced:	1999-2004
Number produced:	Approx. 2,500 per year.
Original list price:	$147,775
SCM Price Guide:	$135,000-$170,000
Tune up/major service:	$4,000-$5,000
Distributor cap:	None
Chassis number:	Stamped in the floorboard behind the driver's seat
Engine number:	In middle of V on top of engine
Club:	Ferrari Club of America, P.O. Box 720597, Atlanta, GA 30358
Web site:	www.ferrariclubofamerica.com
Alternatives:	2004 Lamborghini Gallardo, 2000-2004 Aston Martin DB7 Vantage
SCM Investment Grade:	B

1979 Ferrari 512 BB Berlinetta Boxer

Many buyers won't take the risk of unknown mechanical condition on these expensive-to-fix 12-cylinder cars... unless they are such a bargain that lust overcomes logic

Chassis number: 27375

Faced with having to pitch its Daytona front-engined model against the mid-engined Miura and Bora, Ferrari responded with the 365 GTB/4 Berlinetta Boxer in 1973. An entirely new car and the first road-going Ferrari not to have a "V" configuration engine, the Boxer used a 4.4-liter, four-cam, flat-12 derived from the 3-liter Formula 1. The mid-mounted engine/five-speed transaxle was housed in a tubular/monocoque chassis clothed in Pininfarina's elegant Berlinetta coachwork. A new Boxer—the 512 BB—appeared in 1976 with a 4942-cc engine and dry sump. The larger engine provided a useful increase in torque, improving acceleration and driveability. Improvements were also made to the aerodynamics, suspension and tires. And in 1981 it was updated with fuel injection, becoming the 512 BBi.

Bonhams & Brooks

The right-hand drive 512 BB pictured here boasts an engine built by Ferrari specialist Nigel Hudson and incorporating a host of improvements, including LM cams, Mahle pistons, gas-flowed cylinder heads, sports exhaust, and re-jetted carburetors. A maximum 460 horsepower is claimed (approximately 120 more than standard) so a commensurate improvement in performance over the standard car may be expected. The work was carried out in the mid 1980s, after which the present owner purchased the car in 1984. Since then, the car has covered a mere 5,000 miles and only 12,000 total. Additional contemporary upgrades include AP brakes, oil cooler, competition clutch, Compomotive wheels and extended rear wheel arches. Believed accident free, it is in excellent mechanical condition with fair to good interior and benefits from a recent service and belt change. This Boxer has phenomenal performance, yet the vendor claims it is extremely tractable.

Years produced	1974-84 (all types)
Number produced	327 365 BB, 927 512 BB, 1,007 512 BBi
Original price	$35,000 plus DOT/EPA ($10,000-$15,000)
SCM Price Guide	$55,000-$80,000 (BBi $60,000-$90,000)
Tune-up/major service	$3,000; add $2,000 for timing belts
Distributor cap	$300
Chassis #	On frame tube in engine bay
Engine #	Top of engine block
Clubs	Ferrari Club of America, Box 720597, Atlanta, GA 30358; Ferrari Owners Club, 8642 Cleta St., Downey, CA 90241
Web sites	www.ferrariclubofamerica.org; www.FerrariOwnersClub.org
Alternatives	Lamborghini Miura, Maserati Bora

On April 23rd, 2001, Bonhams & Brooks sold this Boxer for $39,200, including buyer's premium, at the RAF Museum in Hendon, England.

How low can Boxers go? Ask the man who bought Lucent at $78 per share. When you review recent prices it is amazing, or distressing, depending on your ownership status, how much they have sunk. A very nice, 13,000-mile, injected Boxer sold at Bonhams & Brooks's December 2000 auction in Switzerland for $44,800. For a car with so much mid-engined performance and aesthetic appeal, why the low price?

My theory is that it's the risk associated with engine problems compared to the total price. For example, you can buy a '60s collectible American car in the $30k to $50k range and if you assume a new engine at $3,000 to $5,000, your risk ratio is 0.1 to perhaps 0.2. As such, it's not a catastrophe if your significant other wants to know why it sounds like there's a can of walnuts rattling under the hood on her first ride.

For most 12-cylinder exotics, a rebuild starts at $20,000 and can go as high as $40,000. So for the $50,000 to $100,000 Italian exotic, the risk ratio is around 0.5. You can lose half your "investment" if your timing belt breaks. Thus, many buyers won't take the risk of unknown mechanical condition on these expensive-to-fix 12-cylinder cars, unless they are such a bargain that lust overcomes logic.

Most of these auction exotics are not championed by a seller who has a notebook full of bills and photos detailing the history. For this Boxer, note the casual catalog statement about "a recent service and belt change." That's reassuring, assuming it was a $5,000 engine-out timing belt change. But what's not reassuring is the description of all the hot-rod stuff done nearly 20 years ago. Imagine the kind of Ferrari owner who needs another 120 horsepower in his already-twitchy car, and puts flares on the rear wheel arches. Why do visions of spiky hair, nose rings and rock-star status come to mind? Would you buy a Ferrari from someone like this?

Many well-documented exotics, with only good stories, sell privately for far more than the examples that show up at auctions with no service history or documentation. The stack of repair bills and photos, backed by a believable owner, are worth real money and peace of mind. (At Barrett-Jackson two years ago, there was a '57 T-Bird owner who stayed with his car for all four days and could convincingly detail and prove everything that was done to it. He hit a home run on the price—it brought $44,500.)

Was this Boxer a good buy? Only time and a thorough mechanical evaluation will tell. But with all the surprises that could surface on this highly modified engine/chassis, this Boxer is either the most fun per dollar this year or a terrible sinkhole. However, as they say in real estate, "Price solves all problems." When a running, driving Boxer gets below $40k, in Ferrari terms, that's almost free. So for some brave bidder, the gamble was worth it.—John Apen

Caveat lector: *The writer is just finishing a major, remove-the-engine service on his 365 Boxer, and has the following recommendations: for frequent driving, buy an injected BBi; for raw excitement, find a 365; for maximum value, buy a carbureted 512. But please, be aware that buying a Boxer without paperwork is akin to playing Russian Roulette with all the chambers loaded.*

(Historic data and photo courtesy of auction company.)

From the July 2001 issue of *SCM*.◆

1980 512 Berlinetta Boxer

Chassis number: 33287

The catalog description went into great detail about it being a fuel-injected car, but it was hard to mistake the four Webers

John Apen

The mid-engined Lamborghini Miura brought Formula One chassis design to the street in the mid-1960s. Ferrari's response was the 365 GTB/4 Berlinetta Boxer, unveiled at the 1971 Turin Auto Show. The first road-going Ferrari not to have a V-configured engine, the Boxer had a four-cam, 4.4-liter flat-12 derived from Ferrari's 3-liter F1 engine. Steering was light, due to the mid-engine layout and a new rack-and-pinion system. The tubular monocoque chassis was clothed in Pininfarina's innovative and elegant coachwork.

A revised Boxer appeared in 1976, the 512 BB. Bore and stroke increases yielded 5 liters of displacement and the larger engine provided a useful increase in torque.

The third Boxer, the 512i, was launched at the fall 1981 Paris Salon with the arrival of fuel injection. Production ended in 1984, after 1,007 fuel-injected cars were built. Throughout its life, the Boxer was never officially imported or sold in the United States.

The SCM *analysis: Road & Track tested a federalized 512 in 1978; 0-60 took 5.5 seconds. They marveled at its ability to keep accelerating, easily running the Boxer beyond 150 mph. "The 512," they concluded, "is the best all-around Sports & GT car we have ever tested... it has it all: speed, handling, lovely shape, well-done cockpit and, most important, a reputation for reliability."*

At Monterey in August 2003, Russo & Steele declared this Boxer sold for $76,680, including buyer's premium. In today's market, this was a strong price for a carbureted 512. Less than two weeks later, this same car was declared a no sale at Kruse's Fall Auburn sale after a high bid of $71,000.

Boxer values tend to languish for a variety of reasons. First, despite the fuel injection on the last 1,007 cars, they were never certified to meet U.S. Department of Transportation or Environmental Protection Agency standards. Some cars made legal by aftermarket converters were butchered, while others were just snuck in to the U.S. and never converted. Ah, the magic of Alabama titles. Regardless, if you're a buyer, the necessary paperwork from the feds is an absolute must.

Second, Boxers are true exotics, with commensurate large repair bills if you buy a car requiring an immediate major service. An engine-out tune-up and timing belt replacement can run over $5,000. Third, to further depress values, over 7,000 flat-12-powered Testarossas, the model that followed the Boxer, were produced. TRs have many refinements and can be bought cheaper. Finally, Boxer production totaled 2,314, which is 50% more than the Daytona and almost seven times that of the 275 GTB/4. Boxers are far from rare birds.

The example here didn't arrive at the Monterey auction preview until late afternoon on the day of the sale. It was driven in by a taciturn individual who handed over a thick notebook in response to questions from onlookers, then went to register. This accomplished, he collected the notebook and left. After that, what you saw was what you bought. There was no further information on the car and the catalog description went into great detail about it being a fuel-injected car, which it was obviously not. This was too early a serial number for an injected Boxer, and besides, its four Webers (looking freshly rebuilt) were hard to mistake for a Bosch K-Jetronic injection system.

Black with black interior, the car was good looking. Cosmetics appeared fine with the exception of the leather dash pulling away from the windshield, a common problem (cost to fix: about $1,500). The paint was nice, but not buffed to show standards. Mileage was extra-low, only 4,832—seemingly too low for the visible pedal and seat wear. Wheels and tires were good, with wheel nuts replacing the standard knock-offs, as mandated by DOT. Impact beams appeared to have been added to the doors. The exhaust system looked original. The engine compartment sparkled and the car started and idled nicely

With the SCM Price Guide*'s estimated top value at $72,500, how do you justify $77k for this less-than-perfect Boxer? The seller's notebook revealed the important information: DOT releases and EPA compliance data, and a thick sheaf of bills for recent services totaling over $15,000. Everything that could be done on an engine-out major service seemed to have been done. (To verify that all the legalization has indeed been vetted, get the serial number and call 202.366.5300. Tell the anonymous DOT answering machine the number and within a few days you will hear back from a knowledgeable DOT expert as to the status. Obviously, this is the kind of thing you need to do before bidding).*

In the case of 33287, the car was imported through New York in 1985 and all the paperwork checked out. So this car appears to be a legal, maybe-low-mileage Boxer that has just had a complete service. With federalization homework done and service records examined, the $77k paid was a reasonable enough amount, especially when you consider this sale took place during the Monterey weekend, when nearly every car seems to go up about 20% in value.—John Apen

(Historical data courtesy of the author.)

From the January 2004 issue of *SCM*.◆

Years produced:	1974-84 (all types)
Number produced:	365 BB, 327; 512 BB, 927; 512 BBi, 1,007
Original price:	$42,000 plus $10,000-$15,000 for DOT/EPA compliance
SCM Price Guide:	512 BB, $55,000-$72,500; 512 BBi, $60,000-$80,000
Tune-up/major service:	$3,000; add $2,000 for timing belts
Distributor cap:	$300
Chassis #:	on frame tube in engine bay
Engine #:	top of engine block
Club:	Ferrari Club of America, Box 720597, Atlanta, GA 30358; Ferrari Owner's Club, 8642 Cleta St., Downey, CA 90241
Web site:	www.ferrariclubofamerica.org; www.FerrariOwnersClub.org
Alternatives:	1985-1991 Ferrari Testarossa, 1966-1969 Lamborghini Miura, 1971-1980 Maserati Bora
SCM Investment Grade:	B

1989 Testarossa Berlinetta

Chassis number: 80060
Engine number: F113B16305

A warning to sellers: don't expect your average Ferrari to get urbane collectors excited

Ferrari's flagship model until recently, the Testarossa revived a famous name when it arrived in 1984. Testa Rossa (two words denoting the red valve covers) had been applied to what many regard as Ferrari's greatest sports racer. The new "Testarossa" retained its Boxer predecessor's mid-mounted 5-liter flat-12 engine with power now boosted to 390 bhp at 6,300 rpm, courtesy of four-valve heads. Despite the power increase, smoothness and drivability was improved, with a maximum speed of 180 mph.

The Pininfarina-designed side strakes, which feed air to the side-mounted radiators, became one of the most instantly recognizable styling cues. Larger than the 512 BB, its increased width accommodated wider tires and radiators, while the increased wheelbase led to a larger passenger compartment. Because of extensive aluminum body panels, it was lighter than the Boxer.

Supplied new in Denmark, this left-hand drive Euro-spec TR is in excellent condition with just 13,000 accident-free miles. The one-owner car has had all scheduled services performed by Ferrari workshops in three cities. The most recent 12,400-mile service was done in October 2001, while in 1997 all engine belts were changed. The car is offered fresh from cosmetic refurbishment of paint, interior and engine. White with magnolia interior, complete service history and related bills, owner's wallet, handbook and toolkit come with the car. A Pioneer AM/FM with a six-disc CD player and a satellite tracking box is installed.

This car was the first automotive lot of the Bonhams sale held in Gstaad, Switzerland, December 18, 2001. It brought a terrifyingly low (especially if you paid $250,000 for your TR in 1989) $32,070. The auction itself was a glittering event that saw 27 cars sell, for a 79% sales rate, with several cars bringing over-the-top prices from a crowd of major collectors and many prominent European dealers. The F1 Dino steering wheel that Mike Hawthorn clenched in '58 to win the world driving title brought $52,800, double the high estimate, setting a world record for a steering wheel. It cost more than ten of the cars at the sale.

The downside with this moneyed crowd of knowledgeable collectors was that there were few who wanted an ordinary Italian car, as they generally already have a "beater Ferrari." So a warning to sellers: don't expect your average Ferrari to get urbane collectors excited. At Gstaad, this "Miami Vice" special was as out of place as a four-headlight 330 on the Breakers Hotel lawn at the Cavallino Classic.

While the Testarossa is a true supercar, it will never qualify as an "A-grade" collectible. In 1984 its Pininfarina design either elicited praise for its striking looks, or condemnation for some of its perceived excesses. Long waiting lists were common during its first four years and delivery prices were as much as $100,000 over the MSRP of $134,000. But with the crash of the early '90s, the value of TRs has brought a whole new meaning of depreciation to the Ferrari world.

Why isn't the TR collectible? Because of the sheer number made. Over 7,000 left the factory at Maranello, more than any other Ferrari model before or since.

Furthermore, there is a downside to the TR's sparkling, seamless performance. The factory-mandated services cost 50% more than those of the V8 cars. Every 30,000 miles or five years, the whole rear subframe with engine is taken out and put on its own special dolly to have a $6,000 service performed. Today, that represents 10% of the value of a $60,000 car, and more than 20% of the price of this car (to see what's involved in this service, visit http://arariti.quirt.com/service for 180 photos).

SCM Investment Grade	C
Years produced	1985-91
Number produced	7,177
Original price	$99,500
SCM Price Guide	$45,000-$55,000
Major service	$4,500, $6,000 with belts
Chassis #	On top of steering column in driver's compartment
Engine #	Rear-center of engine block, non-matching
Club	Ferrari Club of America, Box 720597, Atlanta, GA 30358; Ferrari Owner's Club, 8642 Cleta St., Downey, CA 90241
Web site	www.ferrariclubofamerica.org; www.FerrariOwnersClub.org
Alternatives	Lamborghini Countach, Corvette ZR-1, Porsche 911 Turbo

But why was the sale price of this particular car so low when it had only 13,000 miles and had recently been serviced? First, white is not the color of choice for a TR, the light paint making it look even more like a whale that's been scratching its sides on a coral reef. But far more important were the questions raised by the recent "cosmetic refurbishment of paint, interior and engine" on this nearly new car.

On-site SCM *reporter Richard Hudson-Evans stated that it indeed had been recently repainted and re-trimmed, and this is on a declared "accident-free" car. Had this car suffered an engine fire? One can only guess. TRs are notorious for their catalytic converters going up in flames when a whole bank or several cylinders stop firing due to ignition glitches, and the hot cat overheats as it attempts to digest several liters of raw fuel.*

A recent analysis of wholesale auction transactions at the biggest auction company in the US during the last two years shows 36 TRs sold with a median price of $58,500, with 11 selling below $55,000. So, by typical retail standards, this was a very good buy. However, the new owner shouldn't assume he can make a quick $20k on a flip. Chances are the same reasons that made it a $32k car for him will make it a $32k car for the next buyer. The best bet is to drive the car and hope nothing breaks.—John Apen

(Historic data and photo courtesy of auction company.)

1985 288 GTO Berlinetta

Chassis number: ZFFPA16B000055683
Engine number: 114B062

How well the 288 might have done will never be known; the series was discontinued before the car had a chance to run

Bonhams

Introduced in 1984, the 288 GTO was built for Group B racing, though most of the 272 examples made for homologation were in road-going trim. As happens occasionally, some lucky customers were able to buy a superb road car because others wanted to go to the track.

In standard form, this engine produced a massive 400 bhp with 365 ft/lbs torque at 3,800 rpm. Top speed was 190 miles per hour and 0 to 62 miles per hour could be achieved in less than five seconds. Even so, it was a perfectly tractable road car and even air conditioning was an option.

Moto-Technique was responsible for fitting air conditioning and also for repairing the bodywork when, in April 2001 this car had an argument with the side of a cliff in southern France, fortunately at low speed. The repairs were undertaken without regard to cost and the fastidious vendor describes the condition of the body, and every other element of the car, as "excellent." It is, naturally, finished in Rosso Corsa while the seats are upholstered in black leather. Current mileage stands at just 17,000 kilometers.

Ferrari is jealous of its heritage and only an outstanding car would be allowed to inherit a designation as glorious as "GTO." With only 272 examples of the 288 GTO made, it is the rarest road-going Ferrari of the past 35 years and one of the most desirable of all times.

This vehicle sold for $223,797, including buyer's premium, at the Bonhams Gstaad sale, held December 18, 2001.

The Group B class was a series dominated by well-funded factory teams and followed by a hard-core, mainly European fan base. How well the 288 might have done will never be known, as the series was discontinued before the car had a chance to run.

The 288 project started with a new frame and the car was designed from there. The twin-turbo engine was mounted longitudinally with the transmission attached to the rear. The body was formed from composite material. Virtually every part on the car is unique to the 288, including the suspension, gas tanks, mirrors and all of the trim.

The elegant styling of the 288 retains the delicate lines of the 308 GTB, yet adds a degree of no-nonsense performance. Unfortunately, the similarity leads some enthusiasts to the incorrect conclusion that a 288 is a 308 in wide-body disguise.

Driving a 288 GTO is, for an automotive enthusiast, one of life's ultimate pleasures. It has a fully finished interior with comfortable seats and good air conditioning. The steering is light, the interior noise level is acceptable and the suspension is well suited for grand touring. The engine starts easily, idles smoothly and glides effortlessly throughout the rpm range. Floor the throttle and the 288 emits a scream that goes from mild to hair-raising as the rpms increase and the turbos reach full boost. The tires rip at the pavement, barely retaining adhesion, and scenery turns to a blur. The sensation is a combination of brute force coupled with the taut control offered by the excellent Ferrari tubular chassis.

Years produced	1984-85
Number produced	272
Original list price	$80,000
SCM Price Guide	$275,000-$375,000
Tune-up/major service	$1,000/$4,000
Distributor cap	$125
Chassis #	Under engine cover on right rear corner of frame
Engine #	On top of block, toward the front
Club	Ferrari Club of America, P.O. Box 720597, Atlanta, GA 30358; Ferrari Owner's Club, 8642 Cleta St., Downey, CA 90241
Web site	www.FerrariClubofAmerica.org, www.FerrariOwnersClub.org
Alternatives	Porsche 959, Jaguar XJ220
SCM Investment Grade	B

The "argument with the side of a cliff" history of S/N 55683 significantly hurts its value. Selling the car in a public forum with the accident damage announced, while the proper thing to do, may have hurt its value. Ferrari collectors covet virgins and 55683 is now a deflowered maiden. While it may have been repaired "without regard to cost," money cannot buy originality. The owner's decision to sell the car so soon after its repair was not confidence-inspiring.

In the late '80s, the value of 288s exceeded the million-dollar mark. It quickly dropped as the market receded and has stabilized in the $200,000 to $300,000 range.

"Driving a 288 GTO is, for an automotive enthusiast, one of life's ultimate pleasures."

With this car, if the accident damage was truly repaired to as-new condition, it could bring the new owner a nice profit if hand-sold in an environment where a proper examination of the car could be performed.

The 288 GTO will never achieve the value and notoriety of the 250 GTO due to its absolute lack of competition heritage. And, as mentioned above, their visual similarity to the mass-produced 308 doesn't do their prices any favors. Nonetheless, the 288 GTO is a rare factory supercar that was in fact built to go racing.

The combination of low production numbers, competition intent and prodigious performance has kept the value of the 288 GTO steady. While it's unlikely that prices for these cars will soar, it is equally unlikely that they will ever be worth significantly less than they are today.—Steve Ahlgrim

(Historic data and photo courtesy of the auction company.)

From the July 2002 issue of *SCM*.◆

1991 Ferrari F40

Driving one is a visceral experience, hammering the senses with brutal acceleration, go-kart-quick reflexes and a howling exhaust note that pierces your very being

Chassis number: ZFFMN34A0M0085226

Introduced in Europe in 1987, Ferrari's newest supercar was a shock to the senses. An engineering tour-de-force, the F40 combined raw-edged radical styling with state-of-the-art engine, body and chassis design.

Driving one is a visceral experience, hammering the senses with brutal acceleration, go-kart-quick reflexes and a howling exhaust note that pierces your very being. The experience is addictive, a powerful narcotic for the soul of a driver.

More than anything, it's the car's purpose that underlines the experience. Few concessions are made to creature comforts—no radio, no carpets, no power windows, not even door panels. Instead, racing seats with red Nomex covers clarify the point, which is—of course—absolute uncompromising performance.

Cost-no-object engineering produced a specification that still seems state of the art today, more than 14 years later—such as the carbon fiber and Kevlar reinforced steel space-frame chassis with composite body panels. The car's Evoluzione twin turbo and intercooled, four-cam, port-injected V8 engine is controlled by a race-proven Weber-Marelli engine management system. Formula One-sized wheels and tires benefit from tremendous wind tunnel induced downforce. Few cars today can match its 200-mph top speed; 0 to 60 times were reported in the 3-second range.

The vendor of this US-delivery car is also its original owner. An aficionado of Italian cars, as well as a personal acquaintance of Enzo Ferrari, Mr. Copanos has nonetheless resisted the urge to drive it, choosing to preserve this example in pristine showroom condition—the odometer attests to the fact that it has been driven just 192 miles since new. As a '91 model, it also benefits from the many updates made by the factory since the official introduction of the F40 into the US market the previous year.

This car sold for $344,300, including commission, at the RM Monterey auction, held August 18, 2001.

Years produced	1988-92
Number produced	1,311
Original list price	$399,150
SCM Price Guide	$310,000-$375,000
Tune-up/major service	$3,500-$4,500
Distributor cap	N/A
Chassis #	On the frame in the front compartment under the washer bottle
Engine #	On the top of the engine in the front by the water pump
Club	Ferrari Club of America, PO Box 720597 Atlanta, GA 30358; Ferrari Owner's Club, 8642 Cleta St., Downey, CA 90241
Web site	www.ferrariclubofamerica.com, www.FerrariOwnersClub.org
Alternatives	Porsche 959, McLaren F1, Jaguar XJR-15

The F40 is without a doubt the most exciting street Ferrari to ever come out of Maranello. Its race car level of trim and brutal, turbocharged performance makes even the F50 seem tame. At the same time, the F40 is well mannered, air conditioned and civilized enough to drive around town. Such is its nature — fire and ice in one package.

Laguna Seca Raceway was the scene of my first encounter with an F40 driven in anger. An expertly driven one spanked all of the Ferrari street cars and passed several of the Ferrari race cars. It was elegant yet ferocious, a true descendant of Ferrari's best offerings.

The next day I saw the same F40 with a middle-aged gentleman piloting an older lady through the Fisherman's Wharf area of San Francisco. Pointing and talking, he idled the half-million-dollar tour bus through the congested streets. While the 201-mph Ferrari looked totally out of place performing this pedestrian duty, there was no overheating, fouling of spark plugs or embarrassing displays of supercar temperament. I'm sure the owner's only anxious moments were getting his mother in and out of the deep bucket seats and explaining why he had spent more money on this one car than the total cumulative value of every house she had ever lived in.

Introduced at the height of the 1980s price frenzy, the rampant speculation on the F40 epitomized the era. By the time the F40 hit the US shores the "market" price was already established. While list price was somewhere in the $250k range, European cars were selling for a cool million dollars. American dealers bumped that a bit and started cutting deals. Dealer profits were obscene, but so was the speculators' greed. A Northeastern dealer reportedly built a new showroom on the profit from their two F40s.

Within months of the first F40 deliveries, the collector car market began to collapse. Speculators walked away from their deposits as the market price slipped under their contracted prices. Dealers adjusted the contracts as the prices fell, but by the time the last new F40s were delivered, they could be bought at list price.

F40s are not rare by Ferrari standards. It was implied that the F40 would be a limited-production model, but with 1,311 cars built, F40 production exceeded every Ferrari model built before it except the Testarossas, Dinos and 308 series cars. As a comparison, there were 1,291 Daytonas, 350 275 GTB/4s and only 272 288 GTOs produced.

Despite its relatively large production, the F40 remains a highly sought-after car. There are very few on the market at any given time. Its dual-purpose race car/collector car status ensures customers for both driver-quality and collector-quality cars. The F40 is a special car that should remain valuable for the foreseeable future. The $344,300 paid for John Copanos's F40 was a shade less than it might bring today, proving that even in Monterey, and even when spending nearly 350 large, you can still get a bit of a bargain.
—Steve Ahlgrim

(Historic data courtesy of auction company.)

From the March 2002 issue of *SCM*.◆

1997 F50

Chassis number: 104799

A guy who can write a $500,000 check can probably just as easily write a $600,000 check

"Fifty years of racing, fifty years of winning, fifty years of hard work." With these words, Luca Montezemolo, head of Ferrari S.p.A., introduced the F50 at the Auto Museum in Geneva, Switzerland, in conjunction with the 63rd annual International Automobile Show, on March 6, 1995.

Using technology from Ferrari's Formula One V12, the new, normally aspirated 4.7-liter engine featured a crankcase made of nodular cast iron, Nikasil-coated liners and titanium connecting rods. Maximum power was 520 hp at 8,500 rpm. The engine itself was safe to over 10,000 rpm. The weight of the V12 was a mere 436 pounds.

Top speed was given as being 202 mph and 0-60 could be covered in 3.7 seconds. The standing mile could be accomplished in 30.3 seconds. Some commentators described the F50 as a Ferrari Formula One machine with a second seat and a sports car body.

The chassis was made entirely of aerospace carbon fiber and weighed a lithe 225 pounds. For the first time in a Ferrari road car, the engine/gearbox/differential assembly acted as a load-bearing structure within the chassis.

The body of the F50 was developed in the wind tunnel. Subframes were bolted to the chassis to support the bodywork, which was made of carbon fiber/Kevlar and Nomex honeycomb materials.

As a small publicity stunt, Ferrari announced that just 349 cars would be built—one less than the market demanded. The first ten cars went to Europe, while deliveries to the US started in July 1995. It was thought that only 50 cars would be sold to America.

The price of the F50 was $475,000 plus taxes.

This F50 has received the best of care, each service performed fully and on time. It runs flawlessly with no indication of mechanical wear. It has required some paint repairs for stone chips and other road rash. The interior, while no longer perfect, remains in excellent condition.

This car sold for $528,000, including buyer's premium, at RM's Monterey auction, held August 16 to 17, 2002.

The F50 was the evolution of the immensely popular F40. The F40 had demonstrated incredible performance, outrageous styling and everyday-driver reliability. With more than 1,300 cars built, the F40 could boast proven salability with a broad base of parts and service support. The F50 proved itself a worthy successor, albeit with a softer edge.

The Louisiana-based seller of S/N 104799 was a veteran F50 owner and a very serious collector. His prior holdings included a million-dollar F50 GT and a red 1995 F50. This car shared a garage with the Holy Grail of many enthusiasts, a Cobra Daytona coupe. The sale of S/N 104799 cleared a space for the next toy, the $6.5m Ferrari 330 TR/LM that he purchased at the RM auction on Saturday night.

RM Auctions

Rather than hoarding his precious treasures in a private museum, the seller regularly exercises his stable. He has been seen driving his cars throughout the bayou country and drove this F50 daily, racking up more than 37,000 miles.

Years produced	1995-97
Number produced	349
Original list price	$475,000
SCM Price Guide	$650,000-$750,000
Tune-up/major service	$6,000
Distributor cap	N/A
Chassis #	Chassis plate riveted to the bulkhead in the front compartment
Engine #	Front left side of block
Clubs	Ferrari Club of America, P.O. Box 720597, Atlanta, GA 30358; Ferrari Owner's Club, 8642 Cleta St., Downey, CA 90241
Web site	www.ferrariclubofamerica.org; www.ferrariownersclub.org
Alternatives	Ferrari F40, McLaren F1, Bugatti EB 110
SCM Investment Grade	A

RM and the vendor should be quite pleased with the auction result. While the car was unquestionably valuable, it could have been a most difficult sale. 40,000 miles is more than ten times the mileage on most F50s. While the mileage shouldn't affect the mechanical performance, it does muddy the perceived value of the car. At the half-a-million mark buyers can be pretty fussy. A guy who can write a $500,000 check can probably just as easily write a $600,000 check. Given the option, many of the buyers would much rather pay top dollar for a premium car than save a few bucks on a lesser example.

A fresh-out-of-the-box F50 is likely a $650,000 car. In May a much lower mileage F50 sold at a Monaco auction for $401,271, a very good buy. At $528,000, RM found the high side of an optimistic $450,000 to $550,000 presale estimate. (It appears the SCM *Price Guide of $650,000 to $750,000 probably needs to be adjusted downward.)*

While some say that the car brought an above-market price, the buyer was able to score a relatively rare car with an unusual benefit. He might have bought the only F50 on the planet that can really be driven without hurting its value. It might cost $50,000 in resale value to put 10,000 miles on a 5,000-mile F50, but there may be no difference in the value between a 40,000-mile and a 50,000-mile F50. That sweetens this deal, and for an owner/enthusiast who plans on really using his car, makes the price paid seem more reasonable.—Steve Ahlgrim ◆

(Historical and descriptive information provided by RM Auctions.)

From the December 2002 issue of *SCM*.

A $2,000 Hose Job

For $250, you can probably buy the parts and magic "overhaul in a can" potions that will keep your Impala on the road nearly forever... repairs to the Ferrari can cost enough to cause a quick trip to the home equity loan broker

Just as we get used to the toll taken by the passage of years, from carrying reading glasses to keeping a bottle of Advil by the bedside, owners of older Ferraris have grown accustomed to the idiosyncrasies and weaknesses of their cars. To these long-term owners, the Ferrari they have owned for many years is a great car, starts right up, and doesn't leak much oil.

Chances are, however, that they have put fewer and fewer miles on their car as time has passed. Often when someone decides to part with a prized Ferrari, it may not have been started or driven for months or years. And just as likely, chances are the new owner, excited by his new toy, wants to start driving it as often as he can.

And that's where the problems can start.

Ferraris, like all cars, age. Anyone buying a 1972 Chevy Impala expects a worn suspension, soft shocks, minor engine leaks, a clunking differential, and air conditioning long overdue for a recharge. But for the $2,500 the car will cost, you've got pretty decent basic transportation that may go another 50,000 miles before it needs serious attention.

Someone buying a 1972 Dino will be spending well over $65,000, yet their "new/used" car will have the same inherent age-related problems as our hypothetical Chevy Impala does. But there's a major difference. For $250, you can probably buy the parts and magic "overhaul in a can" potions that will keep your Impala on the road nearly forever. The repairs to the Ferrari can cost enough to cause a quick trip to the home equity loan broker.

Virtually every unrestored Ferrari over 20 years old needs a variety of simple maintenance activities performed, in addition to the typical tune-up, brake pad replacement and so on. Shock absorber seals, suspension bushings, brake hoses and water hoses are made of rubber or rubber-related components, and rubber deteriorates with age. Water pumps tend to start leaking as well, and engines often need to be pulled and resealed to stop the inevitable oil leaks.

For instance, I recently sold a verified one-owner, red with tan, US model 246 GTS with only 38,750 original miles. This Dino had seen very little use during the past decade, had great panel fits and paint, and ran well. Upon detailed inspection, the list of needed repairs was long and included radiator and heater hoses that were as hard as hockey pucks. It would cost $2,000 to replace them as the hoses run through the center of the car. Also needing work were flaccid front shocks ($1,000); a radiator long overdue for a recore ($800); radiator fans that desperately needed to be rebuilt ($600); a cracked headlight switch ($1,000 if you can find one, or have one built out of used parts); an abused first gear synchro ($4,500); an inoperable horn ($300); dragging front brakes ($1,000); a master cylinder that had lost one of its two circuits ($2,000); multiple engine leaks ($7,500); rusted-through header heat shields (included in the engine-out reseal); inoperative air conditioning ($1,000); warped door panels ($1,500) and a minor rip in the driver seat ($2,500—you have to do both seats so all the panels match). The initial estimate to do all the above was well over $20,000.

And this was a very nice car.

Then there was the "while you're at it" (and it's already apart) wish list, which included replacing the clutch, powder-coating the suspension, re-plating the calipers, a major service and a rebuild of the heating and cooling system. This easily adds another $10,000 to the repair estimate, and suddenly our straight, non-rusted, no-bad-stories, one-owner Dino seems like a potential parts car.

Bonhams & Brooks

How about $2,000 for new heater hoses?

After the usual negotiations a compromise was reached, an equitable split for repairs was made; a purchase agreement was signed and payment was made. The seller felt like he got a fair price given the things the car needed, and the buyer felt like the reduction he received allowed him to have some money to apply towards the repairs immediately necessary to get the car back on the road, and for it to perform reliably.

All of the above simply reinforces why I am a relentless advocate of thorough pre-purchase inspections as a part of any used Ferrari acquisition.

None of the age-related problems above should be deal-killers. However, pre-purchase inspections may turn up major crash damage that has been repaired poorly, bent frames that have been repaired badly, or a sick engine that needs a mandatory rebuild. And unless you're buying something for parts, no old serial-production Ferrari with those kinds of issues is worth having.

After an inspection, I usually recommend to the seller and the buyer that they reach a percentage split agreement on the estimated cost of repairs. Split agreements work well because the buyers aren't nearly as eager to have every aging part on the car replaced if they are paying part of the bill.

However, pre-purchase inspections may turn up real deal-killers, including major crash damage that has been repaired poorly, bent frames that have been repaired badly, or a sick engine that needs a mandatory rebuild.

I have found that the two key elements to a successful purchase are first, a pre-purchase inspection that tells you exactly what you are dealing with, and second, the understanding on the buyer's part that these are just used cars, and like all used cars, will have things that will need to be dealt with when they arrive in your garage. Expect your used Dino to act like a Lexus and you'll be disappointed. Expect it to need an infusion of love, affection and a few dollars to start behaving itself, and you'll be rewarded with a terrific ride.—*Michael Sheehan*

From the January 2003 issue of *SCM*.◆

The ABCs of 348s, 355s and 360s

Try driving your 355 with a lean cylinder and your $5,000 exhaust manifold replacement will shortly become a $25k engine rebuild

Made famous by its regular appearances in the television show "Magnum, P.I.," the 308/328 is probably the most recognizable Ferrari of all time. But despite its pleasing Pininfarina lines, by 1989 it was time for something new.

Its successor, the Ferrari 348, was introduced that year and offered major improvements in creature comforts and performance. It was the first Ferrari built without a conventional tube chassis, and the first mass-produced Ferrari to feature an in-line engine and transmission arrangement. It brought Ferrari into the age of modern electronics, had more-than-adequate air conditioning and provided world-class performance.

But not all were satisfied with the 348. Its styling was considered bland at best, with some comparing its wedge-shaped design to that of a Toyota MR2 fitted with big tires and a horse on the nose. Also, the 348 had more than its share of growing pains, including a weak gearbox in the early cars that had a tendency to self-destruct. Three major gearbox updates were offered in an effort to resolve the various problems. In addition, the 348 flywheel is made of 30 different parts, including springs and washers, with the assembly packed in grease, in an attempt to dampen the harmonic vibrations of the engine. As you can imagine, it's a nightmare (or perhaps a flat-rate mechanic's dream) to disassemble as part of a resurfacing during a clutch replacement. With a new flywheel priced at $3,200, the double-disc clutch priced at $1,800, a throwout bearing priced at $600 and $450 for labor, a clutch replacement on a 348 can quickly become a very expensive venture.

Additionally, the electronics on the early systems were a hornet's nest of defective ECUs, failure-prone $1,400 alternators and recalcitrant starters. Due to their overtaxed alternators, 348s should only be started with fully charged batteries. The puny alternator will often fry itself as it attempts to charge a low battery. For those who don't want to pay Ferrari $1,400 for a new alternator, a rebuild is a more modest $250. Furthermore, the early Bosch Motronic 2.5 engine management system was troublesome, whereas the later Motronic 2.7 version offered better performance and improved engine management.

While the basic engine is relatively bulletproof, the 348 is the only Ferrari to feature a single serpentine timing belt for all four camshafts, causing rapid wear that can result in belt failure and very expensive valve-train damage. The long single-cam timing belt makes degreeing the cams, part of the major engine service, a nightmarishly onerous event, as any adjustment affects everything else connected to it. Adding to the complications, a 30,000-mile major service requires the engine to be removed from the car, not an inexpensive operation. Figure $5,000 for the "engine out" major service.

The 348 improved as it evolved. The 348 Spyder, introduced in 1994, featured more leg room, the improved 2.7 Motronic engine system, thicker castings on the rear wheels giving a full additional inch of offset per side and improved high-speed stability. Listed at 300 horsepower from the factory, an aftermarket computer chip update and a Tubi exhaust will easily give 340 horsepower, offering substantial performance for, at least in the Ferrari world, not a lot of bucks.

Over 6'2"? You may find yourself impaled on the steering wheel.

When 348 shopping, run fast and far from any car that hints at deferred maintenance. The 348 is one of the few cars that you want to come with a stack of receipts for updates in the glovebox. As 348s improved each year, newer is better with the 1994 being the top of the line. Best bet on a 348 is the 1994 Spyder with an updated gearbox. For a decent car showing less than 15,000 miles, pay $75,000.

The 355 series, introduced in 1995 and built through 1999, offered the Ferrari buyer a vast improvement over the troublesome 348. The 355s have only two major problem areas: faulty exhaust manifolds and valve guides that tend to wear rapidly. For those not used to the world of Ferrari prices, an exhaust manifold for a 355 is $4,000, not including labor. Can't afford a $5,000 bill to repair the exhaust manifold, you say? Try driving your 355 with a lean cylinder and your $5,000 exhaust manifold replacement will shortly become a $25k engine rebuild, due to the too-lean fuel mixture frying the piston and cylinder liner. Like the 348, any major engine work on the 355 requires a $5,000 engine-out service.

The 355 Spyder top can also be problematic since the windows must automatically drop, the seats must move forward, the car must be in neutral and the emergency brake must be on for the power top to work properly. Make the mistake of being over 6'2" and you may find yourself impaled on the steering wheel of your 355 as the seat goes through its automatic forward motion required to drop the top.

Current asking prices for 1995-99 355 Spyders are in the $120,000 to $140,000 range. Bargain hard, as you may be the only buyer out there. After all, once you get past $150,000 you're well into 360 Modena coupe land, and a far superior car even if the top doesn't go down.

Very few service problems have been reported for 360s other than the usual oil leaks that seem to accompany any car from Modena. Breaking with tradition, the 360 can be serviced with the engine in the car, access provided by a removable panel behind the rear seats.

360s, especially Spyders, are still on the price bubble, and may stay there until the next V8 model comes out. Coupes are selling in the $150,000 to $185,000 range, and Spyders are still an astronomical $250,000 for US models. Gray-market cars are a little cheaper, at $135,000 for coupes and $200,000 for Spyders, but you lose your warranty, and remember that the very things that made the car less expensive when you bought it will make it worth less when you go to sell.—*Michael Sheehan*

From the November 2002 issue of *SCM*.◆

The Modenas Are Falling!

After all, it's still $80k over window sticker for what is just a used car

Paraphrasing Oscar Hammerstein II from "Showboat," "Fish gotta swim, birds gotta fly, and I'm gonna watch new Ferraris depreciate till I die." One of the extraordinary things about the "instant collectible" market is its predictability. Over the past few decades, we have watched Plymouth Prowlers, Ferrari Testarossas, Dodge Vipers and 328s run up the slope of inflated values, then free-fall off the cliff towards "just a car" pricing.

This month, we'll take a brief look at the market conditions for "gold chain cars," specifically 360 Modena Spyders. Next month, we'll visit the world of blue-chip collectible Ferraris, where important cars continue to bring strong prices.

Comparing a 250 SWB or even a Daytona to a 360 Spyder is uninformative at best and ludicrous at worst. All serial-production Ferraris built after 1990 are still depreciating except for the limited-production F40 and F50, which have gone up in value. Consider that 16 years after 308 QV production stopped, they are now fully depreciated. Ferrari 328s have a little farther to fall, and 360 Spyders are going to be worth less every year until 2017 (roughly). By then, they will be as ancient as a current 308 and their performance will pale when compared to the latest, greatest iteration from Ferrari 16 years from now.

The current slowdown of the economy has caused the pages of *Ferrari Market Letter* to be inundated with ads for late-model Ferraris. This is an easily predicted market correction. When first introduced in April, MSRP for a new 360 Spyder was $180k. The first few out the door sold on the secondary market for $375k, a premium of almost $200k. Within a month, the richest and least patient kids on the block had one parked in their (probably marble-surfaced) driveway, so supply increased and prices went down to $350k.

Christie's

Steadily dropping in price.

Now that several hundred have been delivered to the US, these cars have steadily dropped in price at a rate of about $20k a month, and are now down to about $260k. While this may be a substantial decline, it was to be expected as more cars came on the market. And, after all, it's still $80k over window sticker for what is just a used car. I wouldn't be surprised to see them trading at MSRP within three months.

"If you're trying to sell a contract on a yet-to-be-delivered 360 for $100k over sticker, or expect to get your money back on a car you paid $300k for, I suggest you get in line behind the whiners who bought 3Com stock last year and are demanding that their brokers get them their purchase price back."

If you're trying to sell a contract on a yet-to-be-delivered 360 for $100k over sticker, or expect to get your money back on a car you paid $300k for, I suggest you get in line behind the whiners who bought 3Com stock last year and are demanding that their brokers get them their purchase price back.

From my perspective as a trader, I expect a continued, precipitous decline in the over-inflated prices of late-model Ferraris. After all, remember when 1989 328s were $125,000 cars and Testarossas from the same year were bringing $250,000 and more?

There's no lack of demand for unusual, rare older cars. As long as interest rates remain low, now is a good time to buy. —*Michael Sheehan*

From the December 2001 issue of *SCM*.◆

328 GTS or Testarossa?

The 1986–89 Testarossa offers the best ride for the buck in the Ferrari world today

The bargain-hunters in the Ferrari world seem to be obsessed with the price similarities of the 1986-89 328 GTS and the 1986-89 Testarossa. Endless comparisons ensue: V8 versus V12; classic versus trendy styling; Targa versus coupe. Which is the better car and which is the better investment?

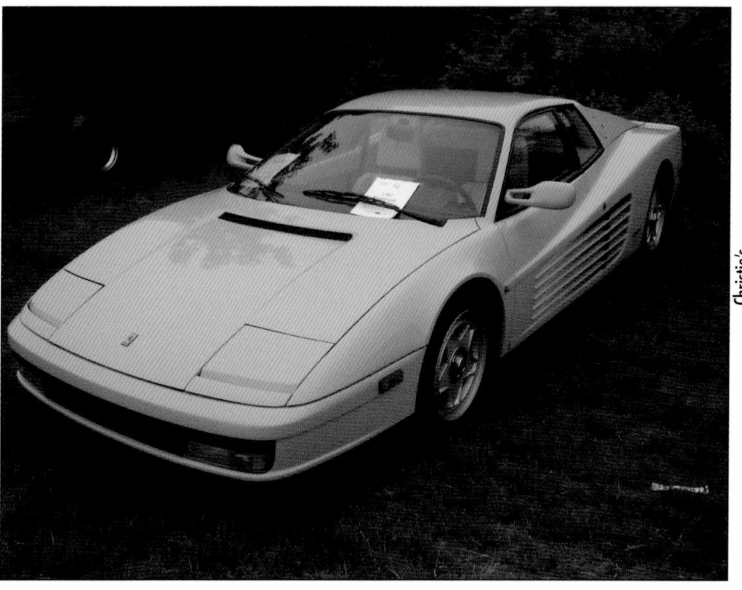

Christie's

The 328 GTS is popular today. A 1986 328 GTS with 30,000 miles, a recent service and all records can be found for $40,000 to $45,000 while a 1989 328 GTS with recent service and 10,000 miles or less will bring $60,000 to $65,000 because this was the last production year and the only year with ABS brakes. Instantly recognizable as a Ferrari (of supreme importance to most first-time buyers), 328s are relatively light and nimble, and have classic Pininfarina lines (as opposed to the Toyota MR2 with horsie badges called the 348). As the last of the V8s that don't require the engine to come out for service, a 30,000-mile service is usually under $3,000, whereas the same service in the later 348/355/360 cars can top $6,000.

A 328 will give years of low-cost entertaining driving potential and, possibly best of all, it can be done with the Targa roof stowed. On the negative side, the 328 is the last evolution of the 308 series, which was Ferrari's "entry-level" car for the first-time buyer. What you end up with in terms of performance and comfort is a 25-year-old design with, by modern standards, only adequate acceleration, braking and A/C and heater capabilities.

The 1986–89 Testarossa, in this humble scribe's opinion, offers the best ride for the buck in the Ferrari world today. Yes, it's a big car with heavy controls under 15 mph, but who drives a Ferrari under 15 mph besides the valet at Spago (at least when he knows you are watching)? They have acres of torque, effortless performance and a triple-digit cruising-speed capability that will put you in jail in all fifty states.

Like the 328, they are instantly recognizable as Ferraris and are very user-friendly, with excellent creature comforts. A 1986 TR with 30,000 miles and all services done can be bought in the low $50,000 range (avoid those that have not had the oil and water pump drive updates). A late 1988 or 1989 with about 10,000 miles will bring $75,000 to $85,000. If you're over 6' 3" the Testarossa will fit you like a glove. Conversely, 5' 10" is really the effective comfort limit for a 328 owner. On the negative side, maintenance on the TR is higher than on the 328, with a major service running from $5,000 to $6,000.

What can the prospective buyer expect five years out, from equivalent cars (a 10,000-mile 1989 328 GTS and a 1989 Testarossa, both in resale red with tan, no bad stories, purchased today and driven 3,000 miles a year)? The 328 GTS will be about $10,000 to $15,000 cheaper today, but will be worth the same or more as a TR in five years. Maintenance on the Testarossa will always be more expensive, and as the value of the cars declines, the cost of service (which will only go up) proportionately becomes a larger part of the car's worth.

"Yes, it's a big car with heavy controls under 15 mph, but who drives a Ferrari under 15 mph besides the valet at Spago—at least when he knows you're watching?"

Emotionally, the body shape of the Testarossa already seems dated, unlike the more classic, svelte, even sexy shape of the 328 GTS. Finally, the lack of a Targa on the TR is a real value-downer. The 328 GTS and the Testarossa had production runs in the thousands and most aren't candidates to be long-term investments like the esoteric SWBs or TdFs. On the other hand, in five years you will be able to find decent 328s and TRs in the low $30s, while SWBs may be cracking the $2m mark.

Both 328s and TRs provide ultra-exotic performance at a Camry price, but for overall driving and esthetic pleasure, coupled with market value, my vote goes to the 328.—*Michael Sheehan*

From the June 2001 issue of *SCM*.◆

Not Sale-Proof Anymore

While a lot of the Ferrari market has been in the toilet for the past decade, the prices of truly exceptional cars have continued a relentless climb

Son-of-a-gun, once again the Ferrari market is hot. Recent dealer sales and auctions have shown very high prices for cars that were difficult to sell as recently as a few months ago.

Barrett-Jackson

Generally, high-volume models such as the Boxers and TRs are more or less fully depreciated and slow to sell, but even in this somnambulant corner of the market, the sun has started to shine. 1979 512 BB S/N 30235 was offered by a well-known Canadian broker on eBay in May of this year and bid to only $42,000 with a buy-it-now price of $65,000. The same 512 BB was put back on eBay in June and was bid to and sold for $66,100. I think Boxers are an enormous amount of car for the money, and while $66,100 is really still too cheap, it's a lot better than $42,000.

Vintage event–friendly cars, usable for European vintage racing and rallies—such as alloy-bodied Boanos, Lussos and early 275 GTBs—continue to enjoy a strong market and rising prices because of the European interest and the weak dollar. Steel-bodied Boano S/N 0641 GT, restored to a very high standard and finished in black with a bronze top, has just sold in the $225,000 range. A year ago, I would have expected this car to sell in the $145,000 range. Alloy-bodied Boano S/N 0613 came out of Japan early this year, was freshened up, went through several dealers' hands and sold to an end-user for just under $300,000, a recent high for a no-race-history alloy Boano. Last year at this time, it would have struggled to bring $200,000. Yes, folks, these are real and significant gains in value.

Poor old Daytonas are finally getting a little pop of their own. In June of 2000, 365 GTB/4 Daytona S/N 14819 was advertised on eBay at a buy-it-now price of under $95,000. After not selling, it went to a dealer in Orange County for well under $95,000. There, it was refurbished to attractive if not concours-winning standards, and in June of this year sold at the Barrett-Jackson Petersen Museum auction in L.A. for an impressive $145,800.

In conversations with dealers around the country, their informal consensus is that there is room in the US market for about six Daytonas a month to be sold at retail, for strong money. When you get more than six cars offered, a mini-negative price war sets in, and the results can be discouraging for a seller. It does appear the flow of panic-sellers of Daytonas has slowed down, and perhaps with the stock market ticking back up, collectors aren't quite so worried about turning their four-wheeled toys into money.

At the same Barrett-Jackson auction at the Petersen, 400 Superamerica S/N 3949 SA sold for a staggering $432,000. Even though it was a one-family-owned car with covered headlights, finished nicely in red with black with red piping, the price paid is a new public-sale record, in this decade, for a 400 LWB Superamerica.

The previous three 400 Superamericas in the *SCM* Gold database were all sold by RM, 3931 SA making $363,000 in August, 2002 at Monterey, and 4271 SA bringing $357,500 at the Waldorf-Astoria, NYC, in September of 2002, and being sold again for $341,000 in March at the Amelia Island, Florida, auction.

Higher up the food chain, 250 LM S/N 6105, a good older restoration with decent but not particularly significant club racing history, came out of Texas in March and was sold to a well-known European dealer in the low $2,000,000 range. It crossed the Atlantic, duty was paid, and, in June, was sold to a new owner in France for well over $2,500,000. By comparison, only last year 250 LM S/N 5845 sold to a well-known European dealer for substantially back of $2,000,000. He restored it, and it is on the market in Europe for well over $3,000,000.

At the upper end of the Ferrari market stratosphere, in late June Swiss collector René Maspoli sold his 500 Mondial Berlinetta Pinin Farina S/N 0452 MD and his 250 MM Pinin Farina-bodied Berlinetta S/N 0344 MM together to an Italian collector who paid 4,000,000 Swiss Francs, or US $3,050,000, for the pair, much more than I would have thought they would bring. If I had to value each car, in terms of this sale, I would put a number of $1,525,000 on each.

This 500 Mondial is an old friend. As an historical aside, in 1987, on October 13, I bought this same car from a collector in Florida for $300,000, and sold the car on November 18, 1987, to a Japanese collector for $475,000. Proving that not all Japanese collectors lost out, the Japanese owner sold the car back to me on July 5, 1988, for $570,000, and I sold it to a well-known Swiss dealer/broker for $589,000, who then sold it to Maspoli. The exact number he paid isn't known, but I would hazard that it was in the $650,000 range.

Admittedly, $650,000 to $1,250,000 over a 15-year period isn't exactly a skyrocketing rate of return (about 4.6%, compounded annually), but it beats a lot of other financial instruments in today's market.

On the new-car side, 360 Spyders have stabilized, selling for about $50,000 over their window sticker price of $200,000. My dealer friends tell me that while they estimate the market could absorb six Daytonas a month, nationwide, the 360 Spyder is so sought after that every Ferrari dealer in the country could probably sell six of them each, a month, without impacting the market.

I would suggest that if you have a Ferrari to sell, now is the time. And if you're buying now, yes, you'll pay a little more than if you wait until the freezing February winds are blowing across Lake Michigan. But ask yourself, isn't it really worth something, maybe a lot, to have a car and drive it, top-down, when the weather is good? Somehow looking at it in the garage, under a car cover, just isn't the same. *—Michael Sheehan*

From the September 2003 issue of *SCM*.◆

Ferrari Arbitrage

A tradition of driving like a bat out of hell means European cars get more heavy use in six months than most American Ferraris will get in a lifetime

In today's age of instant information, and the growing globalization of the economy, one could surmise that prices of Ferraris would be standardized worldwide. For example, when RM, Christie's or Bonhams has a sale, SCM GOLD-level members receive an e-mail within 72 hours of the sale, notifying them of the prices paid. In the face of this kind of value information, it's hard to imagine that someone could sell equivalent cars for much more, or that they would be willing to take substantially less than the auctions are getting.

However, because of fluctuations in currency rates, differences in importation and tax laws and the ups and downs of economies around the world, Ferrari prices do vary. This variance provides a buying opportunity for enthusiasts and a livelihood for those brokers who trade globally.

For instance, the low-mile, no-stories F40 that is worth as much as $350,000 in the US would only bring $250,000, at most, in Germany or Japan. And if your precious winged wonder has traveled, say, 15,000 kms and has a few rock chips on the nose (the horror), the perfection-loving Americans will discount the car to less than $300,000, buyers in Germany are likely to pay only $220,000 for it, and it has suddenly become sale-proof in Japan.

While the market for new Ferraris such as the 360, 550 and 575 in Japan is reasonably strong, with these cars selling at list price, the market for used Ferraris from the 512 BB up to the 355 is very weak. Meanwhile, the market in Japan for collector cars before the Boxer essentially no longer exists.

We note in passing that Japan is the ultimate example of how the car market changes over time. In the 1980s it was believed that the thousands of Ferraris, Maseratis and other exotics that went to Japan would never return. In addition to cars, the Japanese began real estate "binge buying," snapping up prestigious tracts like Pebble Beach and Rockefeller Center.

Then the unthinkable happened. Japan started sliding into a recession in 1990, and each year it seems to get deeper and darker. Large car collections were broken up and sent back overseas at a deep discount. Pebble Beach and the Rock were sold to American investors, at a substantial loss. Commercial real estate in Tokyo is, in some instances, valued at 90% less than it was a decade ago. A strong yen, aggressive lending by banks and buoyant consumer confidence are just a memory, and Japan's pre-eminence in the collector car world has vaporized.

Late-model used Ferraris are much cheaper in Europe than the US. This weakness makes for some very attractive buys. Be aware, however, with any European Ferrari, that they are far more likely to have been run hard and put away wet than their American counterparts. The lax enforcement of speed limits on the Autostrada, coupled with a tradition of driving like a bat out of hell—even when cruising to the local trattoria—means these cars can get more heavy use in six months than most American Ferraris will get in a lifetime.

As the European auctions show, late 1980s TRs in Europe are absurdly cheap, with low-mileage clean cars selling in the $40,000 range—sometimes less than a 328 GTS. Unfortunately, once a European enthusiast factors in gasoline at $4 a gallon, insurance and exorbitant vehicle registration and use fees, these cars are no longer a bargain for a local user. And their prices aren't far enough below those in the US to make them worth importing.

Just a $25k spread between Euro and US four-cams

As far as classics, you should be able to find a very nice carbureted Boxer in, perhaps, Germany, at around $50,000. Less than $100,000 is the right number for a Daytona with no apparent needs.

The US remains the strongest market for new cars, and also a major profit center for most of the European manufacturers. While Mercedes, BMW, Ferrari, et al. now build "world cars," the world cars sold in the US are much more expensive than virtually identical cars sold in Europe. This in part is what creates the thriving market for one- to five-year-old gray-market 550s and 360s here.

The US market for 15- to 20-year-old enthusiast Ferraris, from the 512 BBs up to the 355, is robust. A first-line Boxer can bring up to $75,000 if hand sold to the proper enthusiast, while even 355 F1 Spyders—now suffering in the shadows as the 360 takes over as the flavor of the month—are still strong at $125,000 for brilliant examples. Modena 360 Spyders are holding strong with prices above $260,000 not uncommon (against an MSRP of $180,000).

While the US market for 275 GTB/4s and similar-era cars is closer to the rest of the world, car for car, you can still get more money by selling here. A good four-cam is worth $300,000 stateside, about $25,000 more than Europe. Similarly, a Daytona that struggles to get $100k in Japan will easily sell for $115,000 or more over here.

If you're thinking about exploiting these value differences, be sure to factor in the costs of acquiring a car overseas and shipping it back. Also, for those cars less than 25 years old (and therefore subject to EPA and DOT regulations), realize that specialist companies will charge $25,000 and more to find, federalize and deliver a late-model European or Japanese Ferrari to your US door.

Also, with a gray market car, you generally don't have the same warranty assurances and dealer support you get by buying US-spec cars. It's often said that there is no such thing as a free lunch—if you choose to save a bundle by buying a late-model Ferrari overseas, be aware that if you have any serious problems, you may find yourself adrift at sea in a very leaky boat.
—Michael Sheehan

From the July 2002 issue of *SCM*.◆

The 512 BB LM

Put an updated 512 BB LM into a time machine and return it to the 1979 Le Mans race—it would be a much better car

Ferrari's philosophy has always been to incorporate, when possible, their racing technology into their road cars. In the early 1970s, the flat-12 "Boxer" technology used in the early 1970s Ferrari Formula One and Ferrari 312 PB sports racers found its way into Ferrari's flagship 12-cylinder sports cars, the 365 GT4 BB (Berlinetta Boxer) and the 512 BB/BBi that followed.

There was no factory effort to campaign the 365 GT4 BB, for it was simply too big and heavy, and the engine sat too high over the transaxle for competitive racing. The rival Porsche RSR Carrera of 1974-75 was already a highly developed race car that excelled in endurance racing.

With the introduction of the 5-liter 512 BB engine, and with substantial encouragement from wealthy privateers who wanted to race a Ferrari GT car (and who were willing to pay $80,000 plus spares to own a Ferrari-built race car), Ferrari produced a series of 25 silhouette race cars based on the 512 BB. Called the BB LMs, the first three were introduced at the 1979 Daytona 24-hour race.

These cars benefited from all new Pininfarina-designed and wind-tunnel tested bodywork. They were 16 inches longer than the production 512 BBs, with smooth bodylines and fender fairings. The roofline extended to the tail, thanks to a plexiglass rear window, and a rear wing added down-force. Ten-inch wide front wheels and 13-inch wide rears put the rubber to the ground.

But all of these modifications were too little—and too late. While the 1979 Ferrari 512 BB LM's Lucas-injected flat-12 produced a claimed 480 horsepower, the engineers at Porsche had evolved the Porsche 935 IMSA into a 700-plus horsepower twin-turbo rocket. With brakes from the 917, the 935 IMSA was able to out-brake the 512 BB LM into the corners, go through the corners faster (thanks to wider tires and lighter weight), and then leave the Ferrari a speck in the mirror on the straights. Non-competitive in 1979, the 512 BB LM was even less competitive by the end of its racing career in 1983.

In the mid-late 1980s, 512 BB LMs became a popular choice for the Ferrari club member who wanted a factory-built race car and could afford the $75,000 price tag. The Ferrari market madness of the late 1980s soon escalated 512 BB LM prices, with 512 BB LM S/N 35527 selling for $1,300,000 at the Coys Nürburgring auction in August 1989 and S/N 29505 selling for $1,000,000 at the Orion Solo Ferrari auction in Monaco in November 1989.

In 1996, Jean Sage and Jacques Swatters started the Shell Historic Ferrari Challenge in Europe, creating an event where one could see and be seen driving a historic racing Ferrari, with eligibility restricted to Ferraris up to the 365 GTB/4C Competition Daytonas of 1974. Thanks to a worldwide economic boom and stock markets rising almost everywhere, the Historic Ferrari Challenge quickly became very popular, with hundreds of entrants eager to participate in a Ferrari factory-sanctioned series. As a result, prices of eligible competition Ferraris started climbing.

In 1998 Ferrari of North America hired David Seibert, organizer of the American 348 and 355 Challenge, to add a US Historic Ferrari Challenge to the 348-355 Challenge race weekend. The US organizers included models up to the 512 BB LM to offer more owners a chance to exercise their cars. Ferrari owners, always looking for the unfair advantage that would allow them to trounce their wealthy buddies on the track, discovered immediately that the 512 BB LM was the car to have if you wanted to win in the US Ferrari Historic series. But as you can imagine, no BB LM owner would think of racing his car today without spending mountains of money to make it faster and more reliable than it ever was when new.

Still a speck in a 935's mirror.

The BB LM engine was rated at 480 horsepower in 1979 but recent dyno tests have shown 460 horsepower to be a more realistic number. Today's engine builders add titanium connecting rods, titanium valves, valve springs from an IRL car and many hours of cylinder head porting work. This, combined with a modern, equal-length, pulse extractor exhaust system and a triple-disc Quarter Master clutch, can result in 520 honest horsepower from the same engine tested on the same dyno.

When originally raced, brakes were one of the weak spots. Consequently, the original cast (as in heavy) 15-inch wheels and Girling brake calipers have been replaced with much lighter 16-inch modular wheels, modern, lighter brake rotors and bigger and better four-puck Brembo calipers. The transaxles, another problem area on the 512 BB LMs, are now updated with new main shafts and transfer shafts made from space-age materials, closer ratio gears and modern racing syncro rings.

While a well-driven 512 S, 512 M or 612 Can-Am Ferrari should easily dominate the US Historic Ferrari Challenge, none have been entered on a regular basis. Today's 512 BB LMs are very fast, easy to drive, dependable race cars. After all these years, they are winners at last—at least in the US Ferrari Historic Challenge.

If it were possible to put a modern, evolved 512 BB LM into a time machine and return it to the 1979 Le Mans race, it would be a much better car now—in every way—than when it was new.

Sadly, on the Mulsanne straight, it would still be just a speck in the rearview mirrors of the 700-horsepower Porsche 935s. Which is partly why the Ferrari-only Historic Challenge was created in the first place. If the big guy from Stuttgart wearing the silver jumpsuit keeps beating you up, just don't let him play in your sandbox anymore.—*Michael Sheehan*

From the March 2003 issue of *SCM*.◆

Michelotto, Ferrari's Tuner

The result was great success, with Ferrari winning at the 24 Hours of Daytona, the 12 Hours of Sebring and at almost every other racetrack in the IMSA, World SportsCar and European ISRS series

Just as AMG is the factory "tuner" for Mercedes, the Kremer Bros. have long been the factory race arm for Porsche, and Jack Roush Racing is the official racing arm for Ford's NASCAR series, Michelotto is the race shop for the Ferrari factory GT and sports prototype racing efforts.

Michelotto began as an authorized Ferrari dealer in Padova, a small town only 50 miles up the road from Venice. In the late 1970s Michelotto started building and race-preparing lightweight 308s for Ferrari France and multiple Italian privateers. While fewer than 20 of these lightweight 308 rally cars were built, they were very successful and hugely popular with rally fans who were thrilled to see Ferraris in competition.

In the early '80s, Michelotto was asked by Ferrari to do the development work for the 288 GTO, and ultimately to build a series of ultra-sophisticated 288 GTO race cars called the 288 GTO Evoluziones. Only six Evoluziones were constructed, and they ended up in the hands of some of the world's most famous collectors, including the Sultan of Brunei.

In the late '80s Ferrari retained Michelotto to develop the replacement for the 288 GTO, the F40. Ten working prototypes were built and used for many thousands of miles of road testing, performance and suspension evaluations. After the introduction of the F40, Ferrari re-entered GT racing and had Michelotto build a series of 19 ultra-high-performance F40 LMs for America's IMSA and Europe's GTC series. Michelotto also built an additional seven F40 GTs for the Italian Supercar Championship and another seven F40 LM GTEs for the BPR GT series.

In 1993 Ferrari made the decision to re-enter sports prototype racing with the 333 SP, the first Ferrari sports racer in almost 20 years. After the first cars were built, the construction and race support were entrusted to Michelotto. The result was great success, with Ferrari winning at the 24 Hours of Daytona, the 12 Hours of Sebring and at almost every other racetrack in the IMSA, World SportsCar and European ISRS series. The 333 SP was not only a successful race winner but also very user friendly, with over 40 cars built, some as recently as 2001, for race teams and for private collectors.

Michelotto's most recent racer is the 360 GT, built for the ALMS, the FIA GT series events and the traditional endurance events such as Daytona, Sebring and Le Mans. In 2001, its first year of racing, the 360 GT won the FIA GT class championship.

While the prices of used race cars usually plummet, Michelotto-built cars—due to the number of venues in which they continue to be competitive—are still highly valued. For instance, while a stock 308 is a "how many do you want for $25,000" car, a Michelotto 308 will cost between $150,000 to $200,000, and that's twice what it was worth four years ago.

F40 LM sold for $398,163 at Poulain Le Fur's 2000 Monaco auction

Michelotto 308, worth as much as eight stock 308s.

In America, a stock, no-bad-stories F40 will set you back around $300,000, while you'll need at least $400,000 to slide behind the wheel of a Michelotto F40 LM, GT or GTE. 333 SPs are still strong at $650,000 to $750,000, and don't seem to be depreciating like a normal used race car should. In fact, the winner of the 1998 Daytona 24 Hours and the 12 Hours of Sebring, S/N 19, sold for $1,000,000 two years ago and would still be worth the same today.

"It can be safely said that if you are a collector of any modern Ferrari GT or sports prototype race car, you are a Michelotto collector."

It can be safely said that if you are a collector of any modern Ferrari GT or sports prototype race car, you are a Michelotto collector.

If you are in the market for a Michelotto-built or modified car, be sure to check with Michelotto to verify any claimed provenance. All of the serial numbers of the Michelotto cars are available, and well documented. Contact: Sig. Luigo Dindo, Michelotto G & C S.n.c., Via Chiesanuova, 27, 35136 Padova, Italy.—Michael Sheehan

From the August 2002 issue of *SCM*.◆

If It Sounds Too Good to Be True...

When I mentioned that I believed this to be a stolen car, the price was dropped to $300,000

Where's Carfax when you need it?

European model F50 S/N 103794 was the 37th F50 built, in silver metallic with a black interior and yellow seats. It was delivered new on November 28, 1995, in Austria to Jean-Robert Grellet. It was resold by Grellet on December 19, 1998, for 608,500 Swiss Francs to dealer François Degand. Degand then sold the car to England.

On June 8, 2001, this F50, now repainted in red, was shown at the Bond Street Association-sponsored FOC UK meeting by its third owner, John Hunt, a British property manager. In October, 2001, Hunt drove the car to Italy for a vacation. According to police reports, the F50 was stolen from a supposedly highly secured hotel parking lot in Lake Como during the early morning hours of Sunday, October 21. At the time, its odometer showed 20,000 miles.

Less than 60 days later, in early January of this year, the same F50 was offered by a well-known broker. The car now showed only 4,000 miles, and was being offered for $420,000, which is about 5% below the going rate. The hard top and case, the owner's manual and other books, and the service records were all missing.

Following my inquiry about the car, 17 quality photos were supplied by e-mail, showing the chassis number on the frame and steering column, and the assembly number under the hood. There was no question this was the same stolen F50, priced slightly below market but not "under-market" enough to arouse suspicions. The car was with a large exotic car dealer in central Japan. When I mentioned that I believed this to be a stolen car, the price was dropped to $300,000.

"In the US, one might expect a swarm of law-enforcement agencies to descend upon the dealership, with the car returning to its rightful owner and the perpetrators being hauled off to the slammer. The rules in Japan, in my experience, are different."

In the US, one might expect a swarm of law-enforcement agencies to descend upon the dealership, with the car returning to its rightful owner and the perpetrators being hauled off to the slammer. The rules in Japan, in my experience, are different.

Getting a stolen car imported into Japan is relatively easy, as Japanese customs officials don't check serial numbers on imported cars against Interpol records. Once in Japan, a foreign car can be registered with virtually any kind of paperwork, so local registration is another exercise in rubber stamping. Should a car be determined to be stolen, the local police are reluctant to do anything to aid in its recovery. And there are no laws in Japan requiring that a car stolen internationally be exported back to its rightful owner. So, once in Japan, a stolen Ferrari is virtually unrecoverable.

Additionally, in my experience dealers there are masters at simply ignoring a problem in the hope it will go away. If a dealer finds he unknowingly, or otherwise, has ended up with a stolen car, he simply puts it into a warehouse for a few years and waits for whatever token police investigation might occur to die a quiet death. He then brings the car back into the light of day and sells it without fanfare.

One of the local collectors commented to us, "Getting this issue resolved here is virtually impossible. Everybody (with their hands in someone else's pocket) keeps at least one eye closed... The only hope is to get an American lawyer who may be familiar with the way things are dealt with here. But to be frank, even if anything should materialize from this, the process will take a very, very long time."

The process of trying to recover this F50 has begun. The Japanese dealer network has been advised that the car is stolen, thereby making it more difficult to sell; the Japanese police have been notified, if for no other reason than to put some token pressure on the dealer who has the car; and a Japanese law firm has been engaged, to put pressure on the police and the local DMV and auto dealer licensing agency. Obviously, the company that originally insured the F50 when it was stolen has a great interest in this process.

Consequently, if offered a car by a dealer outside the US, exercise due diligence before sending your money. *—Michael Sheehan*

From the May 2002 issue of *SCM*.◆

Importing an F50: A Comedy in Two Acts

No problems were expected; after all, what better defines a race car than "a car that has raced"

In 1998 Ian Hetherington, an English software mogul, decided to race his Euro model F50 in the Ferrari Maranello Challenge. He raced Ferrari F50 S/N 103496 in six of the twelve Maranello Ferrari Challenge races in preparation for an assault on the 1999 championship.

For 1999 Hetherington and F50 S/N 103496 returned for 13 of the 14 rounds of the championship. With three first and three second-place finishes, they ended the season second overall, missing the championship by a single point.

You're sure it's a race car?

S/N 103496 returned for the 2000 Championship and competed in all 14 rounds, with two firsts at Donington, another at Silverstone, two firsts at Oulton Park, and a first and then a second at Le Mans, and was the overall winner of the 2000 Championship.

S/N 103496 also participated in the Porsche vs. Ferrari Challenge, a different series, competing against hot rod 930/935/936s in 1998 and 1999, often finishing as the fastest Ferrari.

On October 2000, S/N 103496 was sold to a retired American driver who still owns a substantial collection of cars he once raced in the IMSA series. On November 1, in preparation for its early November arrival in the US, a package detailing the race history of this car, with many supporting photos, was prepared and sent on to the EPA and DOT requesting approval as a race car entry, exempting the car from the usual EPA and DOT regulations. No problems were expected; after all, what better defines a race car than "a car that has raced." And with 39 races, F50 S/N 103496 would seem to more than define "race car."

On November 2, DOT requested proof that the new owner was a qualified race driver. Simple enough; copies of his racing licenses and detailed photos of the car provided by Mortimer, Houghton, and Turner Ltd., the authorized Ferrari dealer which had supplied the car, were sent to the EPA and DOT. We also retained Lance Beyer, a former lawyer for DOT with many years of experience dealing with them.

On November 3, after review of the photos, DOT requested a statement from MHT Ltd. confirming that the car was a race car, had raced in 39 separate races, and that its intrinsic value was as a race car and not a street car. MHT Ferrari supplied the appropriate letter.

On November 9, F50 S/N 103496 arrived at Miami airport but remained in Customs awaiting DOT and EPA approval.

On November 15, DOT contacted Ferrari of North America and asked if Ferrari had ever built an F50 race car. FNA replied in the negative and so we were advised by DOT that, since Ferrari had never built an F50 race car, this car could not be recognized as a race car. DOT was then supplied with copies detailing the presentation of the first F50 GT (which had received DOT/EPA exemptions).DOT accepted that their source at FNA had erred and another hurdle was cleared.

DOT next decided they needed a letter from Specialised Cars, the company that prepared this car for racing, listing the work done and stating its position that this car is indeed a race car. On November 17, the letter was supplied and approved. Two more weeks gone.

DOT then decided they needed a "stronger" letter, which was dutifully supplied on November 20. DOT next decided they needed confirmation from the race organizer that Specialised Cars was qualified to do the work described in their letter outlining the conversion of F50 S/N 103496 from a street car to a race car. On December 8, DOT was supplied with a letter from John Swift, director of the Maranello Challenge Series.

DOT asked for a letter from the Maranello Challenge sponsor, Maranello Concessionaires, that Specialised Cars was qualified to prepare race cars and confirmation that this car was recognized as a race car. Thanks to John Newman, General Manager of Ferrari UK, the letter was supplied on December 8.

I asked Art Zafiropoulo, owner of F50 GT S/N 001, to provide the import paperwork showing his F50 GT's importation under the race car exemption. This was sent to EPA and DOT.

Now past thirty days in storage with US Customs, it was necessary to put the car into bonded storage rather than have customs seize the car for lack of clearance paperwork. The costs of importation climbed.

On January 2, DOT next decided they needed "current" photos detailing the many modifications made to convert the car to racing standards. On January 8, with special permission from US Customs, Al Roberts of Shelton Ferrari photographed the car in a dark and dusty warehouse and sent the requested photos to DOT.

Our attorney was able to narrow down DOT's concern to one area, that of intent. DOT's mindset was "what was the main intent of the manufacturer when the car was built?" In layman's talk, we "only" needed to prove the car was re-manufactured as a race car, and DOT would approve the car.

On January 25, we supplied DOT with a very detailed letter from Specialised Cars outlining the costs of remanufacturing this car as a race car and the greater costs needed to re-convert it back to a street car, making its use as a street car financially impractical.

On February 1, DOT asked Al Roberts of Shelton Ferrari to go back and take better photos showing the ride height by putting a ruler up to the bottom of the car, along with clear photos of the fuel filler opening. Additionally they also wanted a letter from Shelton Ferrari repeating what was already stated by Specialised Cars in England.

February 8, Tom Shelton of Shelton Sports cars provided a detailed cost analysis letter to DOT about the costs of re-conversion.

The next day, DOT agreed to release the car.

February 22, DOT typed the letter releasing the car. End of Act One.

Next month, Act Two: EPA wants to know if a can of Coke will fit under the F50.—*Michael Sheehan*

From the July 2001 issue of *SCM*.◆

Importing an F50: Part II

If a standard Coke can will roll under a car, it cannot be a race car; if a Coke cannot roll under a car, it must be a race car

In the past issue of *Sports Car Market*, we reviewed the Byzantine process of importing a Ferrari F50, S/N 103496, which had been converted to racing specs and was last year's winner of the European Maranello Challenge. After a mere three-and-a-half months, DOT decided our F50 was indeed a race car and acceptable for importation into the US under the race car exemption.

Whew! Passed the "racey-looking" dashboard test.

After receiving the release letter from the DOT on February 22nd of this year we expected the EPA to rubber stamp DOT's decision. This proved to be supremely optimistic on our part; EPA decided to ask the same questions as DOT, in rephrased or reworded bureau-babble.

For instance, while DOT had wanted an explanation of the work done to convert this car to a race car, EPA on February 2 asked for a breakdown of the estimated cost to convert the car back to a street car. This is because DOT is concerned about the intent of the car's manufacturer, while EPA focuses on the road-ability of the vehicle.

On February 6, Specialised Cars, in England, which had prepared the car for racing, provided a detailed letter outlining the substantial cost to convert the car back to a street car. They also stated that, because of its history, converting this well-raced F50 into a street car would be financial folly.

On March 18, the EPA asked why the car sat high off the ground. On March 19, Mortimer, Houghton and Turner (MHT), an authorized Ferrari dealer in England who sold us the F50, supplied a letter explaining that the car was raised as high as possible on its adjustable suspension and fitted with the taller rain tires to prevent damage in shipping. The EPA was not satisfied with this explanation. They decided that the car had to be lower to be accepted as a race car.

On March 28, our esteemed attorney, Lance Beyer (lbeyer1@rochester.rr.com), who specializes in matters relating to vehicle importation, insisted EPA give us a definitive ruling on how low is low enough. John Guy, an engineer with the EPA, then devised the "Coke-can" test. If a standard Coke can will roll under a car, it cannot be a race car; if a Coke cannot roll under a car, it must be a race car.

On March 30, US Customs allowed the F50 to be taken to Shelton Ferrari of Fort Lauderdale, Florida, to be lowered from its transportation settings and pass the Coke-can test. Shelton lowered the suspension and fit racing slicks into place, lowering the car by 3 inches. Digital photos of the car passing the Coke can test were dutifully submitted to EPA.

On April 23, EPA stated that since digital photos can be altered they needed "hard" photos of the F50 passing the Coke can test, along with a statement from Shelton Ferrari affirming the car to be in race condition, the tires to be at racing pressure and to have had no additional weight added. Glossy 5 x 7 photos and the appropriate cover letter were sent to EPA.

May 15, the car passed the famous Coke can test, but was kicked sideways to Len Lazarus at the EPA, and he expressed his concern that this F50 looked just like any other F50 and that the EPA had already turned down previous requests to import F50s as race cars. Lazarus wanted photos substantiating that the car had a "racy looking" dashboard and interior. Once again, new copies of photos already supplied to both the DOT and the EPA were obtained from MHT Ferrari in England and dutifully re-supplied to the EPA.

On May 29, the F50 passed the "racy looking" dashboard test, but still had to pass a roll cage test, since the EPA had decided that real race cars have roll cages, not roll hoops. Attorney Beyer discovered that the EPA had already allowed entry to two F50 GTs under the race car exemption, and asked if we were to build a roll bar to match the bar fitted to the F50 GTs already imported, would this final test appease the EPA?

On June 2, the EPA denied they ever allowed the two F50 GTs to be imported, as they had no records of these cars. Therefore, these cars must have been smuggled. We advised the EPA that we had already sent exhaustive information on the two F50 GTs already imported but were told "the file is too thick" to take the time to go through. If we wished to prove the two F50 GTs were legally imported, we must re-send the paperwork on these cars to the EPA. We resubmitted the Customs and DOT paperwork, and the EPA subsequently agreed that two F50 GTs were indeed legally entered.

On June 7, EPA agreed to allow F50 S/N 103496 entry if we matched race car features, especially the roll cage, of the two "race versions" already approved and imported.

On June 15, we forwarded e-mail and detailed digital photos from Art Zafiropoulo, owner of F50 GT S/N 001, concerning the roll cage in his car. On June 18, Len Lazarus reviewed the EPA's importation file on the Zafiropoulo car. He agreed the EPA would generate a final "this is what you have to do to gain approval" letter.

As of July 15, we have still not received this letter. Their ineptitude and malice have cost my client months in delays, not to mention storage, customs and rather staggering (although hard-earned) legal fees, as well as any refurbishing costs required due to the months spent in storage.

I would like to be able to write a happy ending to this story. But given past experiences, I expect to receive a letter with a new set of repetitive, unjustified and expensive-to-meet demands any day now. From our perspective, a reasonable test to determine whether an F50 is actually a race car would be to see how quickly it could roll over a group of EPA bureaucrats.—*Michael Sheehan*

From the August 2001 issue of *SCM*.◆

The Bad Boys: F40, F50 and Enzo

Any of the three is a safe place to park some money, and taking one for a drive will surely be more fun than investing in hog bellies or pork futures

Most of the Ferraris built in the last two decades have one thing in common with Toyota Camrys: After they leave the showroom floor, they become depreciating used cars. But three Ferraris built during that period stand out as having appreciated in value, the F40 and the F50, and the Enzo continues to sell well over its sticker price of $650,000, at least for now.

Enzo: values holding steady at the moment.

With only 210 factory-built, U.S.-spec F40s, 56 U.S.-spec F50s, and a probable 70 U.S.-spec Enzos scheduled to be built, these are the most exclusive Ferraris of their eras (1989-1992, 1995-1996 and 2003-2004, respectively). When new, all were presold to those with the right connections to be at the top of lengthy waiting lists, and the financial wherewithal to pay from $300,000 to well over a million dollars for a car that they would, in all probability, rarely use.

When the F40, with its dramatic rear wing and promises of ultra-high performance, was announced, Ferrari fanatics, along with dealers and brokers, made the market look like feeding time at a shark exhibit. Despite a list price of around $300,000, the first few F40s were sold for over $1 million. Then prices dropped, bottoming out in the late 1990s at approximately $250,000-$275,000, before climbing to today's $325,000-$375,000 level for an ultra low-mileage (under 1,000 miles) example.

With a twin-turbocharged V8 spitting out 478 hp, the F40's 0-60 mph time is a mere 3.8 seconds and top speed is 196 mph. Even more, they look nasty and brutish like a proper supercar should.

A new F50 listed for about $450,000, but could only be leased, not purchased. Reportedly, Ferrari wanted to control the rampant price speculation, which they felt was affecting their credibility, and to protect themselves against product liability lawsuits.

As they came off lease and were sold into the secondary market, prices started to rise and never stopped. Today, an under-1,000-mile, well-documented and properly serviced U.S.-model F50 will easily bring $675,000. They have a 4.7-liter V12 that puts out 520 hp, achieve 0-60 mph in 3.7 seconds, and have a top speed of 202 mph.

The new bad boy on the block is the Enzo, Ferrari's attempt to combine *Star Wars* styling with a real Formula One transmission that includes launch control. Other F1-derived features include ride-height control technology, active integrated aerodynamics, and built-in rear underbody diffusers or "tunnels." Performance continues to climb. The 5998-cc, 660-hp V12 will rocket the Enzo from 0-60 mph in 3.6 seconds, and the top speed is 217.5 mph.

While the list price is about $650,000, the first few to change hands brought $1.2 million. However, the "bids" in the trade are dropping and the real sell price will probably be under $1 million by early next year.

Service problems on both the F40 and F50 are minimal, even when buying a 1,000-mile "garage queen," but count on spending $5,000-plus in deferred maintenance on either an F40 or an F50.

The F40 cam-belt tensioner bearings tend to tighten up, causing the outside of the cam belt to scuff and gall against the tensioner, which leads to belt failure. The F40 bellhousing is magnesium and emits gases that will cause the clutch hydraulics to fail. Also, as F40s are now 10 years old, they are all are due for a complete water hose and rubber component replacement, regardless of miles.

The major problem with the F50 is its all-electronic instrument cluster. Prior to purchase, the car should be run through its entire start-up and electronics check sequence. If some part of the dashboard electronics is defective (not an uncommon occurrence), an authorized dealer will ship the dash back to Italy for a six-month, $10,000 repair. For those who would like faster service at a lower price, an independent Ferrari shop in the U.S. rebuilds the dashes at half the price and with a much faster turnaround.

The F50s also had a factory recall for a defective front main seal, and any car with ultra low miles may not have had the update. Finally, the belly pan on the F50 tends to hide leaks by holding dripping fluids, so it must be checked before purchase for pools of problems.

So far the Enzo has had five factory recalls related to a cooling fan update, the oil tank level dipstick, the front moveable flap connection, the F1 gearbox oil tank cap and the engine oil drain plug. All are covered under warranty.

Unlike vintage Ferraris, there should be no hidden problems on a no-accident, no-stories F40, F50 or Enzo. On the two earlier cars, whatever problems there are should be resolved by a $10,000 check-up (lunch money for those who can afford to own these cars). As for the Enzo, Ferrari will fix it for you under warranty.

Just as the performance-oriented, limited-production SWBs, TdFs and 275 GTBs have achieved a collectible status, these limited production late model cars will always be among the top tier of Ferraris. Of the three, I would suggest that at the current time the F40 is the best investment, as it has hit bottom and rebounded. The F50 seems relatively stable but fully priced, while the Enzo will undoubtedly fall some—if not much—in the near future. But over time, any of the three is a safe place to park some money, and taking one for a drive will surely be more fun than counting a handful stock certificates.

—*Michael Sheehan*

From the February 2004 Issue of *SCM*.◆

F40 & F50: Bucking the Trend

Sold new to those with the financial wherewithal to pay $300,000 to over a million for a car they would in all probability never use

While 360 Berlinettas and Spyders, 456 GTs and 550 Maranellos and Barchettas are dropping in price, F40s and F50s are increasing in value. Why? 360s, 456s and 550s are all mass-production Ferraris, with more coming off the production line every day. As supply meets demand, their prices come down. Further, many of these cars are driven on a daily basis, racking up the miles. With time they become "just used cars," albeit very exotic, exclusive and state-of-the-art used cars.

But F40s and F50s are entirely different animals. There were only about 200 factory-built US-spec F40s and around fifty US-spec F50s. They were the most exclusive Ferraris of their eras ('80-'91 and '95-'97). When new, all were sold to those with the right connections to be at the top of the lengthy waiting lists, and the financial wherewithal to pay $300,000 to over a million dollars for a car that they would, in all probability, rarely use.

All markets seek a level. Despite a list price of around $300k, the first few F40s were sold for over $1m. Prices dropped, bottoming out in the late 1990s at approximately $250k-$275k, before climbing to today's $300k-$350k level.

A new F50 listed for about $450k, but could only be leased, not purchased. As they came off lease, prices started to rise and never stopped. Today, a very low-mileage (under 1,000), well-documented and properly serviced F50 will easily bring a mind-boggling $750k. With only fifty US cars built, this is the price of exclusivity.

Service problems on both the F40 and F50 are minimal, even when buying a 500-mile "garage queen." The F40 tensioner bearings tend to tighten up, causing the outside of the cam belt to scuff and gall against the tensioner, leading to belt failure; the bellhousing is magnesium and consequently emits gases that will cause the clutch hydraulics to fail.

The major problem with the F50 is its all-electronic instrument cluster. Prior to purchase, the car should be run through its entire start-up and electronics check sequence. If some part of the dashboard is defective—not an uncommon occurrence—the dash must go back to Italy for a six-month, $10,000 repair. For those not married to their local authorized Ferrari dealer, an independent Ferrari shop in the US rebuilds the dashes at one-half the price and with a much faster turnaround. The F50s had a factory recall for a defective front main seal, and any car with ultra low miles may not have had the update. Finally, the belly pan on the F50 tends to hide leaks by holding dripping fluids and must be checked for pools of problems before purchase.

F40: Your best investment at the moment.

The Prancing Horse Bad Boys are driving F50s.

On both the F40 and F50, excluding F50 dash nightmares, a preventative trip to your favorite Ferrari expert and a check for $5,000 to $10,000 will resolve all of the hangar queen problems. And if you think $5,000 to $10,000 is a lot of money, you're right, but not when you are considering spending $500,000 or more on a car. Besides, as the saying goes, if you have to ask…

I see no reason, barring global recession, that the prices of F40s or F50s will do anything but increase, albeit more slowly as we come to the end of the current market adjustment. For collectors of means interested in modern supercars, these are the ultimate Ferraris. —*Michael Sheehan*

From the January 2002 issue of *SCM*.◆

V6 Mid-Engine

#252-**1971 FERRARI 246 GT Dino Coupe**. S/N 2422. Red/black. LHD. Odo: 57,231 km. Mid-production Dino, hence "clapper" type wipers and slightly different bumpers with optional nudge-bar. Electric windows. Two owners from new. Largely still original, paint good, some microblistering to driver's side A-post. Interior, wheels, engine bay all good. Period Philips radio. Cond: 2-. **SOLD AT $62,216.** *$6,400 above top estimate paid, full retail in Europe, where 246 GTs are more highly prized than in the topless crazy US. Of course, Europeans actually drive their cars at speed, where the coupe is a vastly superior automobile.* ***Bonhams Europe, Gstaad, CH, 12/03.***

#508-**1972 FERRARI 246 GT Dino Coupe**. Body by Pininfarina. S/N 05050. Eng. #05050. Red/black. LHD. Odo: 32,655 miles. Fairly recent $32,000 restoration, repaint and brightwork perfect. Leather crazed, engine bay presentation only fair. Cond: 1-. **SOLD AT $61,236.** *Strong price for a coupe; we've seen GTSs, albeit in lesser condition, sell for about this amount in the US. Of course, as the Europeans actually use their cars, they do put a slightly higher value on the superior-driving closed car.* ***Bonhams, Goodwood, UK, 7/11.***

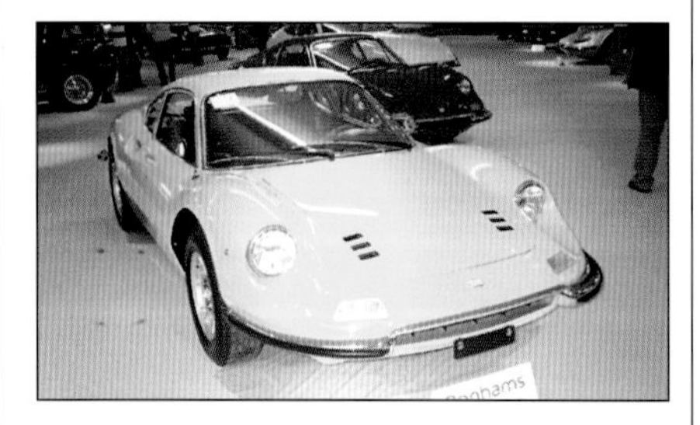

#257-**1972 FERRARI 246 GT Dino Coupe**. S/N 6024. Yellow/black. LHD. Odo: 54,699 km. One owner since 1975. Power windows. Restored at some time, repaint only "externally" OK. Brightwork and wheels good, engine bay clean. Voxson 8-track, Momo wheel. Cond: 2+. **SOLD AT $68,435.** *Top retail valued at $4,700 above high estimate. Slightly too much for condition, I thought, but yellow cars seemed to do well at this event.* ***Bonhams Europe, Gstaad, CH, 12/03.***

#473-**1973 FERRARI 246 GTS Targa**. S/N 04784. Red/black leather. LHD. Odo: 77,994 miles. Quickie masked respray, bubbles on driver's door, scratches on Targa top, worn carpeting. Used hard and put away wet. Cond: 3-. **SOLD AT $59,400.** *A very scary car that can only be categorized as a driver Ferrari that is a ticking time bomb. Ferraris are so incredibly expensive to refurbish that I would suggest the buyer take out a big ad in a European magazine, offering it for sale, to take advantage of the strong Euro. A very easy car to go underwater with.* ***Kruse, Dallas, TX, 11/03***

#46-**1973 FERRARI 246 GTS Dino Spyder**. Body by Scaglietti. S/N 5480. Fly yellow/black leather. LHD. Odo: 34,602 miles. Restored "some years ago" before going to Japanese collection. Books and owner's pouch. No mention of any mechanical restoration. Chassis semi-detailed, lower body panels gloss instead of original flat black. Dash appears original, correct fabric. Cond: 2. **SOLD AT $105,750.** *Again, high price for a cosmetically excellent car with no claims or documentation as to mechanical work. On the other hand, isn't that what Monterey auctions are all about? See a toy you like and just buy it. You'll remember the car more than the price.* ***Christie's, Pebble Beach, CA, 8/03.***

#53-**1974 FERRARI 246 GTS Dino Targa**. S/N 07756. Fly yellow/black leather. LHD. Odo: 79,813 km. Very nice paint marred by at least one ding, good chrome. Let down by interior details that, although not hateful, have some issues with fading chrome, small tear in dash, scarred paint at ignition key. Blaupunkt AM/FM, air conditioning. Cond: 3. **SOLD AT $67,100.** *Right on the money, perhaps even a decent buy for an end user. About 70% of the needed repairs are of the weekend-fix style, but repairing a tear in the dash is best left to the professionals.* ***RM Auctions, Meadow Brook, MI, 8/03.***

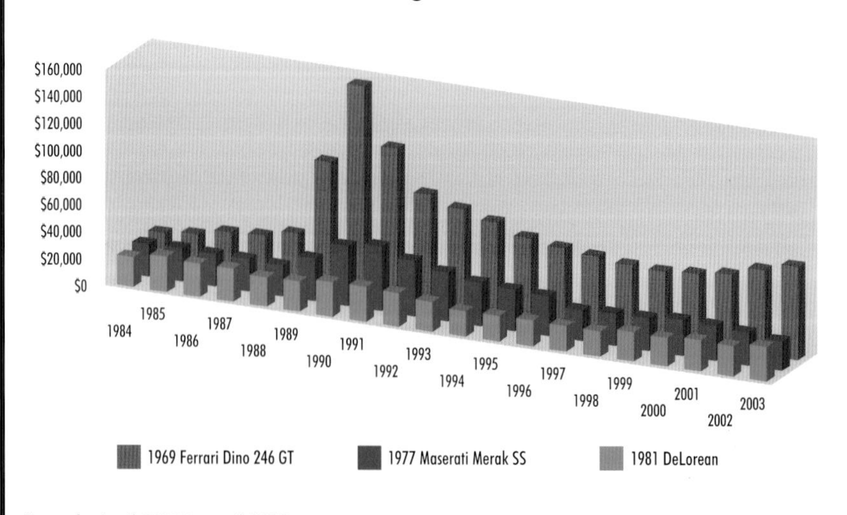

From the April 2002 issue of *SCM*.

V8 Mid-Engine

#251-**1976 FERRARI 308 GTB Fiberglass Coupe**. S/N 19275. Lime Green/black. LHD. Odo: 7,935 km. Early plastic car. Original kms (4,700 miles). One owner, last on road 1989, all still original. Paint mainly excellent, driver's door edge chips, minor crazing to driver's side leather. Engine bay dull but original. Instruction label still dangling from Borletti clock. Cond: 1-. **Sold At $36,598.** *$8,700 over top estimate paid for totally unmolested and unrepeatable time-warp car. These plastic, cabureted cars are real rocket ships—but buyers hated a fiberglass Ferrari, so they soon became steel. About that "Laugh-in" Color...* ***Bonhams Europe, Gstaad, CH, 12/03.***

#130-**1976 FERRARI 308 GTB Coupe**. Fieberglass Body by Pininfarina. S/N 19965. Eng. #19965. Rosso Rubino/tan. RHD. Odo: 7,016 miles. Air conditioning, genuine low mileage. All original (even tires and unused spare!) paint and interior excellent, alloys dull and marked, engine clean. Cond: 1-. **SOLD AT $45,713.** *Exceptional example of Ferrari's first V8-engined GT in early version's corrosion-free fiberglass thoroughly deserved over mid-estimate valuation.* ***Bonhams, Goodwood Circuit, UK, 9/03.***

#11-**1979 FERRARI 308 GTS Targa**. S/N F106AS 30625. Black/red. LHD. Your basic as-raced 308, with graphics. M&R race harness seat belts. Dry sump. Good glass, paint shows a few scratches but is of good quality. Roll cage, tires appear to have a few track miles left. Cond: 4+. **SOLD AT $25,850.** *If club racing is your desire, finding and buying a fully equipped, as-raced, prepared example at auction can represent a bargain over buying a used-up example and converting it on your own. Competitive? Most likely not, but looks great on the trailer.* ***Christie's, New York, NY, 6/03.***

#10120-**1980 FERRARI 308 GTS Coupe**. Body by Pininfarina. S/N FFAA02AEA0032967. Red/black leather. LHD. Odo: 74,694 miles. Body in average condition: no major dings and paint still glossy. But the interior shows use; driver's seat separating. Engine bay is very dirty but no oil leaks apparent. Engine sounds all right but who knows when last tuned—no records. Cond: 3. **SOLD AT $18,600.** *308s are bargain basement Ferraris—many were made and the prices are good. The early models can cost a lot to set straight. The bidding on this car reflected the fact that it was the proverbial "pig in a poke" with no known history.* ***Silver Auctions, Tacoma, WA, 9/03.***

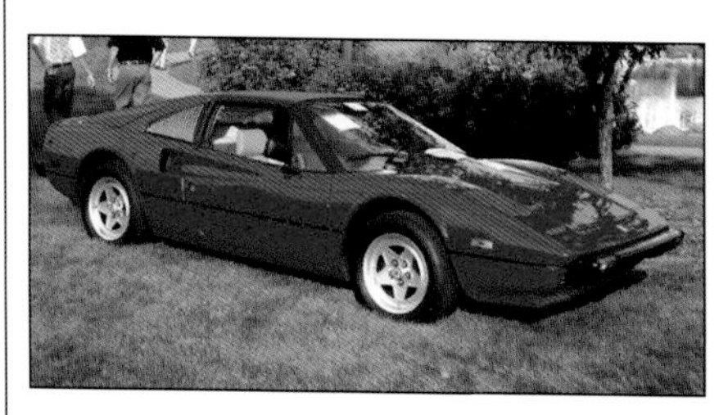

#276-**1981 FERRARI 308 GTSi Targa Coupe**. S/N ZFFAA02A0B0034581. Red/tan leather. LHD. Odo: 8,599 miles. "Dealer installed turbo." Air conditioning. Some windshield sealant pulling loose. Gorgeous original paint with only a few nicks on the vent panels. Minor door panel wear on the tops. Originally owned by the manager of the band Cheap Trick. Cond: 2. **SOLD AT $39,900.** *Rock- star provenance, combined with non-stock turbocharger equals "proceed with extreme caution." Even with minimal miles, expect previous maximum use. Welcome to my nightmare, don't bother to call the Dream Police.* ***Mecum Auctioneers, Elhart Lake, WI, 7/03.***

The Twenty Year Picture

Maserati BiTurbo, Lotus Esprit Turbo, Ferrari 308 GTBi QV

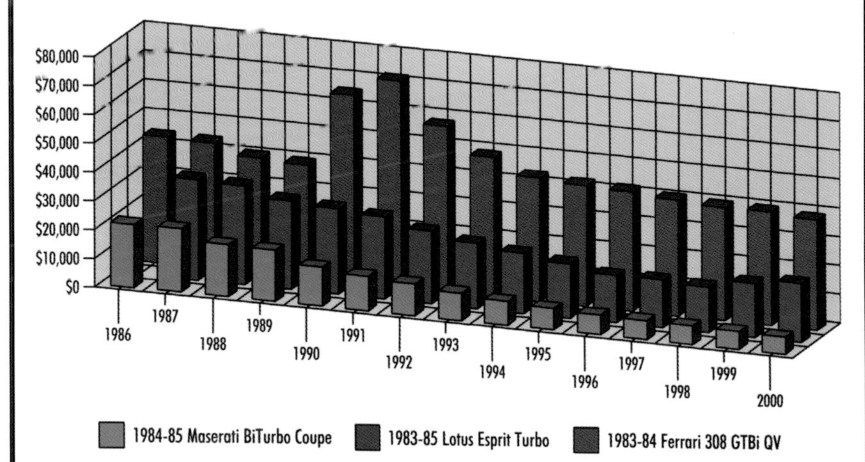

(Prices are for cars in excellent condition. Data provided courtesy of CPI. Additional data compiled from SCM archives.)

This month value guide is courtesy of Cars of Particular Interest. CPI is the pocket guide most often used by credit unions and banks when dealing with loan values of collectible domestic and imported cars. From the March 2000 issue of *SCM.*

#045-**1986 FERRARI 328 GTS** Targa. S/N ZFFXA20A2G0060955. Red/tan leather. LHD. Odo: 8,571 miles. Very nice original paint. Gasket between windshield and Targa top worn and cracked. Leather surrounding the shifter coming apart; tops of door lock plungers chewed up. Some fading of the plastic switch plates on the console. Late-model Alpine stereo system. Cond: 2. **SOLD AT $31,763.** *Declared sold for indicated amount on Friday afternoon. Crossed the block again on Saturday, declared sold for $28,980. Somewhere within the ether of the auction world, this is your basic $30k Ferrari. With good service records, a small bargain. But don't you think that if the seller had them, they would have been on display? So call this price fair.* ***Silver, Fountain Hills, AZ, 1/04.***

#128-**1987 FERRARI MONDIAL Cabriolet**. Black/tan. LHD. Odo: 30,230 miles. Cigarette burn on driver's door panel, interior wear consistent with mileage. Average paint. Overall, just a car with few minuses or pluses. And I didn't see any info about the 30,000-mile service. Cond: 3+. **SOLD AT $34,020.** *In the world of Ferraris, low miles and meticulous care are the buyer's mantras, and this example did nothing to instill confidence on the part of a buyer. Unless the prescribed maintenance has been performed, this could be a time bomb waiting to explode.* ***Russo and Steele, Monterey, CA, 8/03.***

#5493-S095-**1987 FERRARI MONDIAL Convertible**. S/N ZFFXCA7H0068391. Black/tan. LHD. Odo: 31,559 miles. 3.2 liter. Paint chips on headlight doors and front end. Some paint waviness and orange peel on right side. Small paint chips on windshield. Driver's seat dry and starting to show cracking. Sony tape deck with remote CD changer and amp in trunk. Cond: 2. **SOLD AT $32,400.** *If the servicing was kept up to date then this car was priced right on the money. If not, add $5,000 to the real price.* ***Russo and Steele, Scottsdale, AZ, 1/04.***

#719A-**1987 FERRARI MONDIAL 3.2 Cabriolet**. S/N ZFFWC238000068037. Dark blue/tan. LHD. Odo: 39,245 km. Fresh Michelin tires. Has wear to the interior to be expected by miles indicated, some repaint work showing to front bumpers, possible elsewhere. AM/FM cassette, air conditioned, blackout trim shows no fade as often seen on Stateside cars—perhaps there is a silver lining in all those grey clouds outside. Cond: 3+. **Sold At $32,220.** *It's going to take awhile (like maybe forever) before the markets learn to love (or at least stop hating) the Mondial. Buy the one you want in the color you want, look for the best example with the best service records and history, and a recent cam-belt change. This was a small bargain for a 3.2.* ***Coys, London, UK, 12/03.***

#272-**1988 FERRARI 328 GTS Targa**. S/N 77436. Black/magnolia. LHD. Odo: 3,813 km. Original kms (2,287 miles). Original paint still mainly good, minor marks to front, alloys very good. Driver's seat leather slightly grubby and cracking, cam belts freshly renewed in September 2003. Late-build car with ABS. Cond: 2-. **Sold At $41,353.** *Virtually minimum reserve met, which is retail money in UK for 328 GTS targa-top. A very good deal for the buyer, and a handsome color to boot. Changed cam belts a nice $3,000 bonus.* ***Bonhams Europe, Gstaad, CH, 12/03.***

#5470-**1991 FERRARI MONDIAL Convertible**. S/N ZFFFK33A5L00879390. Red/tan. LHD. Odo: 13,884 miles. All panel gaps good and even. Paint worn thin on black trims and a few door edge chips but otherwise good. Rear flexible window shows scratches. Carpets are dirty but don't appear worn. JVC stereo. Engine bay is as-driven clean. Cond: 2. **SOLD AT $43,000.** *Declared sold at R&S Monterey 2003 for $52,380. Ex-Kurt Russell and Goldie Hawn ownership. Drop top and four seats (even Goldie wouldn't fit in the back one though). That price seemed high, this price is about right. Lots of fun here, but not loved in the marketplace.* ***Russo and Steele, Scottsdale, AZ, 1/04.***

#176-**1991 FERRARI MONDIAL T Convertible**. S/N 2FFK33A5L0087939. Red/tan. LHD. Odo: 13,581 miles. Original owners Kurt Russell and Goldie Hawn. 30k service performed. Eight-inch scratch on driver's front fender touched up. Maintained and detailed with a perfect interior. If you have to have a Mondial, this is exactly what you want. Cond: 1-. **SOLD AT $52,380.** *While I was sitting in the driver's seat writing up this car, a rat jumped out from under the passenger seat (a Hollywood agent in disguise?) and lodged itself under the dash. Let's hope the new owner sees this report and rectifies the rodent stowaway.* ***Russo and Steele, Monterey, CA, 8/03.***

#256-**1995 FERRARI 348 Spyder**. S/N ZFFRG43A9S0099338. Fly Yellow/black leather LHD. Odo: 16,612 miles. Heavier than expected wear on driver's seat outboard bolster and leather steering wheel rim. Large number of paint chips unattended to on the nose. Top in near perfect condition. Heavily dealer prepped. Cond: 2. **SOLD AT $57,225.** *Having just had its scheduled service, was bought well. Just don't expect to turn it for a profit, as it is still a late model used car.* ***Mecum Auctioneers, Elhart Lake, WI, 7/03.***

83-**1996 FERRARI 355 GTS Coupe**. Body by Pininfarina. S/N 105104. Eng. #42421. Red/magnolia. LHD. Odo: 36,500 miles. Genuine mileage with full service history by four owners (already!) Happily both cambelts and clutch changed 2,500 miles ago. Body, paint, interior are all original and excellent, leather only lightly soiled. Cond: 1-. **SOLD AT $83,480.** *$3,320 over top estimate reflected more than one suitor wanting to become the car's fifth owner. The 355 drives so much better than the 348, and is much cheaper than the trendy 360. They are good buys.* ***H&H, Buxton, UK, 10/03.***

#481-**1998 FERRARI F355 Coupe**. S/N ZFFXR48A3W0111581. Silver/red leather. LHD. Odo: 2,688 miles. A very nice low-mileage example that has only minor cosmetic flaws any car that had been driven would have. Slight scratches on convertible top window, but the condition is commensurate with the mileage. Cond: 1-. **SOLD AT $103,140.** *A market-correct price for an F355 in this condition, and an ideal way to buy a Ferrari, as the original owner has taken the major depreciation hit. Since most F355s are red, this silver example was a welcome change. Well bought.* ***Kruse, Dallas, TX, 11/03.***

#706-**1999 FERRARI 355 Convertible**. S/N ZFFXR48A9X0115975. Yellow/black vinyl, yellow piping. LHD. Odo: 11,538 miles. Paint in good shape, interior also looks good. Engine sounds strong. A few dings on the doors but nothing major. Top was never displayed so its condition is unknown. Cond: 3. **SOLD AT $131,250.** *This is big money for a 355 convertible, and points out that it's not just hot rod buyers in the audience in Reno.* ***Silver Auctions, Reno, NV, 8/03.***

#148-**2000 FERRARI 360 Modena Berlinetta**. S/N 121894. Red/tan. LHD. Odo: 1,837 miles. Still in short supply with a waiting list at most dealers, here was a chance to buy a virtually new car and drive it home the next day. Purchased in 2001 and barely used, stunning. Cond: 1-. **SOLD AT $159,500.** *No hassles and no bargaining with sales people. Apparently worth the slight market premium, but below low estimate of $160,000. MSRP in 2000 was $138,225; in 2003, $150,060.* ***RM Auctions, Monterey, CA, 8/03.***

Flat-12 Mid-Engine

#282-**1974 FERRARI 365 GT4/BB Boxer Coupe**. S/N 17927. Red/magnolia. LHD. Odo: 42,993 km. One of 367 built. Repaint in original color excellent. Wheels mint, original interior quite good, though slightly soiled and crumpled. Detailed engine bay. Handsome. Cond: 2+. **SOLD AT $90,383.** *Some like the 365s the best of all the Boxers, with their peakier engines. More popular in Europe than the US, partly because there was never a US-legal model. As they become exempt from many states, smog regulations due to age, we may see slight growth in popularity and value stateside.* ***Bonhams Europe, Gstaad, CH, 12/03.***

#261-**1975 FERRARI 365 GT4/BB Boxer Coupe**. S/N 18299. Red/beige. LHD. Odo: 49,442 km. Originally dark blue with black sills. Post-1989 repaint and color change very good, apart from chip to driver's side wheel-arch. Original seats grubby and shiny, wheels marked. Cond: 2-. **SOLD AT $59,470.** *Not as nice as Lot #282, hence lower price paid, which valued car correctly. Too bad it's not blue any longer—Boxers are handsome in that color.* ***Bonhams Europe, Gstaad, CH, 12/03.***

#277-**1980 FERRARI 512 BB/LM Silhouette Competition Coupe**. S/N 30559. Red/black. LHD. 14th of only 29 512BB/LMs built and first Series II. Presented as raced by NART. Fresh repaint excellent, comp spec interior with only one bucket. Passenger seating area completely taken up by fuse/switch board, roll-cage side bar paint very chipped. Minor racing history, but well documented. Cond: 2+. **SOLD AT $353,761.** *Well under $460,300 lower estimate was surprisingly accepted from French buyer who has therefore given this particular car public valuation. Will never be hugely competitive in vintage racing, but will always be popular and relatively cheap to run.* ***Bonhams Europe, Gstaad, CH, 12/03.***

#256-**1980 FERRARI 512 BB Coupe**. S/N 30865. Red/tan. LHD. Odo: 9,069 km. Genuine low mileage by one owner (Lepeltier). Very original. Speed chips to front, rear alloys marked, some wear to driver's seat. Pioneer radio/cassette. Tire pressure sticker still on windshield, original XWX tires. Time-warp car. Cond: 2. **SOLD AT $77,214.** *$11,900 over high estimate was still less than $90,283 and $59,470 paid for earlier 365 BB models #282 and #261. 512s, even still-in-the-wrapper examples like this, just don't command the prices of the 365. Might have been worth a touch more in the US, where everyone always seems to want the model with the biggest engine.* ***Bonhams Europe, Gstaad, CH, 12/03.***

#94-**1983 FERRARI 512 BBi Boxer Berlinetta**. S/N ZFFJA09B00044231. Red/tan leather. LHD. Odo: 16,546 miles. Wear to driver's seat bolster, some dryness to all leather that could be caught if treated now. Michelin TRX radials, Pioneer AM/FM cassette with matching equalizer. Paint shows well with some touched-up chips. Cond: 3. **SOLD AT $71,500.** *Sounds like current market money to me. At one time the Boxer was the Ferrari to have, but as with all fashion trends, it fell off a cliff after the next set of models arrived. It is crawling back now, so the bargains are drying up.* ***RM Auctions, Meadow Brook, MI, 8/03.***

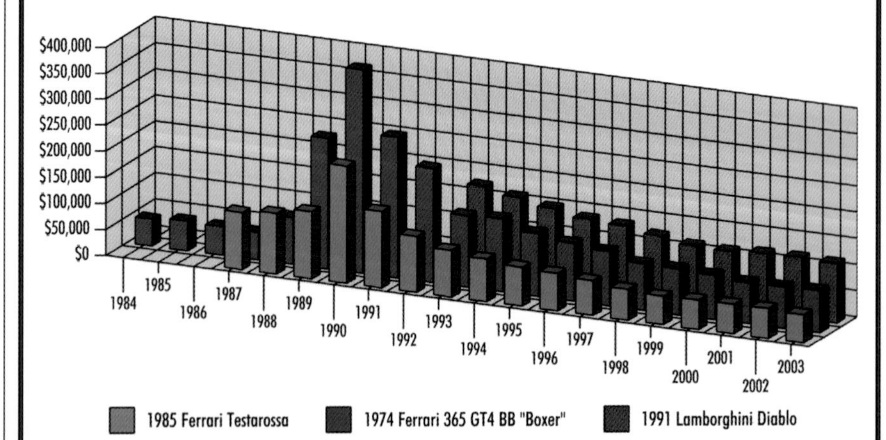

This month value guide is courtesy of Cars of Particular Interest. CPI is the pocket guide most often used by credit unions and banks when dealing with loan values of collectible domestic and imported cars.
From the September 2003 issue of *SCM*.

#36-**1986 FERRARI TESTAROSSA Coupe**. S/N 70000065901. Eng. #729. Red/tan. RHD. Odo: 28,494 miles. Absolutely genuine mileage and RHD. Original paint excellent, interior slightly grubby, wheels mint. New tires and carpets. Said to drive very well. Cond: 1-. **SOLD AT $53,310.** *Minimum required was forthcoming. Even with expensive-to-change cam belts, Testarossas at this money do seem cheap. But like all glamor cars, once their moment in the sun has passed, their value plummets. Everyone wants a 360 or a 550 now.* ***H&H Classic Auctions, Buxton, UK, 12/03.***

#62-**1986 FERRARI TESTAROSSA Coupe**. S/N ZFFTA17T0G0061513. Yellow/tan leather. LHD. Odo: 14,017 miles. Euro delivery, private import. Seats had good re-dye, are hard and need dye again. Leather dash has marks scarring, console has same. More beat-up interior than I have seen in any TR. Rust bleeding off cheese-grater sides. Three of four wheels scarred. Cond: 4. **SOLD AT $45,100.** *Seems cheap? Don't get me started on this one—almost the poster car for what can go wrong to a Testarossa when no one is looking. One side shows more rust than the other—damage repair or is that the side that was dragged in the ocean?* ***Kensington, Bridehampton, NY, 7/03.***

#545-**1987 FERRARI TESTAROSSA Coupe**. Body by Pininfarina. S/N 0067455. Black/black. RHD. Odo: 14,337 miles. Genuine UK mileage with full service history including 2000 cam-belt change during sole ownership of *Top Gun* movie director Tony Scott. Original paint good with few marks, seat retrim excellent, windshield renewed, six-stack CD. Cond: 2+. **SOLD AT $52,164.** *As long as you like your Ferraris in black, this low-mileage, one-owner, well-maintained RHD Testarossa was well bought for mid-estimate price paid. TRs are finally settling in the $50k-$60k range for good cars, $40k-$50k for scary ones. You do the math.* ***Bonhams, Goodwood, UK, 7/11.***

#27-**1987 FERRARI TESTAROSSA Coupe**. Body by Pininfarina. S/N 67557. Eng. #00114. Red/red. LHD. Odo: 28,583 miles. Another 1987 Dutch Motor Show stand car. Again, still all original with only minor cosmetic wear and a cambelts change in 2002. Cond: 1- **SOLD AT $45,485.** *Again, low mileage and unspoiled originality was responsible for high estimate being reached. Interesting that the low estimate was just $34k—the lowest I've seen yet for a nice car. I keep thinking they just can't be worth any less, and then...* ***Christie's, Apeldoorn, Holland, 8/03.***

#104-**1988 FERRARI TESTAROSSA Coupe**. S/N 73391. Eng. #00564. Red/black. RHD. Odo: 6,600 miles. One owner and original miles claimed, sold from estate. Still original paint flat, with chips. Front corner scuffed, much seat belt wear to driver's seat bolster, dash top distressed, wheels good. Light damage to bodywork on rear three-quarters, dents on roof, bumpers dinged from parking, dash sunbleached. Sat outdoors since May 1999. Cond: 3-. **SOLD AT $44,462.** *Considerable wear and tear did not deter new owner paying $18,662 over guide price. Attractive "25 SHY" registration plate may have helped. There will be no good, or cheap, surprises with this car.* ***Christie's, London, UK, 12/03.***

PART III
Random Thoughts

Who do you sue if your Ferrari gets attacked by mice when it's in a storage facility? And if your uncle was the Sultan of Brunei, which collectible Ferrari should be first on your list?

Those and other topics make up the "Random Thoughts" chapter of this book. You'll also find an extensive comparison between Ferraris and Lamborghinis, and recommendations on what's hot and what's not in the Ferrari world today. And to wrap it all up, there's a comprehensive price guide, along with our appreciation predictions and an investment grade for every model.

We hope you've enjoyed the read, and that when you set out on your hunt for your first, or your next, Ferrari, that the information in *Keith Martin on Collecting Ferrari* will make you a more thoughtful buyer. What we're all really after is the best possible car, at the best possible price, that will give us thousands of pleasurable miles. And hopefully when it comes time to sell, maybe even make a little money.

After all, isn't that what collecting is all about?
—*Keith Martin*◆

Even Dealers Get Stung

We all want to talk ourselves into a good deal, and often continue to do so even though warning signs begin to pop up

We all want to talk ourselves into a good deal, and often continue to do so even as warning signs begin to pop up. Sometimes dealers have problems too. I got a call last week from Peter Sweeney of Forza Motors in Connecticut. He and his partner deal mainly in Italian exotics below $100,000.

They had recently purchased a red/tan 1985 Ferrari 308 GTSi QV for resale from a "friend," sight unseen as a result of the owner's assurance that the vehicle was superb in every respect. They did run an Internet Carfax report, which indicated a clean title and no damage history.

When they took delivery of the vehicle, it appeared to be in pretty good shape, but they were disappointed to learn that it needed a clutch. They were also surprised to find that the car, which they understood had always resided in Connecticut, and which was purchased from a Connecticut resident, was titled and registered in New Hampshire.

The New Hampshire title set off alarm bells for Sweeney. New Hampshire is a state, along with Alabama and others, from which it is easy to purchase a "title of convenience" from a title broker. Generally, titles from these states may be obtained for cars when there is some sort of problem in the chain of title that prevents the vehicle from being registered in its home state, such as a salvage title resulting from the vehicle having been declared a total loss due to accident or other damage.

When the seller was questioned, he said there was no problem with the car and he had only obtained the New Hampshire title to avoid Connecticut sales tax. Although the situation was not ideal, Sweeney believed him, particularly because the Carfax report was clear of any damage history.

To prepare the vehicle for sale, Sweeney had a Connecticut state inspection done, eliminating a possible snag in case a purchaser from Connecticut (or another state with strict emissions laws) was interested in the vehicle. After the 308 passed inspection, Peter put it on eBay for auction and waited for the bids to pour in.

What came pouring instead were irate e-mails condemning him for failing to disclose that the vehicle had been wrecked and had a salvage title from Connecticut. Prospective bidders had been checking Carfax, which now declared this car to have a branded title. Just what was Sweeney trying to pull, they asked.

Understandably he was dumbfounded. He rechecked Carfax, and sure enough *this time* the vehicle was shown as having a Connecticut salvage title, having been totaled in 1986.

Apparently, the data Carfax purchased from the state of Connecticut only included records back to a certain date, or *records with recent activity.* The recent Connecticut inspection had informed the DMV's computer systems that there was activity on an archived record, which then "activated" the 308's history. As a result, the salvage title was reported to Carfax. As Sweeney had already looked at a Carfax report (although outdated, unknown to him), he had no reason to contact them again. Of course, interested buyers certainly did.

Where does this leave Sweeney? He is legally required to disclose the latent defect (salvage/branded title) if he sells the car, and this will be difficult because it can not be registered in Connecticut until the car is certified to have met all safety and emission requirements. Sweeney will unfortunately have to pursue legal action against the seller. He will take a loss on the car, which he may or may not recoup from the lawsuit.

Salvage titles aren't much help to a seller.

There are several lessons here. The first is to be aware that Carfax is not infallible. A clean Carfax report does not necessarily mean the vehicle has not been damaged, totaled or marred in any other way.

The second is that any purchaser should be extremely suspicious of a vehicle being sold by its owner (as opposed to a dealer or broker) that is registered or titled in a state other than the one in which the vehicle is garaged. If the state where the vehicle is registered is one where emissions laws are less stringent than the one in which the vehicle resides, or if it is a state such as New Hampshire, from which mail-order titles can be obtained, my instinct would be to run away. The easy availability of mail-order "titles of convenience" is often taken advantage of by unscrupulous owners and sellers, and very rarely for innocent reasons.

If you absolutely have to have the vehicle, at the very least call the DMV in the state in which the car sits, give them the VIN and ask if the car has failed inspection, been issued a salvage title or can not be registered in that state for any other reason.

Even if they have no information, have an inspection done looking for past accident damage and make sure the vehicle will pass emissions and inspection in the state in which you plan to register it.

There's an unfortunate red mist that comes with collector car buying, and it can afflict dealers as well as end-users. We all want to talk ourselves into a good deal, and often continue to do so even as warning signs begin to pop up.

Sweeney will probably lose money on this car; he will certainly lose an enormous amount of time and energy. However, if he had been unlucky enough to sell the car, and worse, it had gone to a West Coast buyer who might have paid for transcontinental shipping before the branded title was discovered, Sweeney would be facing a much larger financial outlay.

In this case, his only luck may have been to discover the problems before the car changed hands.—*Alexander Leventhal*

Alex Leventhal is a car collector and attorney in New York. His comments are general in nature, and are not a substitute for a consultation with an attorney.

From the May 2001 issue of *SCM.*◆

My 360's Been Impounded

Ferrari is requiring these cars be sold back to them not to prevent speculation, but to ensure that their dealers, and not the original owner, are the beneficiaries

Ferrari SpA (the factory) and Ferrari North America (FNA—the US importer/distributor) have always been a little eccentric (we might just call it "Italian") in their business dealings. Recall Luigi Chinetti's refusal to sell a car to an undesirable customer, or Enzo Ferrari requiring a Mille Miglia Barchetta to be painted yellow and fitted with a green interior when he learned it was to be delivered to an American actress who intended to drive it on the street.

Of late, however, Ferrari North America has been less charming and more pernicious.

The first series of phone calls I received from Ferrari buyers regarded language that was being put into the purchase contracts for 550 Barchettas, and is now being used in 360 Modena purchases as well. The language requires, in essence, that the purchaser of one of these vehicles, if they wish to sell the car during the first year (or two) of ownership, may sell it back only to the dealer from which it was purchased, and only for the price paid, or less.

Ferrari NA claims that this is being done to prevent speculation. This is, in my opinion, a blatant falsehood. It would appear that FNA simply wishes to restrict the speculation to their authorized dealers. Advertisements for slightly used (luxury tax paid!) Ferraris from authorized dealers asking $100,000 or more *over* sticker are common. It's clear that Ferrari is requiring these cars be sold back to them not to prevent speculation, but to ensure that their dealers, and not the original owner, are the beneficiaries of any extra profits that may be available.

"Be forewarned, however, that the courts do not always look kindly on lawsuits by well-heeled would-be Ferrari buyers who are trying to enforce their right to make a $100,000 or so profit on a car."

What does this mean for owners? If this language is not included in the original purchase agreement but is instead a contract to be signed at delivery, a lawyer's intervention should be able to force delivery without the buyer's signature. If the dealer is requiring this language in the original purchase contract, they cannot easily be forced to sell a car without it.

This is not to say, though, that this language would necessarily be enforceable by FNA in the event that it is breached, as it may unfairly restrain trade. Be forewarned, however, that the courts do not always look kindly on lawsuits by well-heeled would-be Ferrari buyers (speculators?) who are trying to enforce what they perceive is their right to make a $100,000 or so profit on a car.

My most recent phone calls, all of which have had a frantic, desperate tenor, arise from further egregious actions on the part of Ferrari NA. Ferrari recently requested and was granted an injunction by the DOT that *immediately prohibits the US DOT from certifying any European-spec Ferraris that were produced after December 20, 2000.*

Should Ferrari ultimately prevail and the injunction not be lifted, gray-market vehicles currently in the US awaiting certification will have to be exported or crushed. Ferrari's claim is that European-spec cars cannot be made safe for use on US highways, and that they should therefore be barred from importation into the United States.

Will you be driving your new Ferrari to court?

Of course, the only reason that anyone would want to import a Euro-spec Ferrari is that the waiting list for a new US car is two to three years, and that used examples (luxury tax paid!) are being sold for astronomical sums. Just as with Mercedes-Benz autos in the late '80s, since prices of European cars are significantly lower, entrepreneurs can make a profit by buying them, importing them and certifying them, and then selling them in the US.

Since all Ferraris are "world cars," the argument that they are unable to be converted to US specs and that they are unsafe for use on US highways is specious. It seems more likely, particularly in consideration of Ferrari's other recent efforts, discussed above, that Ferrari is once again seeking to protect their profits by making sure only their dealers, and not importers or brokers, can sell Ferraris in the United States.

Will Ferrari ultimately succeed in banning the importation of these vehicles? The prevailing opinion among the knowledgeable is no. These are essentially world cars, and despite Ferrari's assertion to the contrary, they are clearly convertible and safe for US use. In the meantime, however, many small importers and brokers may be bankrupted as they are unable to deliver cars for which they have already paid six figures, imported, converted and are in the process of certifying. In any event, this injunction will have a chilling effect on the importation of gray-market Ferraris, which means that Ferrari NA will have succeeded in protecting its profits.

What does this mean for enthusiasts? Simply, do not, under any circumstances, buy a Euro Ferrari that does not already have its DOT and EPA releases until this mess is sorted out, and obviously don't try to import a Euro Ferrari.

Ultimately, in a capitalist environment, making a profit is a desirable thing. However, it is disappointing to see a company like Ferrari, with its glorious history, stooping to such transparent devices to maximize the profits of its dealers, while denying that same opportunity to those who choose to buy their products.—*Alexander Leventhal*

Alex Leventhal is a car collector and attorney in New York. His comments are general in nature, and are not a substitute for a consultation with an attorney.

From the October 2001 issue of *SCM*.◆

Vermin Coverage

The mechanic was fairly certain that the damage was done by rats—not only from the shape of the teeth marks, but also from the pair of dead rats found in the car

The e-mail message came from a Ferrari owner in New York City who keeps his black/tan 1986 Mondial 3.2 Cab in a garage on 14th Street in Greenwich Village. He purchased the car, used, in 1989 at the height of the market, paying above 1989 MSRP for it. He had been unable to drive his car for several months because he was too busy starting a new dot.com business. Let's just say that his timing, whether in cars or business, was terrible.

Although the Mondial started after its lengthy siesta, it ran erratically, and none of the instruments functioned. The owner assumed that nothing more than a fusebox malfunction was at fault, and he arranged to have the car shipped to his mechanic for repairs, no doubt wishing reliability was the characteristic that his Ferrari shared with a Toyota, rather than styling.

When the owner of the cantankerous Cab heard from his mechanic, he found that his Ferrari had not been affected by a common Italian electrical malfunction. Instead, a rodent had been gnawing on various and sundry electrical components, damaging wiring in the engine compartment and under the dash. The mechanic was fairly certain that the damage was done by *Rattus norvegicus*—rats—not only from the shape of the teeth marks, but also from the pair of dead rats found in the car. He mentioned that this was not unusual in vehicles that sit dormant for large amounts of time, although it was much more common in rural areas than in New York City parking garages. He advised the Mondial owner to contact his insurance company and talk to them about paying what was sure to be a multi-thousand-dollar repair bill.

The news the owner got from his insurance company was almost as depressing as the current market valuation of his new Internet company. His insurance company specifically excluded coverage of losses due to "infestations of vermin."

The response I gave was that things were not as bad as they could have been, as the parking garage was acting as a "bailee for hire." A "bailment" is the legal relationship that arises when one person delivers personal property (in this case, the car) to another party (in this case, the garage) under an agreement that the latter is duty bound to return the identical property to the former, as agreed. A "bailor" is the person who delivers the property, and the "bailee" is the person who accepts the property under the agreement to return it. A "bailee for hire" may be a person or business, such as a parking garage or a coat check, which stores personal property for a fee.

The law of bailments allows that once the bailor (the owner of the car) proves the existence of a bailment and the loss to his vehicle, a presumption of negligence arises. The burden shifts to the bailee (the garage) to prove they provided adequate care for the vehicle. The bailee will be liable for damages to the vehicle at this point, unless they can prove they acted "reasonably under the circumstances" or that the vermin infestation was an "act of God."

Prancing horse on the nose, hungry rat under the hood.

In all likelihood, the owner of the vehicle would prevail against the garage in a lawsuit seeking redress for the damages to the Ferrari, since the garage keeper allowed the car to be chewed apart while he was storing it. The garage keeper would be in a better position if he could show that he put out rat poison, or took other reasonable precautions to keep these hungry rodents away.

"While the law may be on the side of the Mondial owner, the difference between the real world and a hypothetical law-school case is whether the amount to be awarded in case of victory makes the matter worth pursuing in the face of legal fees and court costs."

However, while the law may be on the side of the Mondial owner, as always, the difference between the real world and a hypothetical law-school case is whether the amount to be awarded in case of victory makes the matter worth pursuing in the face of legal fees and court costs. In this case, the Ferrari's repair bill will be high enough, $3,000 to $5,000, that the matter may be worth pursuing, particularly if the garage, or its insurance company, settles quickly. However, if the owner's attorney has to do more than simply write a demand letter, the expense of pursuing the case may well mean that the owner is never made entirely "whole." In other words, he'll still have a net loss, thanks to the rat infestation.

In terms of cars that are stored at home and not in a bailment situation, you should carefully examine your insurance policy and talk to your insurer to get confirmation in writing that your policy does not exclude coverage in the event of loss due to vermin.

Alternatively, you could invest in a cat, and keep it in your garage. Preferably, that cat would be female, as male cats have a way of marking their territory that may make getting into your Ferrari a surprising olfactory experience. If indeed the Mondial owner should choose a feline solution, I suggest he go to the corner bricks-and-mortar pet shop to find an appropriate cat (black with tan paws?), now that pets.com has met its demise.
—Alexander Leventhal

Alexander Leventhal is a car collector and attorney in New York. His comments here are general in nature, and are not a substitute for a consultation with an attorney.

From the February 2002 issue of *SCM*.◆

The Missing Ferrari 360 Spyder

When I asked him how he could send a quarter of a million dollars for a car he had never seen, to a guy he had never met, his reply was, "The guy had a really nice Web site"

A gentleman recently called fearing that he had purchased a car that didn't exist, or in any case was not going to be delivered. The object of his desire was a Ferrari 360 Spyder. Not willing to wait three years for a dealer-delivered car, he located one for sale on the internet.

Price wasn't an object. He had willingly agreed to pay $250k—about $100k over list—and then wired the funds into an alleged "escrow" account. He was told that only by paying in full could he be ensured of immediate delivery.

After the wire was received, the buyer's persistent phone calls to the seller yielded one excuse after another as to why the car could not be delivered. However, he did receive occasional trinkets from the car, including the owner's manuals and a spare set of keys (presumably to appease him), until the seller stopped returning phone calls altogether.

It is worth noting that none of the excuses offered by the seller were what I presume to be the truth, which is that the seller had sold the car to someone else (or many other people) and planned to deliver it to only one of them (at most).

After figuring out that the money was no longer in the "escrow" account and that the seller was not willing to return it, the anxious buyer contacted me. When I asked him how he could send a quarter of a million dollars for a car he had never seen, to a guy he had never met, who lived half way across the country, without any references, inspections, or any other due diligence, his reply was, "The guy had a really nice website…I figured he had to be on the level!"

The buyer expressed a desire to immediately begin a lawsuit against the seller to get his money back. Before we had a discussion about fees, likelihood of success and the practicality of chasing a defendant who may well be judgment-proof, I asked the buyer to tell me the exact events of the transaction in detail.

He mentioned something in passing that turned out to be the difference between fiscal immolation and a sunburn. Just after the buyer had wired the money, long before he had nay indication that the car would not show up, he brought his bill of sale with VIN down to his insurance agent and had the car placed on his policy, just in case something happened in transit. After that, he took constructive possession of the vehicle (remember the trinkets of appeasement). What this means is that he is lucky enough, now that it is clear that the vehicle is not coming, to be in a position to file a police report outlining the situation, and to then report the vehicle "stolen" to his insurance company and provide them with a reference to the police report.

It seems likely that his insurance company will pay on the claim, then pursue the seller to recover their money. Whether they will pay the list price or the "spot" price is debatable, but, frankly, anything is better than nothing at this point. The buyer was remarkably lucky that he put this coverage in place in good faith before anything untoward happened. Had he waited until after he feared the vehicle was lost (bad faith) or not put it in place at all, he would be spending tens of thousands of dollars on litigation that might go nowhere, as opposed to collecting a check from his carrier.

I suppose the first lesson to be learned here is that a nice Web site—even a *really* nice Web site—doesn't necessarily imply the veracity or integrity of the business that publishes it. The second, which has been covered in the pages of this magazine many times before, is that it is never wise to purchase a car from someone without both a pre-purchase inspection and a careful checking of the references of the seller.

Anytime someone takes your money and doesn't deliver the car in question, it is good to have someone other than yourself pay the cost of litigating to get the money back, and, ideally, to spot you the money while they do so. One way to do this is to pay for the car on a credit card (November 2000, "Legal Files," page 60). This is not generally possible with cars in this price range, but the buyer in this case did one thing that has yielded him almost the same result.

By insuring the specific car that he had purchased early in the process (in good faith), he has a pretty good chance of being indemnified for his loss. This certainly does not mean that one can take these kind of risks often, with reliance on indemnification from the insurance carrier. However, it does make it clear that every purchaser should secure coverage at the earliest possible juncture, specifying a VIN and as much other detail as possible, and taking constructive possession as soon as possible, even if it's only an owner's manual or a set of keys, just in case something unforeseen happens. *—Alexander Leventhal*

Alexander Leventhal is a car collector and attorney in New York. His comments here are general in nature, and are not a substitute for consultation with an attorney.

From January 2002 issue of *SCM.* ◆

The Summer Bounce

The unpredictable economy has had little effect on those who can indulge themselves by buying cars from Maranello

In December, 2001, I wrote that the price of Modenas was falling. For those dealers and brokers in the market on a daily basis, a combination of the after-effects of September 11th and snow on the ground in much of the US contributed to a slow-down in sales overall, and a drop in price for the current "flavor of the month" Ferrari, the 360 Modena convertible.

Spring is here, December snows are a memory and, son of a gun, the market is bouncing right back. While a 2001 US-model 360 Spyder went from a December "retail" price of about $260,000 to around $240,000 by March, they are once again around $260,000, maintaining an $80,000 premium over their $180,000 sticker price.

Now that the legal problems with importing 360s have been settled, expect more Euro cars to come on to the market in the next few months. They tend to sell in the $180,000 range, and may affect the price of US cars. However, most 360 Spyder buyers want their cars now, and want them with no questions and no stories, so expect US cars to stay relatively strong.

Older cars like Lussos, 275 GTBs and Daytonas have firmed up considerably, with a good, no-stories Daytona coupe bringing about $135,000, helping to provide a bottom for their much-evolved brethren, the 550 Maranellos. A 1997 Euro-model 550 seems to have hit a bottom price of about $125,000 and, for the summer, should stay in that price range. Meanwhile, a 1997 US car is now around $150,000 and selling well in that price range. Expect these prices to drop modestly later this year.

F40s and F50s remain stable with a US model F40 selling in the $300,000 range for a good car and $350,000 for an exceptionally low-mileage, only-good-stories example. A Euro F50 will bring about $600,000 and a US car will bring $650,000 to $750,000 for an under-500-mile car.

Currently taking it in the shorts is the limited-use 360 Challenge car that sold, when new, for well over its $160,000 sticker—FNA required a $50,000 "sign up" premium to run in the 360 Challenge. The entry list in the 360 Challenge has dropped from 40 plus cars in 2001 to only 20 cars in 2002, and following the decline in demand, prices have slipped from a high of around $200,000 out the door only two years ago to about $140,000 today. A bright spot for 360 Challenge owners is that the SCCA has accepted the 360 Challenge cars for their T1 series, where they will run against Vipers and Corvette Z06s. Hopefully, the option of having much-cheaper-to-run and much-closer-to-home events available will stabilize 360 Challenge prices. However, we all know that there is nothing so unloved as last year's race car.

Generally speaking, the unpredictable economy seems to have had little effect on those who can afford to indulge themselves by buying cars from Maranello. There is still plenty of wealth in the country; otherwise, how could 360 Spyder sales stay so strong? For older cars, there are a host of specialty lease and finance plans available, at record-low interest rates, so a collectible Ferrari has

Paul Jarmyn

$300,000 will get you a very nice F40.

www.MichaelMcCafferty.com

Spyders strong at $260,000.

Daytona Coupes firming up at $135,000

really never been more affordable in terms of true out-of-pocket costs. Further, the prices of most serial-production older Ferraris have really been quite stable for some time, unlike the gyrating stock market, so the terms "safe investment" and "vintage Ferrari" may actually belong, for the first time in a decade, in the same sentence together. —*Michael Sheehen*

From the June 2002 issue of *SCM*.◆

Your First-Time Ferrari

"Get me the best" types are more interested in having bragging rights at Warren Buffet's next Sun Valley get-together than how their cars actually perform

Which is the best Ferrari for a first-time owner? The answer is not simple, because of the financial resources, intended use and old-versus-new preferences of the potential buyer.

Obviously a first-time Ferrari for someone who struggles to justify spending $25,000 for his dream car will be different from the Ferrari for someone who has $1,500,000 to spend on a toy that will sit next to all his other multi-million-dollar baubles.

But regardless of their financial situation, everyone starts somewhere. I've broken the market into six segments, ranging from "You're better off buying a Honda S2000 (i.e. under $25,000)" to the ultimate price tier, what I'll call "My daddy was Bill Gates' personal trainer," or, "The Sultan of Brunei is my uncle."

UNDER $25,000

For less than $25,000, our first-time owner has few options. A very nice 308 GT4 is the choice for those who can live with the cheesewedge-in-search-of-a-mouse Bertone styling. A decent 308 GTBi or GTSi, hopefully one that isn't ingesting a few quarts of oil every 100 miles, is the choice for those who still remember watching *Magnum P.I.* and want a car everyone knows is a Ferrari. If you must have a V12, can live with the "Fiat on steroids" Pininfarina styling and think that having back seats for children is a neat idea, a 365/4 2+2 or a 400 is your choice.

The V12 365/4 2+2 and 400 will be by far the most costly to maintain, the 308 GTB or GTS will offer the most ego strokes and the 308 GT4 is the most fun to drive, as it can be tossed around like a go-kart.

Be aware that with these bargain basement Ferraris, nearly every one will be a study in deferred maintenance, making a pre-purchase inspection mandatory.

I'VE GOT $75K TO SPEND

For up to $75,000, for those who want a V12, we get into the old-versus-new debate of a 330 GTC, 365 2+2 or a 365 GTC/4 versus a 456 GT. Perhaps I'm on the wrong side of 50, but for me the 456 offers comfort and performance far beyond the earlier cars. But the verdict is far from in. To quote David Miller, an *SCM*er from Toronto who e-mailed me this morning, "I prefer the understated styling of the 330 GTC vs. the 456, which kind of screams 'It's a Ferrari!'"

Let he who writes the check make the choice. For V8 fans, the best choice is a late-series 1994-95 348 Spyder. The many problems that plagued the early 348s were resolved by the time the final cars were built.

BUDDY, CAN YOU SPARE $150,000?

Bumping the ante to $150,000, we once again confront the old-versus-new choices of a 365 GTB/4 Daytona versus its modern incarnation, a 550 Maranello.

Buyers are generational, as almost every Daytona buyer is over 40, while the 550, a far more user-friendly car, attracts both the seasoned Ferrari veteran and the prancing-horse newbie. Daytona buyers tend to think the raucous exhaust, heavy low-speed steering and feeble air conditioning (like three mice breathing across an ice cube)

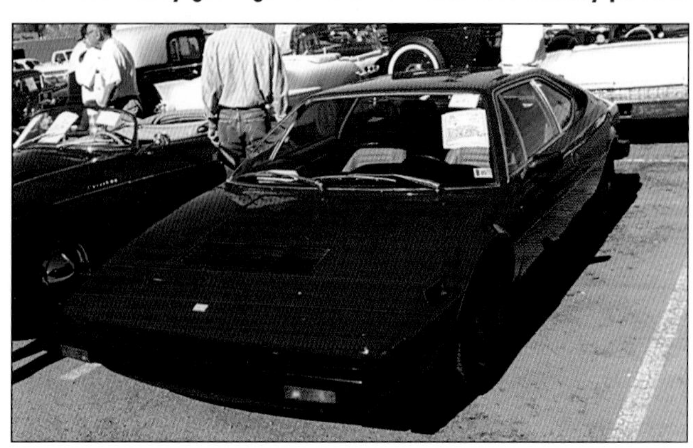

308 GT4: Cheesewedge in search of a mouse.

is their dream come true. 550 owners simply expect that their cars will be at least as reliable and easy to live with as a Honda Accord, except with more expensive tune-up bills. New Ferraris are much better cars than old Ferraris, but are they really better? That's a question best discussed late at night, over a few bottles of cult California cabernets.

One fact is beyond dispute. Good Daytonas simply won't be getting any cheaper, and in fact seem to be on an upswing. 550s, as new as they are, are still depreciating and are going to do so for the next decade.

For those who want a V8, the choices are simple: a 355 Berlinetta or Spyder or a 360 Berlinetta. There's no lack of low-mileage US-model 360 Berlinettas available at under $150,000.

HOW ABOUT HALF A MIL?

Up to $500,000 we are into 275 GTB/4 and 365 GTS/4 Daytona Spyder territory for those who prefer the old cars, and F40s and 550 Barchettas for those want something modern. Value-wise, 275 GTB/4s, Daytona Spyders and F40s have all gone up in value recently. On the other hand, thanks to 30 Euro-model 550 Barchettas being released by the EPA in a 60-day period, all hitting the market at the same time, their values are still sliding downwards.

All of these but the Barchettas are blue-chip collectibles and will garner a prominent position at any Ferrari gathering they are brought to. The 550, as an inventory-clearing special, is still struggling to find its proper valuation in the marketplace.

OKAY, JUST TAKE MY MILLION

A checkbook that has room for six zeros puts us into a serious Ferrari collector car category. Only two "new" cars fall into this very rarified class: F50s and, for those lucky enough to have been on the "A" list, a new Enzo.

Both these new-generation cars have performance that will make an F-16 pilot feel at home, should be relatively easy to live with and have a fairly sustainable market value. However, they will never achieve the status of the '50s and '60s dual-purpose Ferraris that were driven on the street and then raced. The early cars cut their teeth in fierce competition, and their exploits have become legendary. The newer cars are better in every way, except that they are really just F1 poseurs, cars that can go faster and stop better than you can imagine—but for what purpose?

As for collector cars around the million-dollar mark, the appreciation of the Euro has priced some of my favorites out of that category. Last year, I know a fellow who was looking for Mille Miglia-eligible cars (built prior to 1958 and with period history) and picked up a 500 TRC and an 857 Monza. Another acquaintance of mine snagged a 250 TdF and a 250 SWB. All of these cars were under $1,000,000.

But all of these cars have seen 20-percent-plus appreciation in the last six months, through currency swings alone. Today, a first-time million-dollar spender is limited to the coach-built cars such as a 410 or 400 Superamerica or Superfast, or perhaps the 166, 195, 212 or 225. Toss in a 250 alloy Boano with some race history for good measure. The serious racer's choices are limited to a 512 BB LM or, perhaps, a 1965 short-nose 275 GTB/2 "Cliente Competizione."

MY UNCLE IS THE SULTAN OF BRUNEI

It's a little strange to think of a novice collector spending millions of dollars on a car, but we see similar phenomena all the time in the art market. The *nouveaux riche* go to their first auction and buy everything in the catalog that's by a famous painter, just to be able to lord it over their friends. I personally know several collectors, recently rich and recently into cars, who simply tell their brokers, "Get me the best." They are often more interested in having bragging rights at Warren Buffet's next Sun Valley get-together than how their cars actually perform; they're collecting famous Ferraris the way entomologists acquire rare insects and skewer them to a display board.

You too can have a 250 TR, if your uncle's the Sultan.

The hot-button cars for rich collectors today, and this category includes veteran buyers as well as first-timers, are the super-good-history.—*Michael Sheehan*

From the October 2003 issue of *SCM*.◆

Of 13-hp BMWs And 310-hp Ferraris

The 743-cc, 13-horsepower flathead-four engine on my children's 1930 BMW DA-2 Kabriolet is far removed from the 3,432-cc, 310-horsepower double-overhead-cam-four engine of a 1956 Ferrari 860 Monza. And most likely, all four of the BMW's cable-operated drum brakes, each the size of a teacup saucer, would fit handily within a single Grand-Prix-bred brake drum of the Monza that RM sold for over $2 million.

Be that as it may, I must confess that, for the first time, Ferraris weren't the first things on my mind during the Monterey weekend. I entered my kids' BMW into the Pebble Beach Concours and served as their all-in-one driver, mechanic and detailer for a glorious three days.

Mick and Colleen, my 11-year-old twins, enjoyed the 50 mile, uphill and downhill Pebble Beach tour; they were constantly turning around in their seats, amazed at how both the ancient Bentleys and Rolls, as well as the modern Suburbans and Durangos, towered above them. I drove the car flat-out the whole way, which meant, of course, that moms pushing strollers would leave me in their dust when the stoplight turned green.

On Sunday, Colleen, with Mick as her riding mechanic, drove the BMW across the ramp and onto the podium at Pebble, where they collected their third-in-class prize at the concours. I know it's a dad thing, but I must say that watching the two of them, in the little classic, brought me more personal pleasure than anything I had done in my previous 29 years attending the events of the Monterey weekend. Watching Colleen and Mick in the little BMW, collecting their trophy and ribbon, was a once-in-a-lifetime experience.

Of course, I couldn't help but make the rounds of the auctions while I was there. That's a "car-guy" thing, and I'm sure you understand. There were plenty of Ferraris offered during the weekend and, for the most part, they all achieved market prices. While Bonhams & Butterfields' August 15 Quail Lodge auction offered a handful of Ferraris, only two sold. The 250 Pininfarina Series II cabriolet, S/N 3311—which needed everything—sold at $135,000, which seemed high to me given its condition, and the 275 GTS, S/N 7337—which was just a nice old used car—sold at $157,500, fair enough.

Mick & Collen Sheehan

The RM auction had a total of 13 Ferraris, and they got some strong money. A 250 Pininfarina Series II cabriolet, S/N 3407, that was nicely restored brought a surprising $258,501, a demonstration that these early open cars have been too cheap for too long. An alloy-bodied 275 GTB/4, S/N 9609, brought a surprising $621,500—I wonder how long it will be before we see one return to the million-dollar values of 1989. I was surprised when a 288 GTO S/N 56343 sold at $279,400—once million-dollar cars as well, they've been a tough sell the past few years above $250,000.

Of course, the big gun of the weekend was the 860 Monza, S/N 0604, that brought $2,057,001.

While that is a hell of a lot of money in anyone's book, the 860 Monza is a hell of a lot of car, being one of three built. As a factory team car, it won the 1956 Sebring 12-hours race, driven by Fangio and Castelotti, then was sold to Von Neumann and campaigned extensively by Phil Hill in the US. Important enough to be featured in the May 1996 issue of *Road & Track* magazine, 0604 has always commanded a premium price and was last publicly offered in Switzerland in 1999 at $1,800,000. Add in that the new owner is a Dutch antique dealer, who is buying in dollars but paying in Euros, gaining an immediate 10% discount. This is a new world-record price for a four-cylinder Ferrari, but I would have to call this price market correct, and I predict this car will see considerable appreciation during the next five years. It's just too cheap compared to the minimum $6,000,000 or so that a 12-cylinder 250 TR will set you back. But even though the Monza set a new record, it's still definitely not 1989 again. For instance, 330 Michelotti S/N 9083, a one-off targa conversion based on a 330 2+2 chassis, brought $143,000 at RM. Yes, that's plenty for a 330 rebody. But on the other hand, it's nowhere near the $1,800,000 I am told was turned down for the car when it was on the lawn at Pebble, in August of 1989.

Of course, the weekend ended with Christie's, where three Ferraris sold. 330 GTC S/N 11517, in nicely restored condition, brought $156,000, all the money for a non-trophy-winning GTC. A 246 GTS, S/N 5480, brought $105,750, which, for this car, was full retail and then some. Of course, enthusiasts of means don't come to Monterey looking for a bargain, and when they see a bauble they like, they just snap it up. I didn't see many marked-up *SCM* Price Guides in the lounges of the Gulfstream GIVs, Dassault Falcon 2000s and Boeing 737 business jets parked at the Monterey jet center, and I doubt that the new owner of the Dino cares what I think about what he paid. And more power to him.

The sale of the 365 California Spyder, S/N 9889, at $634,500 was proof that auctions do indeed sometimes get "all the money." Of course, even the amount this car sold for is far less than the $1,000,000 that was offered for a very similar car in 1989.

Overall, the lessons offered by this weekend were the same ones we've been seeing the past few years. The market for production GT Ferraris such as a quality 250 PF cabriolet, 330 GTC or 246 continues to rise. Cars with questions will not bring anywhere near the silly prices the same cars brought in the late 1980s, simply because the buyers are far more sophisticated end users, not speculators.

This weekend, it wasn't a Ferrari that elicited the "where-did-that-bid-come-from" prize of the weekend. That went to the 2005 Ford GT sold by Christie's, bought by former Microsoft President Jon Shirley, for three times the projected MSRP, a staggering $557,500. But you know what? The proceeds of the sale above the reserve went to charity, and I don't think Mr. Shirley is particularly worried about his financial position being affected if his GT doesn't hold 100% of its value over the next decade.—*Michael Sheehan*

From the November 2002 issue of *SCM*.◆

Close Doesn't Count

Dear SCM: *I read Mike Sheehan's column in the February issue (page 27) with interest. I would like to enlighten Mr. Sheehan that the 365 Boxer, which he "presumes" sold to the trade, was in fact purchased by a private American (yes, there were others present whom Mr. Sheehan missed). The 246 Dino at $45,000 was by no means cheap for Europe and if the French purchaser thinks he can resell it for $75,000, I wish him luck.*

I also disagree with Mr. Sheehan's comment that the Mondial, 208, 308s and Testarossas were sold for wholesale prices. In fact, only the white Testarossa was purchased by a dealer who bravely outbid several private individuals.

As for the Superfast, this car was sold within the pre-sale estimate, and was indeed flawless, so I was amused to see two lesser cars optimistically advertised in the FML *for $100,000 more. I am not aware of a 500 SF selling at auction for more than the car in Gstaad in recent years.*

As for the 250 GTO, no self-respecting auction house could pass up the chance to sell a car like this. We gave it our best and achieved a genuine record bid, the highest made in a classic car auction in over ten years. If the GTO did not change hands, I think this can be put down as much to world economic uncertainty in the days preceding the sale as anything else. If there had been a bidder present willing to go to $10 million, as Sheehan suggests, was he handcuffed? Sorry, but the logic doesn't add up. I am pleased to say that we are still negotiating to sell the car.

Finally, the ex-Jo Schlesser 250 GT Interim Berlinetta was sold by us shortly after the auction and will be going to an appreciative new home in the UK.—***Simon Kidston, President, Bonhams & Brooks Europe S.A.***

I still maintain that the 246 GT ($45,479), the 365 BB ($53,508) and the Superfast ($265,741) sold below world market rates. Putting on my private treaty hat, in the past few months I have sold cars very similar to those cars for more money.

For example, the Superfast you offered, S/N 6043 SF, was a magnificent example. Like you, "I am not aware of a Superfast selling for more in recent years." However, on August 5, 2000, I sold S/N 6039 SF, a comparable Superfast, for well over $100,000 more than the price achieved in your sale and believe I have several American buyers, who were obviously not at Gstaad, who would have paid more for your car. Perhaps they will now be motivated to attend your Monaco sale.

As for the 250 GTO, the high bidder is a collector well known to both of us, who sincerely wanted the car. I believe he knew that there was no real money against him at his highest bid, and wasn't going to be swayed by a chandelier.

It is a simple law of economics that as prices go higher, as they have in the last five years, the pool of potential buyers shrinks. Combined with world economic uncertainly and the lack of a second buyer to bid the price up, the GTO did not sell. You did indeed "give it your best and achieved a genuine record bid," but close only counts in horseshoes and hand grenades.—*Michael Sheehan*

From the April 2002 issue of *SCM*.◆

Low-Buck Horsies

These cars were designed at a time when kidnapping was rampant in Italy and ostentatious displays of wealth were out...bland and discreet were in, although bland may be too exciting a word to use

Like locusts, e-mails seeking advice about entry-level Ferraris descend daily. Each time *SCM* reports on a 400i or Mondial 8 selling for under $20,000, readers check their Visa card limits and start fantasizing about having a Prancing Horse in their driveway.

It is possible to own a Ferrari for less than $20,000. Of course, you must first forsake a few minor items such as reliability, working air conditioning and low maintenance. In exchange, you get all the cams, pistons and repair bills that go with a "real" Ferrari.

For those who like V8s and can live with offbeat styling, the 308 GT4 and the Mondial are hard to beat. Thousands were made so examples of both can easily be found for under $25k. They are advertised and available virtually anywhere on the planet. Any good mechanic can check them out and give you a detailed mechanical inspection report and any decent body shop can give you a detailed body and "has-it-been-crashed/is it rusty" analysis.

The 1974-79 308 GT4, with 2,826 built, offers great handling, a splitting-wedge style recognizable to most as a Ferrari, adequate driver and passenger comfort, rear seats suitable for very small dogs, a great engine sound, decent luggage storage, perfunctory A/C and heating, and, in the world of Ferraris, low maintenance. They also handle very well and are among the fastest of the carbureted 308 series because of low gearing, bigger cams and limited smog equipment.

The smog issue is a serious one. If you live in an area where a GT4 would have to pass a smog test, only buy a car from your area, with its emissions-equipment intact, and that has recently passed its test. Most GT4s have had their air-injection pumps and thermal reactors removed; finding used equipment, repairing, installing and tuning it can easily be a $5,000 project. And even then you might not please the sniffer.

The 308 GT4 has four Weber carbs and two distributors. A major service is $4,000, a clutch will be $2,000, an engine overhaul in the $20,000 range and a transmission overhaul around $8,000.

The very best Series III 308 GT4s with improved A/C and (usually) a sunroof are below $25,000. Nasty cars will bring $15,000, so you do the math.

If you opt for the 1983-85 Mondial QV Coupe, you'll pay another $5,000. You'll also get improved performance, less chance of a smoky engine and longer engine life due to the improved German-made pistons and rings used on the four-valve engine. A total of 1,848 Mondial QV Coupes were built, making them relatively easy to find in the resale market.

If you prefer the sound, torque and power of a V12, and live in an area with emission testing, your best econo-Ferrari choice is the fuel-injected 1980-84 400i. Its predecessors, the carbureted 1976-80 400 GT 2+2 and the 1972-76 365 GT4 2+2 are much faster, but also much more difficult to tune and smog. These cars were designed at a time when kidnapping was rampant in Italy and ostentatious displays of wealth were out. Bland and discreet were in, although bland may be too exciting a word to use for the lines of the 400 series 2+2s.

The automatics are pigs; the three-speed GM transmission has a first gear that is much too tall for adequate acceleration and a final drive that's too short for any kind of high-speed cruising. The five-speed manuals are much faster, as the low first gear offers the acceleration you expect in a Ferrari and fifth gear will provide effortless cruising that can only be used in Europe or Montana.

Boring everywhere except behind the wheel.

Maintenance on the 400i, aside from the $4,000 tune-ups, $10,000 valve jobs and $25,000 engine overhauls, is high. These models are afflicted with a never-ending list of minor problems, including oil coolers that crack and have to be replaced at $1,000 each, and mufflers that hang too low and get ripped off on speed bumps.

The 400i does offer much improved front seat comfort and leg and headroom over the 308 GT4 and Mondial, back seats that will accommodate those with legs almost 18 inches in length, luggage space adequate for any trip and effortless torque and performance.

My pick of the sub-$20,000 group is the five-speed 400i, unless you live in an emissions-exempt area, in which case I would go with a carbureted 365 or 400, also with a manual gearbox. Many years ago in the mid-1970s, I purchased one of the first 365 GT4 2+2s in the country and picked it up at Bob Wallace's shop in Phoenix. As luck would have it, the California Highway Patrol had chosen, for the only time in its history, to go on strike and I chose that weekend to drive the Ferrari from Phoenix to Orange County.

I can remember cruising effortlessly at 125 mph, glorying in the sound of the 12-cylinder engine. The A/C was more than adequate in the hot Arizona and California desert, visibility was terrific, and even a sustained four-hour blast above 100 mph wasn't tiring. This all goes to show that there is no direct correlation between how much a car costs and how much fun it can be.

I assume that most readers of *SCM* feel life is too short to drive Hondas, at least on the weekends. A psychiatrist would probably find that we all share a hormonal imbalance that allows us to accept and even look forward to the inherent irrationality of owning a Ferrari. Worse, we know that owning one on a budget is even crazier, yet still we yearn.

Buying a cheap Ferrari is like walking through a minefield. If you are very, very careful, and very, very lucky, you will buy a great car for not much money, drive it for a few years, and sell it before any type of major service is due. These cars are cheap precisely because their repair and maintenance bills are so horrendous. Who wants to buy a 400i for $20,000 that needs a $25,000 engine overhaul?

If you're clever, your neighbors will refer to you as "the guy up the street who must have won the lottery because he's driving a Ferrari." If you're not, they'll remember you as "the guy who used to live up the street but ended up selling his house because his Ferrari needed a new engine."—*Michael Sheehan*

From the October 2001 issue of *SCM*.◆

Thumbs Up for the Lusso

Three years ago, you couldn't give a Lusso away. Now great Lussos are bringing two and three times as much as Daytonas

The Ferrari market is a fluid animal, with both classic and modern cars moving in and out of favor. Here's my current read on where the action is.

The flavor of the month is definitely the 250 Lusso. Three years ago, you couldn't give a Lusso away. Now great Lussos are bringing two and three times as much as Daytonas. For example, Bonhams sold a competition-prepared Lusso, S/N 5367GT, with period TdF history, for $424,362 at Gstaad in December of last year. At the same event, a concours-condition street Lusso, S/N 5303GT, sold for $235,897. The two Daytona coupes that sold brought $93,958 and $102,632.

There's a reason for this popularity. The Lusso shares the same engine, transmission, brakes and suspension as the "street"-model 250 SWB. Because it is eligible for the many rallies and touring events now so popular in Europe, the Lusso has become the "alternative" to the 250 SWB, without the million-dollar-plus price.

While the Lusso may weigh 100 kilos more than a steel-bodied 250 SWB, it has a superior Watts-link rear suspension, evolved directly from the 250 GTO. Consequently, a well-prepared Lusso is comparable in performance with a steel-bodied 250 SWB on the track. Further, in my eyes the Lusso is more attractive than the 250 SWB.

With the Euro up more than 25% against the dollar during the past few months, it is not surprising that the few Lussos that come on the market in the US are finding their way to the other side of the Atlantic. And as always, while top cars are bringing top prices, the rustbuckets and Bondobarges are still stuck in the Ferrari dog pound, unsellable at nearly any price.

Demand for the 246 GT and GTS continues to be strong. Their timeless styling, comfortable yet race-car-like cockpits, light steering, braking and shifting all combine with an engine that sounds more powerful than it is. Because the 246 series gives a great illusion of performance and speed, it makes every trip to the grocery store seem like a practice session for Le Mans, without the fear of speeding tickets.

The Dino downside is that these cars are now 30-plus years old and are the poster children for deferred maintenance and the need for a detailed mechanical and body inspection as part of the purchase agreement. Simply put, the older the Ferrari, the greater the need for a thorough inspection.

While Dinos haven't gotten back to the world-record $250,000 paid for one in Monterey during the boom, it's not surprising to see a very nice GTS with chairs and flares come near the $100,000 mark. Coupes are just not very popular in the US, even if they drive better, and seem to move in the $60,000-$70,000 range, again for superb examples. It appears that Dinos will always be high on the list of Ferrari collectibles, and buying one today, even at full market prices, may seem like a shrewd move in 24 months.

The 456 GT and the 550 Maranello are getting close to bargain-basement pricing. A 1995 456 now sells for as little as $75,000, while 550s can be found for $125,000. Both the 456 and the 550 offer state-of-the-art supercar performance and creature comforts for what is, in the Ferrari world, low pricing, especially when compared with their MSRPs ($207,000 for the 456, $208,000 for the 550).

The downside? No question these cars are close to fully depreciated, but … how close? We thought that TRs were cheap at $65,000, and now look at them. Which brings us to…

The 512 BB at $65,000 and the Testarossa at $50,000 have failed the test of time as collectibles. While they are user-friendly and practical to use on a daily basis, and remain the high-performance bargains in the Ferrari world (selling for less than a 246 GT or GTS), no one seems to care.

Of course, while the price of entry may be low, both normal and deferred maintenance can make these supercar bargains into money pits, as the cost of an engine may exceed 50% of the value of the car. If you have to have one of these, buy only a perfect car, and sell it before the next major service comes due.

Lussos are king of the flavor-of-the-month club.

Boxers are still a high-performance bargain, but does anyone care?

A great car for sunny Texas, but questionable in drizzly Seattle.

The award for chasing the market down seems to go to the dozen or so die-hards who continue to advertise Euro 550 Barchettas at prices up to (and even over) $300,000, or US-spec 550 Barchettas at prices over $300,000.

While the 550 Barchetta may be gorgeous when topless, its impractical and very-hard-to-operate folding top makes it less than user-friendly on anything but a sunny day. Then add in the many US model 550 Barchettas on the market and the many soon-to-finally-be-legalized Euro cars about to become available here (another case of speculators seeing higher prices in the US, but by the time their cars have cleared all the necessary importation hurdles, the market here has begun to sag to near-European levels). The correct market price today for a US Barchetta, in my opinion, is a more modest $275,000, while a Euro car would be hard-pressed, once releases were in finally in hand, to bring $245,000.—*Michael Sheehan*

From the May 2003 issue of *SCM*.◆

Ferrari vs. Lamborghini, The Early Years

Ever since the 350GT made its debut in 1964, the Lambo vs. Ferrari comparisons, contrasts and late-night heated discussions have been never-ending

Ferruccio Lamborghini made his first fortune building tractors, and his second producing heating appliances. At age 47 he set out to amass yet another fortune by designing, building and selling the ultimate grand touring auto. Thumbing his nose at Ferrari, located only 40 kilometers down the road, was an extra bonus.

Ever since the 350 GT debuted in 1964, the Lambo vs. Ferrari comparisons, contrasts and late-night heated discussions have been never-ending.

1963 Ferrari 250 GT/L Lusso vs. 1967 Lamborghini 350 GT

Classic Lamborghinis fall into two categories: the early front-engined cars, the 350 GT, 400 2+2 and Espada; and the first two mid-engined supercars, the Miura and the Countach, in all their various incarnations.

The comparable Ferraris from the same period start with the 250 Lusso and go through the Testarossa. While primarily a Ferrari guy, I've driven and owned my share of Lambos, and here's my take on how they stack up against each other, apples to apples (rigatoni to rigatoni?) as much as possible.

We begin with the 1964 350 GT and its logical Ferrari counterpart, the 250 GT Lusso. The Lambo is clearly the technological winner, equipped with a 320-hp, four-cam V12, six two-barrel Webers, ZF five-speed, alloy body, fully independent suspension and a dual booster brake system. The Lusso had only a twin-cam 3.0-liter V12, three Webers, a four-speed tranny, and a steel body. Output was a meager 250 hp.

When new, the Ferrari outsold the 350 GT, 350 to 131. Having owned and driven both, the 350 GT is faster and more comfortable. But the market looks at things differently. A best-in-the-world 350 might get to $135,000, while the equivalent Lusso is going to come close to $275,000.

Why? The Lamborghini's styling is not inspired, with a kind of "dumpling on a pancake" look to the greenhouse/body combination that has not stood the test of time. On the other hand, the Lusso has always been regarded as having singularly elegant styling. Despite being slower, the Lusso offers a more spirited driving experience, and produces the legendary V12 sound that conjures up images of Ferrari's unmatched racing heritage.

Skipping past the 400, which was really just the 350 with tiny back seats added in a meaningless attempt to broaden its market appeal, Lamborghini's next evolutionary leap was the Miura. Introduced in 1966, it was built as the P400 from 1966 to 1970, as the Miura S from 1970 to 1971 and the SV from 1971 to 1973.

The Miura was a visual and technological tour de force, and instantly made every other supercar on the planet obsolete. It had drop-dead gorgeous good looks, a lightweight monocoque "tub," and a highly sophisticated sidewinder 4-liter engine with six Webers that produced 385 hp at 7,850 rpm. All up, with fluids, the Miura weighs in at only 2,800 pounds.

While the S had some improvements over the P400, it was the SV that represented the ultimate incarnation. It featured a much stiffer chassis, a split sump to separate the previously co-mingled engine oil from the transmission oil, and vented disc brakes. It also had nine-inch wide rear wheels encompassed by larger rear fender flares, all in an effort to keep the back end from passing the front, not an uncommon occurrence for Miura drivers whose enthusiasm exceeded their talents.

(Note: Over time, Miuras have become known for setting themselves on fire. The carburetors are mounted directly above the spark plugs, and leak if the floats stick. Thus fuel spills directly onto the hot cylinder heads, leading to instant toasted bull.)

Just as the SV was the best Miura, the Daytona was the most highly developed front-engined V12 Ferrari of the period, making a comparison between the two appropriate.

The Daytona is much heavier at 3,600 pounds, less powerful at 352 hp, sits much higher, and is certainly more subtle in its styling. However, once again the Ferrari outsold the Lambo, 1,279 units to 762 (all Miura models).

Obviously, the entire Miura series was technically more sophisticated, in theory faster, and certainly made a bolder statement than the Daytona. But Miuras suffered from poor build quality, redefined the term "instant rust," are ultra-high maintenance, and lack the panache imbued by the Ferrari racing heritage.

Furthermore, I have never found enough road or courage to begin to find the top speed claimed for any of the Miuras; their reputation for extreme front-end lift at triple-digit speeds has reportedly led to many white-knuckle experiences. I can assure you that the Daytona will walk away from a Miura SV under acceleration.

But while Daytonas may have sold better when new, the SV is clearly the current market winner. A Miura P400 will cost $75,000 to $100,000; a Miura S, $100,000 to $150,000; and

1971 Lamborghini Miura P400 S vs. 1971 Ferrari 365 GTB/4 Daytona

an SV $200,000 to $250,000. Daytonas sell in the $125,000 to $150,000 range. The high value of the SV is partly due to its limited production, with just 150 built, but mostly because its Gandini design will always be regarded as a landmark.

The last of the classic Lambos is the Countach, produced in a variety of versions from 1974 to 1989. It is appropriately compared to the 1974-89 Boxer, and the first-generation Testarossa (1985-91).

1988 Ferrari Boxer vs. 1988 Lamborghini Countach

Once again, when unveiled the Countach was a technical and styling tour de force, although it quickly grew visually cluttered with wings and in the U.S., federal bumpers. The Boxer and even the Testarossa are more conservative mechanically and stylistically. Ferrari won the sales race, selling 3,623 Boxers and over 6,000 Testarossas, while just under 2,000 Countachs left the factory.

While it may seem strange to call a Boxer "user-friendly," in fact the Miura and Countach are both so user-cruel that the Boxer seems like a Mercedes S-Class by comparison. The Lambos are sometimes referred to as 45-minute cars, meaning that before an hour is up, the driver wants out. The three-quarter and rear vision from a Countach is a joke; backing up a Countach is an exercise left to the young and limber, as the driver must open the door, sit on the sill, turn backwards and aim while balancing himself, the gas and the brakes.

Should I even mention that the Countach styling is so outrageous that you feel like a drug dealer the minute you get behind the wheel?

While the Miura and the Countach may spec out better than the Boxer or Testarossa, in real life the Ferraris simply walk away from the Lambos. And the Ferraris are supported by a far more extensive dealer and parts network. Need a clutch in your Boxer or Testarossa? Figure on $3,500 to $4,500. For your Countach, that'll be $10,000 to $12,000. Lamborghini ownership is not for the faint of heart, nor thin of wallet.

Today Boxers sell in the $65,000-$95,000 range, and Testarossas in the $50,000-$65,000 range. Countachs are worth slightly more, with 25th Anniversary Editions bringing close to $100,000 if you find the right buyer on the right day.

So if you're looking for a car that says "look at me," the Miura or the Countach are the ticket. If you actually want to use your exotic—as opposed to visiting it in its dedicated service bay at your local shop—or if you enjoy a few hot laps at the next sports car club track day, I'd stick with the prancing horse.

Next month we'll continue our look at raging bull vs. prancing horse with "From the Diablo to the Present: Multiple Management Shuffles and the Germans Now Run the Show."
—*Michael Sheehan*

From the March 2004 issue of *SCM*.◆

Ferrari vs. Lamborghini, Part II: Lambo Closes the Gap

There's no question that the recent infusion of German technology has been nothing but good

Okay, Lambo fanatics, enough! My mailbox is already overflowing with nastiness about last month's column comparing early Lamborghinis with the equivalent Ferraris. Your passionate defenses notwithstanding, I still maintain that while, from a technical perspective, Lamborghinis were usually more sophisticated than their Ferrari counterparts, in the real world of actually using your exotic, the early Lamborghinis were user-cruel, high-maintenance monsters.

The Testarossa vs. Diablo battle turned the table on Ferrari.

We're going to pick up last month's analysis starting after the turmoil of the 1970s, when Lamborghini passed out of the hands of founder Ferruccio Lamborghini. Through the mid-1980s, the firm was relatively stable, but the need for an all-new product line with major technological and production improvements made it obvious that a financially strong partner was needed. To that end, Chrysler purchased Lamborghini on April 23, 1987, with the clear intent to produce an all-new supercar that would put Lamborghini ahead of its annoying neighbor down the road in Maranello.

Countach production for Europe and Japan ended in May 1990, and the next generation Lamborghini, the all-new Diablo, was unveiled. It was fitted with a 5.7-liter V12 pumping out 485 horsepower, an improved cockpit, softer lines, and the now traditional up-swinging doors. For the first time, a Lamborghini was a "real" supercar—user-friendly, fast, and more subdued than the flashier Ferrari Testarossa.

Over time, the market has voted for the Diablo, valuing a 1991 Diablo at about $90,000, while a 1991 Testarossa sells for about $60,000.

In 1992, Ferrari introduced the 512 TR to better compete. It featured a stiffer chassis and improved brakes, and the engine management system was changed from the Bosch CIS to the superior Motronic 2.7. Today the two cars are market equals, with a 1992 Diablo and 1992 512 TR both worth about $100,000.

Downside to the early Diablo? Clutches *might* last 10,000 miles, but expect 5,000 or less. Replacement will lighten your wallet by $9,000, as it is an engine-out service. A clutch on your Testarossa or 512 TR should easily make 15,000 miles and will set you back only $3,500 to $4,500 to replace. And while the Ferrari needs a 30,000-mile service (at $5,000), the Diablo needs a 15,000-mile service (about $4,000). Of course, you will probably be in for clutch work long before that, so while the engine is out, you may as well get the service done early!

Diablo sales peaked in 1991, the first year of production, and only continual updates helped the model survive. In March 1993, the Diablo VT with all-wheel drive was introduced, equipped with an adjustable suspension, larger front brake scoops, a new double-row cam chain, an improved mechanical chain tensioner, and many minor improvements.

In 1995 Ferrari countered with the much-improved and restyled 512M, narrowing the gap, but clearly leaving Lamborghini as technological leader. Interestingly enough, both the 1994-95 Diablo VT and the 1995 512M have a market value of about $135,000.

In 1994 Lamborghini presented the Diablo SE (Special Edition) to celebrate its 30th anniversary. Equipped with two-wheel drive, many carbon fiber parts, and less sound-deadening material, only 26 cars were built for the U.S. market, making the SE one of the more collectable Lamborghinis.

In the same year, Chrysler Corporation agreed to sell Automobili Lamborghini to an Indonesian consortium, which, over the next eight years continued to "evolve" the Diablo. This led to a series of exclusive limited-edition models, including the Diablo SV from 1997-99; the Diablo VT Roadster from 1996-2000; the Diablo VT 6.0, built from 2000-01; and the carbon-fiber-bodied Diablo VT 6.0 SE in 2001. Each became flashier and faster, and the Diablo continued to be the supercar of choice for rock stars and sports celebrities.

Ferrari went in a different direction, returning to front-engine technology and more subdued styling with the introduction of the 550 Maranello in 1996. While direct performance comparisons are hard to make, a 1997 Diablo SV and a 1997 550 will both bring about $125,000, while a 2001 Diablo VT 6.0 and a 2001 550 Maranello will both bring about $160,000.

Over eleven years, Diablo production topped over 3,000 units in various forms, while Ferrari built about 2,280 512 TRs, about 515 512Ms, and about 3,600 550s in the same time period, for a total of 6,400 more-or-less market-equivalent Ferraris.

Audi entered the picture on July 24, 1998, when an agreement between the shareholders of Lamborghini was reached that ultimately led to Audi s complete take-over of the "Italian" firm. Hundreds of German engineers, technicians, designers and managers went south with the intent of building a new "large" Lamborghini and an all-new "small" car to keep up with Ferrari.

Introduced as a 2002 model, the Lamborghini Murcielago (the large car) continues the traditional gull-wing doors and mid-mounted V12, with an all-new six-speed gearbox mounted in front of the engine and a rear-mounted differential with full-time four-wheel drive. Continuing Lamborghini's exotic one-upsmanship, all external bodywork panels are carbon fiber, with the exception of the steel roof and door panels.

The Murcielago's dry-sump V12 is 6192 cc and delivers 580 horsepower, thanks to a variable-geometry intake system and

Mainline Ferrari styling is becoming more conservative.

variable valve timing. Additionally, the Murcielago features a drive-by-wire electronic throttle control and "active" traction control. With a 0-to-60 mph time of 3.8 seconds and a top speed of just over 200 mph, the Murcielago is indeed a supercar.

Creature comforts are improved over the Diablo by widening the door-opening angle and lowering the side member directly under the door by almost ten inches. Interior room has also been improved by redesigning the roof side members and increasing the size of the footwell.

Priced at $280,000 when new in 2002, a low-mileage Murcielago will bring about $220,000 today, normal depreciation for a "production" super-exotic.

For 2004, Lamborghini has introduced its all-new "small" car, the Gallardo, aimed directly at Ferrari's 360 Modena. Audi/Lamborghini engineers chose to use a structural aluminum space frame for the baby Lambo, giving the car a dry weight of only 3,250 pounds. The permanent-all-wheel-drive Gallardo is powered by a mid-mounted 5-liter, dry-sump V10 producing some 500 horsepower and rocketing to a respectable 193 mph using a six-speed gearbox or the now *de rigeur* paddle shifter. Its 0-to-60 mph time is a staggering 4.2 seconds.

As expected, the Gallardo is higher tech than the 360 Modena, has 25 percent more horsepower (at 493), and an extra 101 pound-feet of torque (with 376). Curb weights are more or less the same, but top speed is 17 mph ahead of the 360. Lamborghini claims the Gallardo is an "everyday supercar" to be compared with a Porsche 911 Turbo as much as a 360 Modena, not just a toy for singles bar cruising. With a sticker price of $172,000 to $185,000, the Gallardo is currently selling at $5,000 to $10,000 over window sticker, a little more than a Modena coupe, but a bit back of the 360 Spyder.

In 2002, Lamborghini built 430 Murcielagos. With early delivery of the Gallardo to Europe, production for 2003 jumped to 1,025 cars. With its current facility and about 700 employees, Lamborghini can build 2,000 cars a year at most. Ferrari's 1,600-plus employees, current manufacturing facilities, and corporate "exclusivity" policy limit total production to just over 4,000 cars per year.

There's no question that over the past 14 years, Lamborghini has closed the gap with Ferrari, and the recent infusion of German technology has been nothing but good. After all, can you imagine a German putting up with an early Lambo's electrics?

While with supercars it's always been a case of, "you pay your money and you make your choices," at least today the choices between Ferrari and Lamborghini are both good ones. —*Michael Sheehan*

From the April 2004 issue of *SCM*.◆

Ferraris You're Guaranteed To Lose Money On

You can't buy a "barn find" for $20,000 and come out ahead, nor can you buy a beater that needs paint for $5,000 and end up a winner

Buy a Ferrari, drive it 10,000 miles and lose $20,000; I hope every one of those two-dollar miles was a great one.

In my position as a purveyor of vintage exotic automobiles (that's a classy way to say used-car salesman), I find myself answering questions all too often that have the words "Ferrari" and "investment" in the same sentence.

Ferraris should be bought for fun and pleasure, with any possible financial upside as a secondary consideration. After all, if you take the family for a ski vacation at Vail and it costs you $10,000, you don't expect to be able to sell the memories of your vacation for $15,000 a year later. If you buy a Ferrari, drive it 10,000 miles and lose $20,000, I would hope that every one of those two-dollar miles was a great one.

Some Ferraris are good financial investments. The 250 GT Lusso has doubled in value, from $125,000 to $250,000 in the past two years, and F40s have gone from a low of $225,000 five years ago to a current $300,000, which sure beats the stock market.

But most Ferraris are just used cars with a great exhaust sound and a horrendous cost of repair. Here are a few that, before you buy them, you might want to practice standing in the corner of your garage tearing up stacks of $100 bills, just to get a sense of what a part of the ownership experience will be like.

"Before you buy them, you might want to practice standing in the corner of your garage tearing up stacks of $100 bills, just to get a sense of what a part of the ownership experience will be like."

At the top of the depreciation list are any of the current production cars, with the exception of the Enzo. A 456M GT or 456M GTA has a window sticker of $240,000, but they can be bought new off the showroom floor today for $190,000 and will be worth $145,000 in less than two years—even less for an automatic or a model in an off color. They are closely followed by the 575M. MSRP today: $240,000. Value in 2006: $175,000 or less.

The newest 550 Maranellos are still dropping at the rate of about $15,000 a year while the 1997 550s are close to fully depreciated.

Modena 360 coupes are still sticker-plus items on the dealer floor. With an MSRP of about $175,000, they still bring a small premium of $5,000-$15,000, but in 2006 these same cars will be worth around $150,000.

Modena Spyders are still commanding a $35,000-plus premium above their $185,000 to $200,000 sticker, but I believe that will be less by the end of 2005. In 2006, I expect a low-miles 2004 Spyder to be selling in the $200,000 range, especially if Ferrari has announced a 360 replacement by then.

Simply put, if you buy a brand new Ferrari, it will depreciate more in the first year than most people make in twelve months. But that's all part of the joy of having a *Cavallino Rampante* in your garage.

The Fiat-era cars—the flat-12 365 BB, 512 BB and BBi, the V12 365 2+2, 400, 400i and 412, along with the V8 308s, 328s and Mondials—are fully depreciated. But many of

these cars are now studies in deferred maintenance and can quickly garner stratospheric repair bills. All scream for a detailed pre-purchase inspection. Buy the right car, lose $5,000 a year and be happy. Buy the wrong car and put your mechanic's kids through college. There is no upside on any of these cars, save for being fun for the first-time Ferrari buyer.

The pre-Fiat era cars, from the Daytonas back to the 250 2+2s or 250 coupes and Cabriolets, range in value from $35,000 for a four-headlight 330 2+2 to $8 million for a GTO. As a rule of thumb, the higher the market value of the car, the harder it is to go wrong. That's because the cost of doing a motor, say $35,000, is essentially the same in a nine-figure GTO as it is in a $50,000 250 GTE.

"The final car on my 'don't go there' list is the 1990-92 348 GTS. The successor to the much-loved 328, it had pathetically bland styling (the ultimate sin in an Italian car) and a host of mechanical problems."

Blow the motor in your GTO, and you can adopt a "What, me worry?" attitude. Puke a rod through the block in your 250 GTE and your best bet is to prowl the junkyards for a 350 Chevy V8.

The worst V12 on the list, financially, is the aforementioned 330 GT. Its four-headlight front end is visually challenged, and values are in the $50,000 range for best-in-the-world examples. You can't buy a "barn find" for $20,000 and come out ahead, nor can you buy a beater that needs paint for $5,000 and end up a winner. In fact, if you buy one that needs a major service for $30,000, you'll still be a loser compared to buying a perfect one.

I also caution staying away from 365 GT 2+2s. Yes, Ferrari fanatics refer to them as elegant cruisers but in fact they are heavy, almost ponderous cars with a bizarre, twin-alternator electrical system (on U.S. models) and a poorly designed load-leveling rear suspension that is best tossed out and replaced by Gabriel air shocks.

Asking prices are in the $50,000 plus range, so if you're worried about investment, frankly, you'd be much better off spending another $25,000 and getting a decent driver 330 GTC. That's a car that will always have a ready market.

The final car on my "don't go there" list is the 1990-92 348 GTS. The successor to the much-loved 328, it had pathetically bland styling (the ultimate sin in an Italian car) and a host of mechanical problems. Couple that with a $50,000 resale value at best, maintenance that never seems to end, and there's nowhere to go but down if you're thinking of buying one of these.

While some of the top-line pre-Fiat cars have appreciated tremendously over time, the only post Fiat cars that have appreciated are the 288 GTO, the F40, the F50 and the Enzos, as these cars are very limited-production, top-of-the-line "art-cars." The rest are just cars.—*Michael Sheehan*

From the 2004 issue of the *SCM Price Guide.*◆

The values below reflect a retail buying and selling range for cars in **very good to near excellent condition**—significantly above a "daily driver" and one step below regional concours; a strong #2 on the accepted 1-6 scale, 1 being the best. These values are set by **sales activity**, primarily in the United States, as well as conversations with owners, dealers and collectors. ***Condition and history are the ultimate determinants of value***. Prices below assume cars with "no stories attached." An automobile priced above our guide is not necessarily overpriced, nor is one priced below automatically a bargain.

The SCM Investment Grade is an A to F scale, which ranks the cars in terms of their long-term desirability. The scale ranges from A-Grade cars, great classics like the 250 GTOs and California Spyders, to F-Grade cars, hopeless sleds of which you'll find very few in the Ferrari marque.◆

FERRARI

	Yrs. Built	No. Made	Price Range Low	Price Range High	Grade	Rating	1 Yr. % Change
166 Spyder Corsa	47-48	8	$900,000	$1,200,000	A	★★★★	20%
166 MM Berlinetta	48-50	12	$1,100,000	$1,400,000	A	★★★★	47%
166 MM Barchetta	48-50	25	$1,100,000	$1,600,000	A	★★★★	n/c
166 Inter	48-51	28	$200,000	$295,000	B	★★★	n/c
195 Inter	50-52	19	$200,000	$295,000	B	★★★	n/c
340 America Closed	51	12	$350,000	$1,000,000	A	★★★★	64%
340 America Open	51	13	$400,000	$550,000	A	★★★★	n/c
340 Mexico	52	4	$1,200,000	$1,400,000	A	★★★★	n/c
342 America Berlinetta	52-53	3	$250,000	$375,000	A	★★★★	n/c
342 America cabriolet	52-53	3	$400,000	$750,000	A	★★★★	n/c
212 Export (Closed)	51-52	9	$200,000	$295,000	B	★★★★	n/c
212 Export (Open)	51-52	8	$300,000	$350,000	B	★★★★	n/c
212 Touring Barchetta	51-52	7	$1,100,000	$1,200,000	A	★★★★	22%
212 Inter	51-52	84	$225,000	$300,000	B	★★★	n/c
225 Sport	52	22	$750,000	$950,000	A	★★★★	n/c
166 MM Berlinetta S2	52-53	4	$850,000	$1,000,000	A	★★★★	9%
340 Spyder S2	52-53	9	$1,100,000	$1,300,000	A	★★★★	41%
250 MM	52-53	13	$1,200,000	$1,500,000	A	★★★★	26%
250 MM Berlinetta	52-53	16	$1,200,000	$1,500,000	A	★★★★	26%
340 MM	53	9	$1,800,000	$2,250,000	A	★★★★	n/c
500 Mondial	53-54	33	$600,000	$1,500,000	A	★★★★	62%
375 MM	53-54	16	$3,250,000	$4,000,000	A	★★★★	n/c
375 MM Berlinetta	53-54	7	$2,750,000	$3,250,000	A	★★★★	n/c
250 Europa Series I	53-54	18	$225,000	$300,000	B	★★★	n/c
375 America	53-54	12	$350,000	$750,000	A	★★★	n/c
375 MM+	54	6	$4,000,000	$5,000,000	A	★★★★	n/c
250 Monza	54	4	$1,700,000	$2,000,000	A	★★★★	n/c
750 Monza	54-55	33	$650,000	$850,000	A	★★★★	n/c
250 Europa Series II	54-55	34	$300,000	$475,000	B	★★★	15%
410 Sport Spyder/coupe	55	4	$2,000,000	$3,000,000	A	★★★★	n/c
860 Monza	55-56	2	$1,600,000	$2,000,000	A	★★★★	13%
500 TR	56	17	$700,000	$900,000	A	★★★	n/c
410 Superamerica	56-59	37	$375,000	$500,000	A	★★★	n/c
250 GT Boano/Elle.	56-58	130	$90,000	$180,000	B	★★★★	n/c
250 GT Tour de France	56-59	77	$950,000	$1,200,000	A	★★★★	16%
(Early Pininfarina-bodied "roundtail" TdFs ['56] will command a premium.)							
*14 louvre comp. car		(8-inc.)	$1,000,000	$1,700,000	A	★★★★	8%
*Zagato-bodied		(5-inc.)	$1,500,000	$1,750,000	A	★★★★	n/c
500 TRC	57	20	$1,200,000	$1,500,000	A	★★★★	8%
250 Testa Rossa (all)	56-61	34	$5,000,000	$7,000,000	A	★★★★	n/c
250 GT PF cabriolet Series I	57-59	40	$550,000	$750,000	A	★★★★	n/c
250 GT PF cabriolet Series II	59-62	200	$175,000	$245,000	B	★★★	45%
250 GT California Spyder LWB	57-60	42	$1,100,000	$1,400,000	A	★★★★	22%
*Alloy-bodied		9	$1,400,000	$1,600,000	A	★★★★	n/c
250 GT California Spyder SWB	60-63	51	$1,800,000	$2,200,000	A	★★★★	21%
*Alloy-bodied		3	$2,500,000	$3,000,000	A	★★★★	28%
250 GT Int. Berlinneta	59	7	$600,000	$900,000	A	★★★★	30%
250 Pininfarina coupe	59-62	350	$550,000	$900,000	B	★★★★	n/c
250 GT SWB (steel)	60-62	122	$950,000	$1,250,000	A	★★★	19%
*Alloy-bodied		inc.	$1,800,000	$2,750,000	A	★★★★	47%
*SEFAC variant	61	23	$2,500,000	$3,000,000	A	★★★★	17%
400 Superamerica	60-64	45	$325,000	$450,000	A	★★★★	n/c
250 GTE 2+2	60-63	955	$35,000	$50,000	C	★★★	n/c
250 GTO	62-64	39	$7,500,000	$9,000,000	A	★★★★	n/c
250 GTL Lusso	62-64	350	$200,000	$350,000	B	★★★★	90%
330 LM Berlinetta	63	4	$5,000,000	$7,000,000	A	★★★★	n/c
330 America	63	50	$35,000	$47,500	B	★★★	n/c
330 GT 2+2	63-68	1,080	$30,000	$45,000	C	★★★	n/c
250 LM (no stories)	64-65	32	$2,500,000	$3,500,000	A	★★★★	n/c
500 Superfast	64-66	36	$300,000	$400,000	A	★★★	n/c
275 GTB/2 SN	64-66	450	$200,000	$225,000	A	★★★★	21%
(Add $25,000 for long nose, $25 for 6 carbs, $25 for alloy body, $5,000 for outside filler cap.							
275 GTB/C SN	65	11	$900,000	$1,100,000	A	★★★★	14%
275 GTB/C Le Mans	65	3	$2,500,000	$5,000,000	A	★★★★	23%
275 GTS	65-66	200	$145,000	$200,000	B	★★★★	8%
275 GTB/C	66	12	$1,200,000	$1,400,000	A	★★★★	27%
275 GTB/4	66-68	280	$350,000	$450,000	A	★★★★	19%
(Add $200,000 for alloy body.							
275 GTB/4 NART Spyder	67-68	10	$1,700,000	$2,000,000	A	★★★★	n/c
330 GTC	66-68	600	$85,000	$145,000	B	★★★	10%
330 GTS	66-68	100	$225,000	$275,000	B	★★★★	16%
365 California Spyder	66-67	14	$475,000	$600,000	A	★★	30%

	Yrs. Built	No. Made	Price Range Low	Price Range High	Grade	Rating	1 Yr. % Change
FERRARI							
206 GT Dino	67-68	144	$65,000	$100,000	B	★★★	n/c
365 GTC	68-70	150	$110,000	$145,000	B	★★★★	9%
365 GT 2+2	68-71	800	$50,000	$65,000	C	★★	10%
365 GTB/4 Daytona coupe	68-73	1,273	$125,000	$145,000	B	★★	4%
365 GTS	69	20	$275,000	$350,000	B	★★★★	4%
365 TB/4C (Fact. Daytona Comp.)	71-73	15 (inc)	$1,100,000	$1,500,000	A	★★★★	n/c
Non-factory Comp. Day.	71-73	5 (inc)	$800,000	$1,200,000	B	★★★★	25%
365 GTS/4 Daytona Spyder	72-73	124	$300,000	$375,000	A	★★★★	n/c
365 GTC/4	71-72	500	$55,000	$75,000	C	★★	n/c
246 GT 'Dino' coupe	69-74	2,609	$45,000	$70,000	B	★★★	n/c
246 GTS Spyder	72-74	1,274	$70,000	$95,000	B	★★★★	n/c
(Add $7,500 for "chairs and flares."							
365 GT4 2+2	72-76	470	$15,000	$25,000	D	★	n/c
365 GT4 BB Boxer	74-76	387	$65,000	$85,000	B	★★★★	11%
308 GT4 2+2	74-79	2,826	$18,000	$22,500	C	★★	n/c
308 GTB (fiberglass)	75-77	712	$30,000	$40,000	C	★★★	n/c
(Add $5,000 for dry sump.)							
308 GTB (steel)	75-79	2,089	$25,000	$30,000	C	★★★	n/c
308 GTS	77-79	3,218	$25,000	$32,500	C	★★★	n/c
512 BB Boxer	76-81	929	$55,000	$72,500	B	★★	n/c
400 2+2 carbureted	76-80	502	$18,500	$24,000	D	★	n/c
(Add $2,500 for 400/400i with manual shift.)							
512 BB LM	79-80	25	$425,000	$525,000	B	★★★★	n/c
308 GTBi	80-82	494	$22,500	$27,500	D	★	n/c
308 GTSi	80-82	1,743	$22,500	$27,500	D	★	n/c
400i	80-84	1,308	$18,000	$22,500	D	★	-8%
Mondial 8 coupe	81-82	708	$15,000	$20,000	D	★	n/c
512 BBi Boxer	82-84	1,007	$60,000	$80,000	B	★★★	-3%
308 GTBi QV	83-85	748	$28,000	$30,000	C	★★★	n/c
308 GTSi QV	83-85	3,042	$28,000	$32,500	C	★★	n/c
Mondial coupe QV	83-85	1,848	$20,000	$24,000	C	★★★	-2%
Mondial cabriolet QV	83-85	629	$25,000	$30,000	C	★★★★	n/c
288 GTO	84-85	272	$250,000	$300,000	B	★	10%
Testarossa	85-87.5	7,200	$40,000	$50,000	C	★	-10%
Testarossa	87.5-91	inc.	$50,000	$70,000	C	★★	new
412	85-89	576	$30,000	$35,000	D	★★	-7%
Mondial 3.2 coupe	86-88	987	$28,000	$32,000	C	★★	-2%
Mondial 3.2 cabriolet	86-88	810	$30,000	$37,000	C	★★★	-4%
328 GTB	86-89	1,345	$35,000	$45,000	B	★★★★	n/c
328 GTS	86-88	6,068	$35,000	$50,000	B	★★★★	n/c
F40	88-91	1,315	$275,000	$375,000	A	★	n/c
328 GTS	89	inc.	$40,000	$60,000	B	★★	n/c
Mondial 't' coupe	89	840	$32,500	$40,000	C	★	n/c
Mondial 't' cabriolet	89-91	1,010	$35,000	$47,500	C	★★	n/c
348 tb	90	2,895	$45,000	$55,000	C	★	-2%
348 ts	90-92	4,230	$50,000	$60,000	C	★★	-2%
512 TR	91-95	2,280	$80,000	$90,000	C	★★	n/c
456 GT Manual	92-03	1,548	$75,000	$95,000	C	★★	-11%
348 Spider	93-95	1,090	$60,000	$70,000	B	★★	n/c
F512 M	94-96	500	$155,000	$170,000	C	★★	18%
F355 Berlinetta	94-99	3,938	$65,000	$75,000	B	★★	-18%
F355 GTS	96-99	2,048	$75,000	$95,000	B	★★	-8%
F355 Spider	95-99	2,663	$95,000	$115,000	B	★★★★	n/c
F50	95-97	349	$675,000	$775,000	A	★	4%
456 GT Automatic	96-03	403	$75,000	$95,000	C	★★	-11%
550 Maranello	96-03	1,600	$115,000	$165,000	B	★★	-7%
355 Serie Fiorano	99	100*	$75,000	$105,000	B	★★	-18%
360 Modena	99-	n/a	$125,000	$150,000	B	★★★	-10%
360 Modena Spyder	01-	n/a	$215,000	$235000	B	★★	-5%
360 Modena Challenge	00-	n/a	$85,000	$110,000	B	★★★	-22%
550 Barchetta Pininfarina	00-03	448	$250,000	$275,000	B	★★★	-22%
Enzo	03-	349	$1,100,000	$1,200,000	B		n/c

*Conserning "cut-car" non-factory, non-NARTS Spyder conversions are valued primarily by the equality of workmanship. In today's market, rarely is a cut car valued more than the coupe it is derived from.

Formula One Cars

	Yrs. Built	No. Made	Low	High	Grade	Rating	1 Yr. % Change
312 "Spaghetti Exhaust"	'60s	12	$800,000	$1,000,000	A	★★★★	n/c
70-80 312 B&T series	68-70	40*	$450,000	$600,000	A	★★	n/c
Turbocharged	81-88	36*	$225,000	$275,000	A		n/c

Ferrari Sports Prototype Racers

	Yrs. Built	No. Made	Low	High	Grade	Rating	1 Yr. % Change
Front-engined V6 (Dinos)	57-60	6*	$2,750,000	$3,750,000	A	★★★★	n/c
(Includes 196, 203, 246, 296 S without stories.)							
Rear-engined V6 & V8 Dinoracers	61-67	25*	$1,450,000	$1,850,000	A	★★★★	n/c
(Includes 166, 196, 246, 286, 268 SPs without stories.)							
Rear-engined V12 racers	63-67	22*	$4,000,000	$9,500,000	A	★★★★	n/c
(Includes 250, 275P, 330P, 330P2, 275P2, 365P, 330P3, 365P2/3, 330P4, 330P3/4 [412P] without series.)							

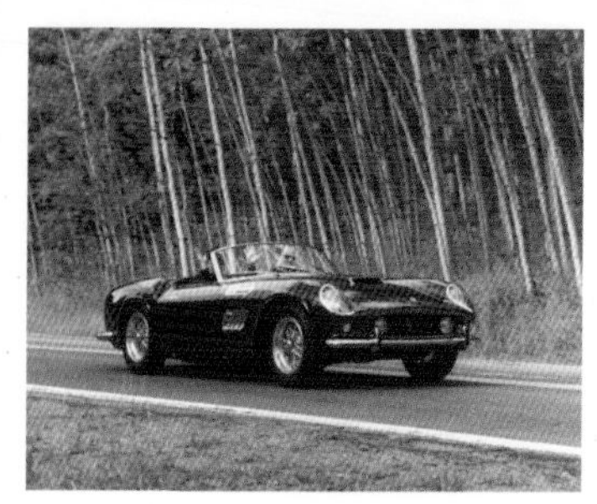

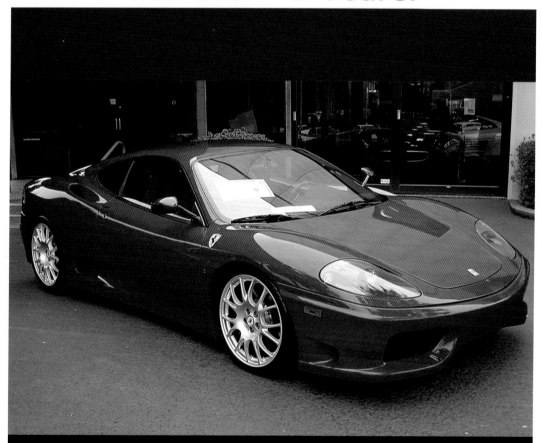

Michael Sheehan's
ferraris-online.com

Michael Sheehan: Ferrari historian, race driver, columnist and exotic car broker.

Meticulous research has made Michael Sheehan recognized for proficiency in all things Ferrari, especially the older, coach-built Ferraris and Ferrari race cars. His experience in restoration, concours and racing provide Mike with first hand knowledge of the strengths and weaknesses of the various Ferrari models, the true expenses involved in repairs, the ability to know how each model Ferrari should perform and which models are appropriate and eligible for your racing, concours or other needs. His connections with thousands of Ferrari owners and watchers keeps Mike abreast of changes of ownership, vehicle status and which cars are "in play." This, coupled with a massive database of these extraordinary automobiles and their owners, enables Mike to quickly find the buyer or seller of the Ferrari of your dreams.

Mike is online at www.ferraris-online.com. Visit us to see many fine Ferraris and other exotics. Learn about the cars that Mike has raced and read his past articles from Ferrari Market Letter, Car and, of course, Sports Car Market. There are plenty of behind the scenes activities that never make it to the site because clients were ready and waiting to purchase particular models. Ferraris are becoming available all of the time, so if you are looking for a specific model, Mike's database and over thirty years of experience can find it for you!

Michael Sheehan in 1957 Ferrari Testa Rossa No. 0732 at the 1988 Mille Miglia Historica

It's what we know, It's what we love.

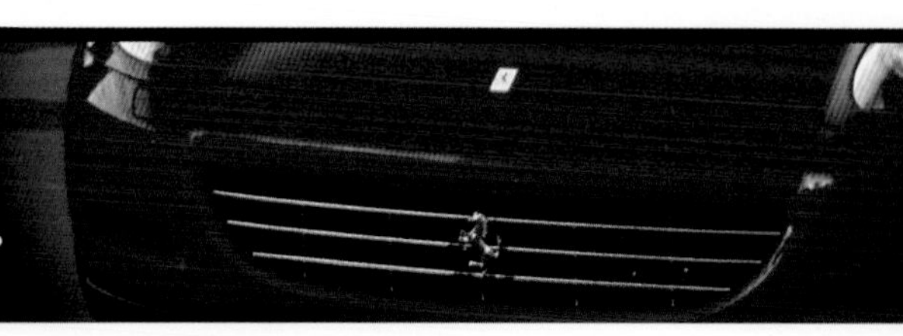

Sales & Leasing

Our sales consultants have the expertise, professionalism, and enthusiasm that makes your research and shopping experience a distinct pleasure. They also have long-established relationships with Ferrari & Maserati factory personnel and extensive experience in the vintage Ferrari & Maserati markets to provide you with all the resources necessary to assure a quality buying experience. In addition, we are proud to feature:

- Consistently large selection of high-quality pre-owned Ferrari cars
- Worldwide contacts to be able to locate specific pre-owned exotic cars
- Thorough inspection of all pre-owned Ferrari & Maserati cars by factory-trained technicians
- Factory Limited Warranty offered on qualified pre-owned Ferrari cars

Service, Parts & Accessories

Our experienced, factory-trained service team is committed to giving your vehicle the quality care and attention it deserves. 100% satisfaction is our highest priority. To this end, we offer a full range of premium quality services including:

- Special enclosed vehicle transport arranged for clients throughout the Midwest by our specially-trained and licensed transport driver
- Experienced, factory-certified technicians
- State-of-the-art electronic diagnosis equipment and software
- Performance of all factory warranty repairs
- Knowledge of all the latest factory updates
- Pre-purchase inspections for third party purchases
- State emissions testing, diagnosis and correction

Since 1975, our parts staff has been the perfect complement to our service team. Our extensive inventory selection ensures quick and accurate availability. We offer free overnight shipping of any out of stock parts for our service clients. Our staff also has worldwide connections for vintage parts and hard-to-find items to find the perfect accessories to enhance your car.

Racing & Restoration

Whether you like to go fast or just look good, we offer a full menu of support and resources to help enthusiasts maximize the enjoyment of their machines, including:

- Racing & track day preparation
- Pre & post track day inspection & servicing
- Ferrari / Maserati Historic Challenge preparation
- Vintage race car preparation and fabrication
- Full mechanical preparation
- Expert Weber carburetion service and rebuilding
- Distributor rebuilding & precision bench testing
- Interior & exterior trimwork
- Precision bodywork, painting & touch-up
- Full service detailing top to bottom
- Paintless dent removal & leather refurbishment

Our craftsmanship and attention to detail have earned our clients numerous Ferrari Club of America major awards, including the Preservation Award, Copa Bella Machina (multiple times), and the National Concourse Platinum Award (multiple times).

Continental has been a factory-authorized Ferrari dealer since 1975. Our experience and knowledge of the Ferrari and Maserati marques is second to none in the Midwest. Our conveniently-located sales and service facility in Hinsdale, Illinois allows easy access from anywhere in Chicagoland or the world via nearby Chicago O'Hare International Airport. Family owned since 1962, Continental has stood the test of time as a leader in the exotic sports car business.

Bonhams 1793

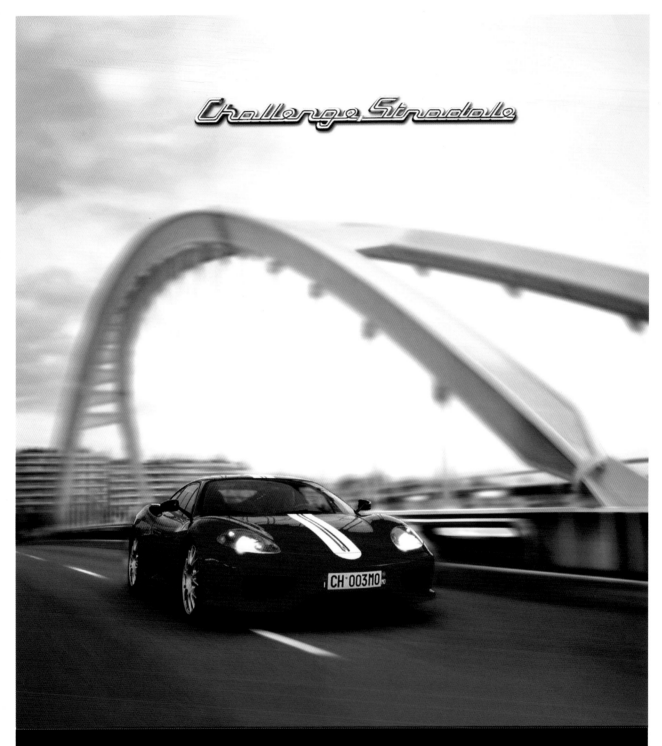

36" Length x 14" Width x 10" Height

THE MILLION DOLLAR CAR COLLECTION

This superb curb-side model of the Ferrari 250 GTO is entirely handmade in England by famous museum model engineers.

The original master for its limited production took over 2,500 hours to complete.

You can now own a miniature 1/5 scale model masterpiece for a fraction of the cost of a real Ferrari.

Email: karenscarworld@aol.com
301 7th Street, Eureka, California 95501
Tel: 707 445 4806 Cell: 707 616 4257 Fax: 707 445 4809

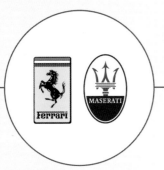

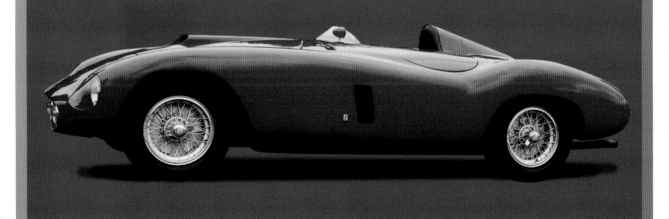

GRIOT'S
GARAGE
Products for your garage
PORTER+CABLE
MACHINE POLISH 3
PAINT CLEANING CLAY
SPEED SHINE
BEST OF SHOW WAX
Everything you need to keep your Ferrari looking and running great.
Have fun in your garage!™
800-345-5789 www.griotsgarage.com

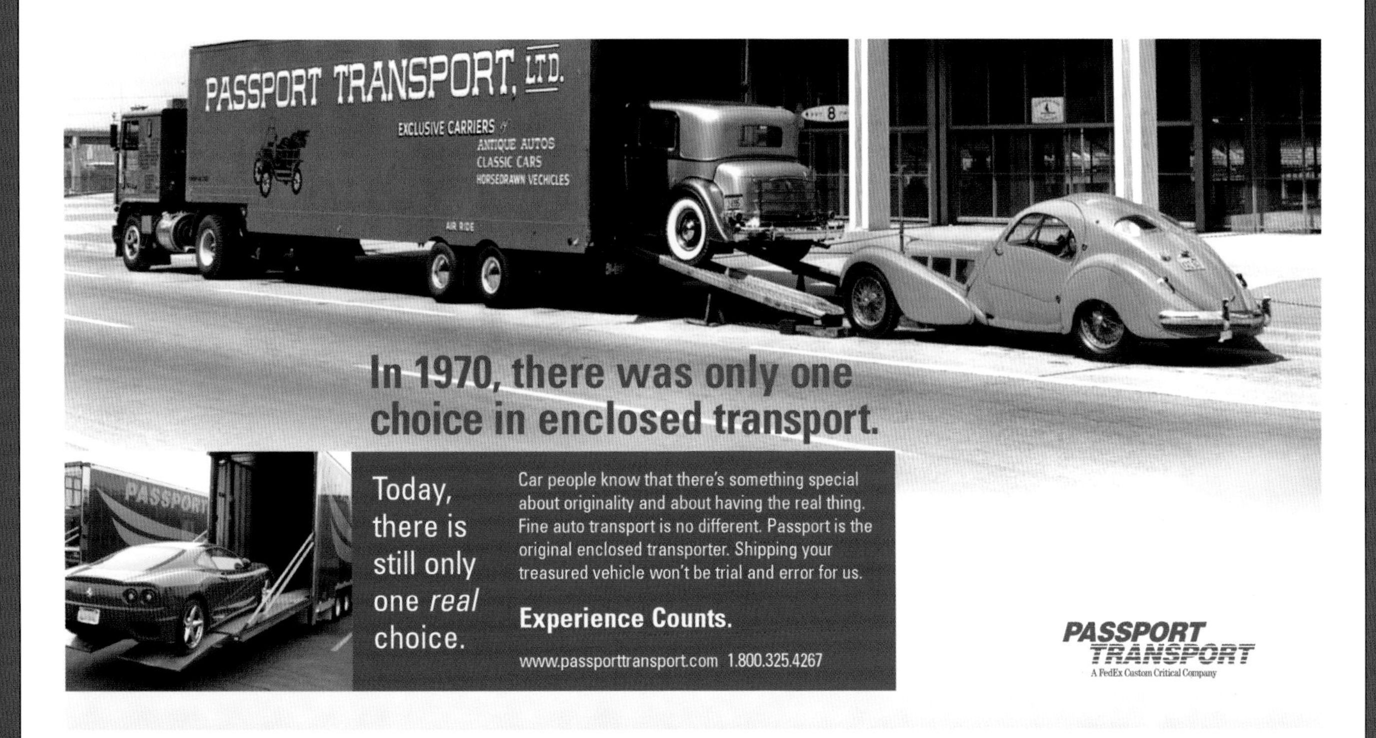
PASSPORT TRANSPORT, LTD.
EXCLUSIVE CARRIERS
ANTIQUE AUTOS
CLASSIC CARS
HORSEDRAWN VECHICLES
In 1970, there was only one choice in enclosed transport.
Today, there is still only one *real* choice.
Car people know that there's something special about originality and about having the real thing. Fine auto transport is no different. Passport is the original enclosed transporter. Shipping your treasured vehicle won't be trial and error for us.
Experience Counts.
www.passporttransport.com 1.800.325.4267
PASSPORT TRANSPORT
A FedEx Custom Critical Company

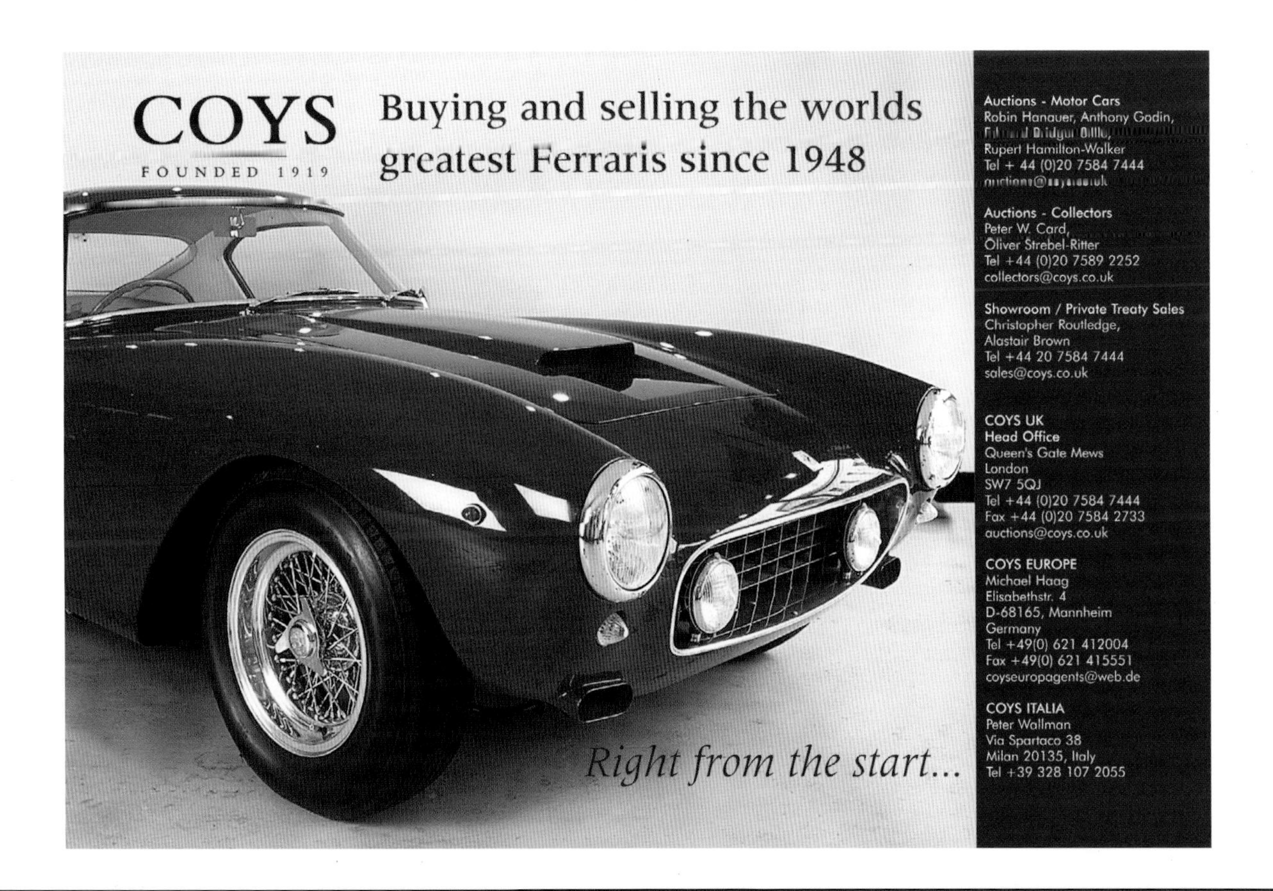
COYS
FOUNDED 1919
Buying and selling the worlds greatest Ferraris since 1948
Right from the start...
Auctions - Motor Cars
Robin Hanauer, Anthony Godin,
Rupert Hamilton-Walker
Tel + 44 (0)20 7584 7444
Auctions - Collectors
Peter W. Card,
Oliver Strebel-Ritter
Tel +44 (0)20 7589 2252
collectors@coys.co.uk
Showroom / Private Treaty Sales
Christopher Routledge,
Alastair Brown
Tel +44 20 7584 7444
sales@coys.co.uk
COYS UK
Head Office
Queen's Gate Mews
London
SW7 5QJ
Tel +44 (0)20 7584 7444
Fax +44 (0)20 7584 2733
auctions@coys.co.uk
COYS EUROPE
Michael Haag
Elisabethstr. 4
D-68165, Mannheim
Germany
Tel +49(0) 621 412004
Fax +49(0) 621 415551
coyseuropagents@web.de
COYS ITALIA
Peter Wallman
Via Spartaco 38
Milan 20135, Italy
Tel +39 328 107 2055

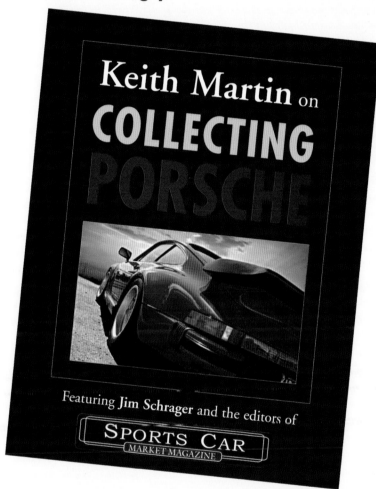

AUCTION COMPANIES

Artcurial-Briest-Poulain-Le Fur. 33-01 42 99 20 20, fax 33-01 42 99 20 21. Maison de vente aux enchères, 7, Rond-Point des Champs Elysées, 75008 Paris. e-mail: artcurial@auction.fr. www.poulainle-fur.com. (FR)
Barrett-Jackson Auction. 480.421.6694, fax 480.421.6697. 3020 North Scottsdale Rd, Scottsdale, AZ 85251. e-mail: info@barrett-jackson.com. www.barrett-jackson.com. (AZ)
Bonhams. 415.391.4000, fax 415.391.4040. 220 San Bruno Avenue, San Francisco, CA 94103; Montpelier St., Knightsbridge, London, SW7 1HH. 44.207.228.8000, fax 44.207.585.0830. www.bonhams.com. (CA)
Branson Collector Car Auction, 800.335.3063, contact Jim Cox, fax 417.336.5616, 1316 W. Hwy. 76, Suite 199, Branson, MO, 65616. www.bransonauction.com. (MO)
Christie's. 310.385.2699, fax 310.385.0246. 360 N. Camden Dr., Beverly Hills, CA 90210. www.christies.com. (CA)
Dana Mecum Auction Company. 815.568.8888, fax 815.568.6615. P.O. Box 422, Marengo, IL 60152. www.mecumauction.com. (IL)
eBay Motors, a part of eBay Inc. List your car for sale for only $40 and pay $40 more when it sells. Visit the "Services" section on www.ebaymotors.com for more details.
H&H Classic Auctions. 44.1925 730630, fax 44.1925 730830 Whitegate Farm, Hatton Lane, Hatton, Cheshire, UK. WA4 4BZ info@classic-auctions.co.uk, www.classic-auctions.com. (UK)
Kruse International. 800.968.4444, fax 260.925.5467.
P.O. Box 190, Auburn, IN 46706. www.kruseinternational.com. (IN)
Kensington Motor Group, Inc. 631.537.1868, fax 631.537.2641. P.O. Box 2277, Sag Harbor, NY 11963. KenMotor@aol.com. (NY)
Palm Springs Auctions Inc. Keith McCormick. 760.320.3290, fax 760.323.7031. 244 N. Indian Canyon Dr., Palm Springs, CA 92262. classiccarauction.com. (CA)
RM Auctions, Inc. 800.211.4371, fax 519.351.1337 One Classic Car Dr., Blenheim, ON NOP 1A0. www.rmauctions.com. (CAN)
Russo and Steele. 602.252.2697, www.russoandsteele.com. (AZ)
Silver Auctions. 800.255.4485, 2020 N. Monroe, Spokane, WA 99205. silver@silverauctions.com; www.silverauctions.com. (WA)
Santiago Collector Car Auctions. 800.994.2816,
fax 405.843.6251. 7321 N. Classen Blvd.,
Oklahoma City, OK 73116. E-mail Rocky: rockydb5@sbcglobal.net. (OK)
Spectrum Auctions. 818.999.0832, fax 818.999.0816. 23295 Ventura Blvd., Woodland Hills, CA 91364. www.spectrumauctions.com. (CA)

APPRAISALS

Dave Brownell's Vintage Auto Appraisals. Phone 802.362.4719; fax 802.362.3007. 25-plus years experience nationwide and internationally. Single cars or entire collections. Brass cars to contemporary supercars. Complete services from pre-purchase to insurance, donation, estate, expert witness. E-mail: dbrownell@sprynet.com. (VT)
Charles W. Clarke. Phone.fax: 860.658.2714. Automotive consultant and appraiser. Hartford, Connecticut area base. State of Connecticut licensed. 40-plus years automotive experience, appraisals and wherewithal to address most any situation. We travel. E-mail: cwc-cars@cox.net. (CT)
Cosmopolitan Motors LLC. 206.467.6531, fax 206.467.6532. Complete appraisal services for any and all vehicles of particular note. Over 1 billion dollars in worldwide experience. We will help you in your time of need: We negotiate for you. Settlements, insurance, disputes, estates, pre-purchase, donations, etc. E-mail: appraisals@cosmopolitanmotors.com. (WA)
USAppraisal. 703.759.9100. 25 years experience with collector automobiles, available nationwide. Call or visit our Web site. David H. Kinney, ASA (Accredited Senior Appraiser, American Society of Appraisers). E-mail: dhkinney@usappraisal.com; www.usappraisal.com. (VA)
Joseph L. Troise Appraisals. 415.332.8183. On-site inspection and evaluation of classic and contemporary cars. Covering northern & mid-California & Tahoe/Reno. Prompt, personal, professional and affordable service for insurance, legal, IRS and pre-purchase inspection. Free phone consultations. joetro@pacbell.net; http://www.oldcarpricing.com. (CA)
Auto Appraisal Group. 800.848.2886. Nationwide, over 50 offices. Certified Appraisals. Pre-purchase inspections, insurance matters, charitable donations, resale values, estates, expert witness. Onsite inspections. Confidential. www.auto-appraisalgroup.com."Not just one man's opinion of value." (VA)
Classic Car Research. 248.557.2880. fax 248.557.3511. 15 years in business, IAAA, for loans, estates, divorce, insurance and pre-purchase. Detroit area, will travel. www.jmkclassiccars.com or kawifreek@msn.com. (MI)
Dean V. Kruse. 260.927.1111, fax 260.920.2222. Certified appraiser with 35 years in the business, appraisals completed for most of nationwide banks and insurance companies. Kruse International auctions more than 10,000 collector cars per year. One car or collections, donators, estates, disputes, pre-purchase inspections, attorneys, buyers, sellers. All inquiries kept confidential. E-mail: dkruse@myvine.com. (IN)
Featherman & Co. Inc. 610.645.5595. Scott Featherman has over 20 years experience and is both a certified IAAA appraiser and ASE master technician. Complete services include appraisals, pre-purchase inspections, expert witness and advisory. Personal, prompt, confidential—available nationwide. E-mail: scott@feathco.com, Web: www.FeathermanCo.com. (PA)

AUTOMOBILIA

Spyder Enterprises: 831.659.5335, fax 831.659.5335 Since 1980, providing serious collectors with the finest selection of authentic, original vintage posters, pre-war thru mid-1960s; mainly focused on Porsche, Ferrari, Mercedes, & racing. Producer of "Automobilia Monterey" August 10-12, 2004. Halon Fire Extinguishers; Porsche 356 leather accessories; Ferrari repro tool kit, 250-330. 38-page list of memorabilia via email at singer356@aol.com or www.vintageautoposters.com. (CA)
www.arteauto.com–l'art et l'automobile gallery and auction house website. 631.329.8580. Our site features drawings, paintings, prints, vintage posters, photos, sculptures, objects, toys, models, books, literature, memorabilia, and more from the beginning of the automobile to date. View online and mail order automobilia auction lots at www.arteauto.com. Email: jvautoart@aol.com. (NY)

BUY.SELL.GENERAL

Cosmopolitan Motors LLC. 206.467.6531, fax 206.467.6532. 2030 8th Ave., Seattle, WA 98121. Experts in collector cars worldwide. Whether buying, selling, evaluating, consigning or appraising, we cut the edge on the current market. Over 1 billion dollars in worldwide experience. Top prices paid; from one car to entire collections, condition and location are no obstacles. "We covet the rare and unusual, whether pedigreed or proletarian." E-mail: sales@cosmopolitanmotors.com. (WA)
eBay Motors, a part of eBay Inc. The World's Online Marketplace. Consistently ranked the best automotive site on the Web by Nielsen.NetRatings. Everyday drivers, collector cars, auto parts and accessories, motorcycles and automobilia. List your car for sale for only $40 and pay $40 more when it sells. Every vehicle transaction is covered by $20,000 in free insurance. Visit the "Services" section on www.ebaymotors.com for more details.
Fantasy Junction. 510.653.7555, fax 510.653.9754, www.fantasyjunction.com, e-mail sales@fantasyjunction.com. Specializing in European collectible autos and racing cars from the 1920s to the 1970s, with over 50 cars in stock. Bruce Trenery has over 25 years experience in this business, based in the East Bay area. Clients and contacts worldwide with satisfaction as the hallmark. 1145 Park Ave., Emeryville, CA 94608. (CA)
Grand Prix Classics. 858.459.3500, fax 858.459.3512. Specialize in the buying, selling trading and consignment of historic sports cars and racing cars. Been in business for 25 years and maintain an inventory of 15 to 20 historic cars. Large extensive poster inventory. Located at 7456 La Jolla Blvd., La Jolla, CA 92037. www.grandprixclassics.com; E-mail: info@grandprixclassics.com. (CA)
Hyman Ltd. 314.524.6000. One of the largest dealers of quality collector cars in the US with over 100 cars in stock. We act as principle in the acquisition of collector cars and are aggressive buyers for complete collections. Our specialties include Europeans sports cars and full classics. We try hard to offer something you have never heard of! Select consignments considered. www.hymanltd.com. (MO)
Oldtimer Garage. 41.31.819 00 00,
fax 41.31.819 51 91. Gurbestrasse 3, CH-3125, Toffen, Bern, Switzerland. www.oldtimergarage.com. (CH)
www.historicalcars.com We Buy-We Sell-We Find. Europe.US.Asia.Far East. If you are looking to buy or sell a vehicle(s) with historic or collector appeal, try us. 30 years of experience, your satisfaction our priority. Any time—Any place—Anywhere. www.historicalcars.com.

CLASSIC CAR TRANSPORT

Cosdel International. 415.777.2000, fax 415.543.5112. Now in its 33rd year of international transport. Complete service, including import.export, customs clearances, DOT and EPA, air/ocean, loading and unloading of containers. Contact Martin Button, e-mail: info@cosdel.com; www.cosdel.com. (CA)

Passport Transport. 800.325.4267, fax 314.878.7295. Classic and specialty cars delivered anywhere in the USA. Special event services, including Pebble Beach, Monterey Historics, Barrett-Jackson, and Auburn. Standard-of-the-industry service since 1970. www.passporttransport.com. (MO)
Intercity Lines, Inc. 800.221.3936, fax 413.436.9422. Rapid, hassle-free, coast-to-coast service. Insured, enclosed transport for your valuable car at affordable prices. State-of-the-art satellite transport tracking. Complete service for vintage races, auctions, relocations. www.intercitylines.com. (MA)
PC BEAR Auto Transport specializing in all types: hobby, collector vehicles, toys, neat old stuff, regular cars, parts, and winching. Life long car nut. Equipment serviced and maintained by me. Clean driving record since 1959 in all states. ICCMC, US DOT insured. I sleep in my truck while transporting. Inspection and check delivery service. Door to door delivery. PC Bear, 135 Broad St., Akron, PA 17501. 717.859-1585. Talk to me anytime. Thank you. (PA)
Concours Transport Systems. 253.973.3987, fax 253.851.4707. Enclosed auto transport nationwide. Lift gate loading, experienced personnel. Classic & exotic cars. Special events—fully insured. Fred Koller, owner. fredkoller@concourstransport.com, www.concourstransport.com. (WA)

COLLECTOR CAR FINANCING

J.J. Best Banc & Company. 800.USA.1965, fax 508.945.6006. The largest national leader on Antique, Classic, Exotic, Rod and Sports Cars with rates starting at 4.99% and long terms from 5 to 12 years. Call, fax or e-mail your application today for quick 10 minute approval. Efficient and professional service is what you deserve so don't hesitate, call us today to be in the driver's seat of your dream car tomorrow. www.jjbest.com. (MA)

COLLECTOR CAR INSURANCE

American Collectors Insurance. 800.360.2277. We've been taking the hassle- and expense-out of insuring collector vehicles since 1976. Get the collector coverage you need, at a price you won't believe! Visit us online for an instant rate quote, www.AmericanCollectors.com, or call toll-free. Available in all states except AK and HI. (NJ)
Hagerty Collector Car Insurance. 800.922.4050. Collector cars aren't like their late-model counterparts. These classics actually appreciate in value so standard market policies that cost significantly more won't do the job. With Hagerty, we'll agree on a fair value and cover you for the full amount. No prorated claims, no hassles, no games. See what Hagerty can do for you! Call. 800.922.4050, or visit our Web site at: www.hagerty.com. (MI)
American Hobbyist Insurance. 800.395.4835. From "brass & wood" antiques to modern day classics, our program accepts a wide range of collector vehicles. Enjoy excellent coverage & low "collector" rates. No strict mileage limitations in most states. Call toll-free or visit us online at AmericanHobbyist.com. (FL)

COLLECTOR CAR LEASING

Premier Financial Services. 203.267.7700, fax 203.267.7773. With over 20 years of experience specializing in exotic, classic and vintage autos, our Lease. Purchase plan is ideal for those who wish to own their vehicle at the end of the term as well as those who like to change cars frequently. Our Simple Interest Early Termination plan allows you the flexibility of financing with the tax advantages of leasing. We make leasing as simple as turning the key. www.WhyNotLease.com. (CT)
Putnam Leasing. 866.90.LEASE (866.905.3273). Never get in a car with strangers. Custom-tailored, lease-to-own financing for your dream car. Easy, fast and dependable. Exclusive leasing agent for Barrett-Jackson, Cavallino and Ferrari Club of America 2004 International Meet. Go with people you trust. Call toll free or visit www.PutnamLeasing.com. (CT)

PHOTOGRAPHY

Bob Dunsmore Racing Photography. PO Box 80008, Multnomah, OR 97280. 503.244.4646. Email: photoraces@aol.com. (OR)

RESTORATION.GENERAL

CARS of Pittsburgh, Inc. 866.877.8866, fax 412.653.3798. Complete classic and custom auto restoration fabrication. Metal repair, polishing, and plating. Pre-purchase inspection, appraisals and title services. The most customer friendly restoration company in the world. See our ad in this issue for more information. 1147 Cochran's Mill Rd., Pittsburgh, PA 15236. davidsteffan@carsofpgh.com, www.carsofpgh.com. (PA)
Guy's Interior Restorations. 503.224.8657, fax 503.223.6953. Award-winning interior restoration. Leather dyeing and color matching. 431 NW 9th, Portland, OR 97209. (OR)

SPORTS AND COMPETITION

Vintage Racing Services, Inc. (ARI/VRS), 203-377-6745, fax 203.386.0486, 1785 Barnum Ave., Stratford, CT 06614. Vintage race car restoration, preparation and race track support at events throughout North America; in Europe and South America by arrangement. Historic Rally Support. www.vintageracingservices.com. (CT)

VINTAGE EVENTS

The Colorado Grand. 1,000 mile tour of western Colorado. Pre-1961 sports cars. Frank Barrett. 970.926.7810, fax 970.926.7835. (CO)

FERRARI/MASERATI/LAMBORGHINI

Ron Tonkin Gran Turismo. Sales, 800.547.4455, 503.255.7560. Service and Parts, 800.944.6483, 503.257.9655. America's oldest and most dedicated Ferrari dealer. New and used exotic cars. Also, huge parts department with fast, fast service. 203 NE 122nd Ave., Portland, OR 97203. (OR)
Garry Roberts & Company. 949.650.2690, fax 949.650.2730. 922 Sunset Dr., Costa Mesa, CA 92627. Specializing in sales of Ferrari and other exotics. Consignments, brokerage services, references available. Extensive computer database. Whether buying or selling, call. (CA)
ItalParts. Fax +31 172 240536. Specializing in Italian car parts and pre-war car parts. 25 years of experience in finding all kinds of parts. Lots of spare parts in stock. Look on my Internet site: www.italparts.com. If you don't find the part there, send us an e-mail: info@italparts.com. Buy Italian engines.parts.cars of pre-war period and '50s and early '60s. (IT)
I constantly collect and sell all Ferraris, Maseratis and Lamborghinis. 310.274.7440, fax 310.274.9809, simonrandy@aol.com. If I don't have what you seek, I can usually find it for you (at low prices). Please, call anytime for straight advice on the market. Finder's fee gladly paid. Randy Simon. (CA)
Re-Originals. 713.849.2400, fax 713.849.2401. THE US source for original, complete seats and covers, bulk upholstery materials, original rubber mats and gaskets, original European taillights, headlights, grilles, windshields. Visit www.reoriginals.com for complete listing. (TX)
Gentry Lane Lamborghini. 416.535.9900, fax 416.535.8152. Also Canada's largest Ferrari parts inventory. Under new ownership. Call today with your needs. Jason Popovich. (ON)
Symbolic Motor Car Company. 858.454.1800, fax 858.454.1890. 7440 La Jolla Blvd., La Jolla, CA 92307. Largest dealer of exotic Ferraris, Jaguars, Alfas and other cars in the world. Always a superb array of important cars on display. Interesting trades always considered. www.symbolicmotors.com. (CA)
Michael Sheehan. 949.646.6086, fax 949.646.6978. Always looking for cars to buy, from rare one-offs to serial production ordinaries. Ferrari, Lamborghini, Lotus—call me first or call me last, I'll make you the best cash offer. Buyers, let me use my 20,000-car database to help you find a car, or verify the history of one you are looking at. www.ferraris-online.com. (CA)
Thomas Shaughnessey Consulting. 949.366.6211, fax 949.366.6827. Professional buyer of Ferraris, primarily '50s, '60s and '70s. Also have extensive Lambo and Maser experience. Additionally deal in Ferrari engines. More than 350 Ferrari wheels in stock. Call today for straight talk and honest advice. San Clemente, CA.
Automotive Restorations, Inc. Vintage Racing Services, Inc. (ARI.VRS), 203.377.6745, fax 203.386.0486, 1785 Barnum Ave., Stratford, CT 06614. Classic, special interest and race cars. Sales, restoration and transportation. www.VintageRacingServices.com, www.AutomotiveRestorations.com. (CT)
FORZA: 860.350.1140, fax 860.350.1148 email forzamot@aol.com. Buyers and sellers of Ferrari, Maserati, Lamborghini and related exotic cars. Call today for friendly, helpful advice. Buyers for cars in any condition, also interested in memorabilia, parts, manuals, books, etc., related to above cars. Willing to compensate for information that leads to purchase. www.forzamotorsports.com. (CT)